NEW HORIZONS IN JOURNALISM

Howard Rusk Long, *General Editor*

ADVISORY BOARD

Irving Dillard, *Professor of Journalism*
Princeton University

James S. Pope, *Former Executive Editor*
Louisville *Courier-Journal* and *Times*

Donald Tyerman, *Former Editor*
The Economist, *London*

LITTLE MACK

JOSEPH B. McCULLAGH

of

The St. Louis *Globe-Democrat*

By **Charles C. Clayton**

Foreword by **Howard Rusk Long**

Southern Illinois University Press   *Carbondale and Edwardsville*

Feffer & Simons, Inc.   *London and Amsterdam*

COPYRIGHT © 1969, *by* Southern Illinois University Press
All rights reserved
Printed in the United States of America
Designed by Andor Braun
Standard Book Number 8093–0399–x
Library of Congress Catalog Card Number 75–76186

CONTENTS

FOREWORD ix
PREFACE xiii

1 From Dublin to St. Louis 1
2 Brilliant War Correspondent 11
3 He Scooped the Nation 41
4 Managing Editor 66
5 The New Journalism 85
6 Controversies and Stunts 109
7 Crusades and Competition 129
8 "Pointed as a Tack" 149
9 Booming St. Louis 167
10 Shrewd Political Observer 184
11 The Twilight Years 202
12 The Right Time to Die 216
13 A Jealous Mistress 224

APPENDIX I 239
APPENDIX II 246
NOTES 251
BIBLIOGRAPHY 259
INDEX 263

LIST OF ILLUSTRATIONS

between pages 14 and 15

Joseph B. McCullagh
Offices of the *Missouri Democrat*
"Temple of Truth"
Notes in McCullagh's Handwriting
Daniel M. Houser

LITTLE MACK
Eugene Field

This talk about the journalists that run the East is bosh,
We've got a Western editor that's little, but, O gosh!
He lives here in Missoora where the people are so set
In ante-bellum notions that they vote for Jackson yet;
But the paper he is running makes the rusty fossils swear,—
The smartest, likeliest paper that is printed anywhere!
And best of all, the paragraphs are pointed as a tack
          And that's because they emanate
              From little Mack.

In architecture he is what you'd call a chunky man,
As if he'd been constructed on the summer cottage plan;
He has a nose like Bonaparte; and round his mobile mouth
Lies all the sensuous languor of the children of the South;
His dealings with reporters who affect a weekly bust
Have given to his violet eyes a shadow of distrust;
In glorious abandon his brown hair wanders back
          From the grand Websterian forehead
              Of little Mack.

No matter what the item is, if there's an item in it,
You bet your life he's on to it and nips it in a minute!
From multifarious nations, countries, monarchies and lands
From Afric's sunny fountains and India's coral strands,
From Greenland's icy mountains and Siloam's shady rills
He gathers in his telegrams, and Houser pays the bills;
What though there be a dearth of news, he has a happy knack
          Of scraping up a lot of scoops,
              Does little Mack.

And learning? Well he knows the folks of every tribe and age
That ever played a part upon this fleeting human stage;
His intellectual system's so extensive and so greedy
That, when it comes to records, he's a walkin' cyclopedy;
For having studied (and digested) all the books a-goin',
It stands to reason he must know about all's worth a-knowin'!
So when a politician with a record's on the track,
        We're apt to hear some history
           From little Mack.

And when a fellow-journalist is broke and needs a twenty,
Who's allus ready to whack up a portion of his plenty?
Who's allus got a wallet that's as full of sordid gain
As his heart is full of kindness and his head is full of brain?
Whose bowels of compassion will in-va-ri-a-bly move
Their owner to those courtesies which plainly, surely prove
That he's the kind of person that never does go back
        On a fellow that's in trouble?
           Why, little Mack!

I've heard 'em tell of Dana, and of Bonner, and of Reid,
Of Johnnie Cockerill, who, I'll own, is very smart indeed;
Yet I don't care what their renown or influence may be,
One metropolitan exchange is quite enough for me!
So keep your Danas, Bonners, Reids, your Cockerills, and the rest,
The woods is full of better men all through this woolly West;
For all that sleek, pretentious, Eastern editorial pack
        We wouldn't swap the shadow of
           Our little Mack!

FOREWORD

Journalism in the United States is an integral part of the industrial revolution, its cash economy, and concentrations of wage earners with money to spend and some degree of functional literacy. When newspaper and magazine proprietors first learned to capture this market for cheap sensationalized reading materials, competition for larger and ever larger audiences launched the drive for an intellectual common denominator continuing to this day with the newcomers of the electronic media now in the van of the race.

Robert Park and Helen MacGill Hughes explain the phenomenon of the yellow press as the logical continuation of folk cultures whose people relied upon the storyteller and the singer for news and entertainment before the printer produced, first the broadside ballad and then the penny newspaper. Biographers and historians, among whom Frank Luther Mott is preeminent, tell how Benjamin Day copied practices, already demonstrated in England, to produce the first successful, popular newspaper in New York City; how James Gordon Bennett perfected editorial techniques and pushed on to greater triumphs; how other titans, such as Greeley, Raymond, Dana, Bennett the younger, Pulitzer, Hearst, Ochs, and Patterson, with a leg up from the merchants of consumer goods, moved New York publishers from the back room to the board room.

But the story of American journalism is far from told. Not enough is known about the individuals in the supporting cast surrounding each of the great figures, nor how the contributions of obscure subordinates enhanced imposing reputations and great newspaper fortunes. Were innovators really the innovators, or did they bring to perfection little known and only partially successful experiments pioneered by others? Conflicting claims and patent disputes are common enough in industry to support a thesis that not all idea men in the realm of journalistic endeavors were properly rewarded or even remembered. One can wonder if New York really was the seed bed of all things progressive in American journalism, as some who reside east of the Hudson seem prepared to believe. Joseph Pulitzer, the upstart from the banks of the Mississippi, for such as these, came to life only after he had breathed new fire into the decadent New York newspaper press. William Randolph Hearst, who served his creative apprenticeship in the Bay Area, before attempting to run Pulitzer out of town, really was not a Californian until he withdrew to San Simeon in the twilight of his career. Henry Watterson, William Rockhill Nelson, E. W. Scripps, Henry Grady, all were obscure peasants in the provinces. Except for the Manhattan beach head consolidated by the Patterson branch of the family, even the Medill-Patterson-McCormick clan of Chicago was lacking in solid achievement. Or so it seems from reading the secondary materials on the shelves of the libraries.

Only a few months ago a biography by Justin E. Walsh rescued from oblivion the constructive portion of the reputation created by Wilbur F. Storey, editor-publisher of the Chicago *Times,* who for more than twenty years ruled the journalistic roosts of that city. Storey, an arch villain by any standard, it turns out, with all his faults, was a superb newsman and innovator of many of the more respectable standard practices found in the newspapers of today.

Although his man had acquired neither the color nor the evil reputation of the Walsh protagonist, Charles C. Clayton, in his book, seeks to perform the same service for Joseph B. McCullagh. In fact the antithetical and the parallel characteristics of the two men are striking. Storey gloried in his godlessness and delighted in spreading filth through the columns of the *Times*. When Storey lacked news he told his reporters to fabricate it. Walsh also credits Storey with setting new standards of news reporting by organizing a large and far-flung network of reporters so well administered that no other paper was consistently ahead of the *Times* with the news.

Professor Clayton credits McCullagh with a substantial number of firsts in American journalism, including the first formal interview with a president of the United States (Andrew Johnson), the concept of Massive Team Coverage of National Presidential Conventions, and with putting together for the St. Louis *Globe-Democrat* the first great system of news coverage undertaken by a single newspaper. In contrast with Storey, "Little Mack" was personally retiring, deeply concerned with the moral tone of his newspaper, and determined that his reporters, local or distant, should record only factual material.

Readers of the McCullagh biography, inevitably, will compare the

FOREWORD

claims for the two editors. This may only demonstrate the parallelism of invention, or it may serve as circumstantial evidence that McCullagh learned some of his trade from Storey during a short stint in Chicago as editor of the rival Chicago *Republican.*

Wholly aside from this comparison and the questions thus raised, is the observation that many of the innovations of McCullagh's *Globe-Democrat* were picked up by Joseph Pulitzer whose greater sense of showmanship exploited the ideas of "Little Mack" far beyond the scope of the latter's use of them. It may be too much to say that the genius of Joseph B. McCullagh failed to come to full flower until Joseph Pulitzer stormed into New York with his bag full of St. Louis newspaper tricks. Nevertheless, Professor Clayton (now at work on a biography of William Rockhill Nelson, creator of The Kansas City *Star*) is convinced that the journalists of the midland contributed as much to the development of the daily newspaper as they received from their contemporaries in New York.

Howard Rusk Long

Southern Illinois University
February 18, 1969

PREFACE

My interest in Joseph B. McCullagh was aroused shortly after I joined the staff of the St. Louis *Globe-Democrat* in 1925. There were still a few old-timers who had known "The Chief" in "The Temple of Truth," McCullagh's favorite description of the massive eight-story building on the southwest corner of Sixth and Pine Streets.

Even in 1925, twenty-nine years after McCullagh's tragic death, he had become a legendary and enigmatic figure. Those who had known him remembered him in terms of anecdotes rather than in recognition of his significant contributions to American journalism. One of those who worked for him was the late Mrs. Julia Underwood, known around the office as "Saint Julia." For many years until her retirement at seventy, she served as the Religious Editor. She remembered McCullagh as a kindly and somewhat shy man, who had encouraged her as a young lady, to work as a general assignment reporter in a period when few women were accepted in the news room.

Another was Charles S. Webb, a benign copy editor, relegated by that time to reading time copy on the morning shift. The late Casper S. Yost, who had served as one of McCullagh's assistants in his later years, was then editor of the editorial page, a rather aloof gentleman of the old school, who until his retirement wrote all of his editorials in long-hand. There were a few printers left who remembered McCullagh. The late Stephen Tammany, who became my close personal friend, and who delighted in amateur theatricals, had been an apprentice printer in the 1890's. George E. Windegger, foreman of the composing room during the first quarter of this century, remembered McCullagh and provided some of the anecdotes in this book. Windegger retired in 1926 and is still living in Eureka, Missouri.

In December 1931 the *Globe-Democrat* moved to new quarters, having outgrown "The Temple of Truth" which seemed so spacious in McCullagh's time. Built during the depression, the new building occupied a full block, bounded by Twelfth Boulevard, Franklin Avenue, and High and Wash Streets. The six-story structure, with two more levels below ground, was hailed at the time as one of the most modern newspaper plants in the world. Samuel I. Newhouse, who purchased the *Globe-Democrat* in 1955, sold the building to the St. Louis *Post-Dispatch* and now history has come full circle. The *Globe-Democrat,* which printed the first issue of the *Post-Dispatch,* is now printed under contract by the *Post-Dispatch.*

Like so many historic landmarks, "The Temple of Truth" has been razed to make room for a parking lot, and the ghost of "Little Mack" no longer wades through stacks of exchanges.

Today all that is left at the *Globe-Democrat* is a copy of one of the few photographs ever made of one of the great editors in American journalism; this hangs in the office of Hamilton Thornton, now editor of the editorial page. There are two or three yellowed clippings in the "morgue." The reticence which McCullagh maintained so zealously during his life, has become a shroud which has buried his memory in obscurity. Even in 1925 there was little recognition of the impressive list of new ideas with which he sparked the development of the "new journalism" in the last three decades of the nineteenth century. Historians of journalism in this century tend to ignore him completely, or at most, to dismiss him with a paragraph. In view of the national recognition accorded McCullagh during his lifetime, I began to wonder why he was so quickly forgotten. This biographical study is the result of my continuing interest in the enigma of McCullagh.

Few in American journalism could do as many things so well. Horace Greeley was a noted editorial writer and a successful publisher, but he was never known as a reporter. James Gordon Bennett was an outstanding newsman, and also successful as a publisher, but he is not remembered for his editorials. The same judgment can be applied to Charles Dana. Joseph Pulitzer and William Randolph Hearst were successful publishers, but neither is remembered as a great reporter or editorial writer.

McCullagh was first of all a great reporter. He was recognized as one of the brilliant correspondents during the Civil War. He won national attention as a Washington correspondent. He was acknowledged as an influential editorial writer and as a master of the editorial paragraph he had few equals. While he was content to leave most of the duties of a publisher to others, his influence in the business office was considerable. He demonstrated the importance of liberal editorial budgets in building a newspaper. He understood how to win and hold circulation and he was a pioneering in advertising and circulation promotion.

Most of all he was a leader in the transition of American newspapers from partisan journalism to the "new journalism" with its emphasis on political independence and impartial reporting. His use of the interview as a news gathering technique, his new ideas in covering political conventions, his promotion of journalistic stunts and campaigns, and his effective use of the newspaper in community programs and reforms all were widely copied by men who later were given credit for initiating them.

It is my hope that this book will contribute to the establishment of Joseph B. McCullagh in his rightful place as one of the great editors and newsmen in American journalism. I would be remiss if I did not acknowledge with gratitude those who have encouraged and assisted me in this task. Foremost on the list to whom I am indebted is my wife, a loyal assistant and my severest critic. Dr. Howard R. Long, chairman of the Department of Journalism at Southern Illinois University, gave encouragement, support, and suggestions. Peter Liu, one of my students, both at Chengchi University in Formosa and at Southern Illinois University, served me well as my research assistant. I received valuable assistance from the staff of the Reference Department of the St. Louis Public Library, the Southern Illinois University Library, and from the staff of the Missouri Historical Society. To all of them, and to many others, I am sincerely grateful.

Charles C. Clayton

Carbondale, Ill.
December, 1968

LITTLE MACK

JOSEPH B. McCULLAGH

of
   The St. Louis *Globe-Democrat*

FROM DUBLIN TO ST. LOUIS

1

One of the fascinating facets of the character of Joseph Burbridge McCullagh is the reticence he maintained concerning his personal life. His passion for anonymity persisted even to the grave. The man Charles Dana, the brilliant editor of the old New York *Sun* described as the greatest reporter he had ever known, and who was acknowledged to be one of the outstanding editors of his time, lies in an unmarked grave in Bellefontaine Cemetery in St. Louis.

On the morning after his death, his successor as editor of the St. Louis *Globe-Democrat,* Captain Henry King, wrote only this brief tribute for the editorial page:

The editorial associates of the late Joseph B. McCullagh, managing editor of the *Globe-Democrat,* feel that they are but following his desire, if it could be known, in making announcement of his unexpected and tragic death without any formal eulogy or extended comment. He was always averse to the use of his own name in his own paper, or in any other, for that matter, and preferred to let his work speak for him. That work is well known to the public, which has been interested and profited by it. He was in the thick of events during some of the most stirring and important periods of the country's history and never failed to render timely and effective service. In a professional sense he belonged to the order of great editors. He began as a boy at the bottom of the ladder, and climbed step by step to the top. All departments and all details of a newspaper were thoroughly known to him. He was devoted to his work and allowed nothing to divert him from it. The philosophy of his career was ceaseless diligence and his diligence was directed by the kind of ability that uniformly does the right thing at the right time in the right way. He achieved marked success, in short, by legitimate means, and his death is a substantial loss to journalism and to the city in which he so long lived and labored.

Approximately two-hundred words were all the newspaper he had made one of the greatest in the nation, gave to his praise. One may speculate that had Mr. McCullagh been able to edit his eulogy, his incisive blue pencil would have reduced it to less than a stick of type.

We know he was born in Dublin, Ireland, in November 1842; the exact date remains a mystery. Presumably he gave the information in the *Encyclopedia of St. Louis History,* which states his parents were John and Sarah McCullagh, and that he was one of eight sons and eight daughters. The 1842 Dublin City Directory lists John McCullagh, shoemaker, at 4 Mary Street in St. Mary's Catholic Parish. It is believed, however, his family was Presbyterian. We know nothing of his boyhood. Probably his parents struggled to provide for their large family. What formal education he received ended by the time he was ten.

Times were hard in Ireland during that period. Three years after he was born the "potato famine" began in 1845 and resulted in the wave of Irish immigration to the United States. Young McCullagh was eleven years old when he decided to join many of his countrymen in seeking a new life in America. Undoubtedly his decision was prompted by the desire to ease the burden of his parents by leaving them one less mouth to feed, as well as by the lack of opportunity in Dublin.

Lacking money to pay for his passage, he signed on as a cabin boy on a sailing vessel and landed penniless in New York City in 1853. Whether it was by design or merely his first chance for work we can only speculate, but in any event his first employment set the course his life would take. He became an apprentice printer for the *Freeman's Journal* in New York City and learned to set type. Of the next five years little is known, but he must have learned his trade well, for when he was sixteen he came to St. Louis.

There is no inkling of how he made the journey west. Probably he came by train, but there were no bridges across the Mississippi River in 1858 and the railroad terminal was in Alton, Illinois, some twenty miles upstream. Passengers for St. Louis crossed the river by ferry. St. Louis may have seemed tame after New York City but it was a flourishing and wide open city. The census of 1860 gave it a population of 160,000. It was the "Gateway to the West," a role commemorated today on the riverfront by the Gateway Arch which soars some six-hundred feet of concrete and stainless steel. Steamboats still lined the levee and industry had begun to expand. The city could boast of nineteen flour mills and twelve iron foundries and there were numerous breweries.

Another traveler who arrived about the same time, recalled later that he was surprised to find the saloons open on Sunday and the city was proud of being known as a "wide open town." Most of the city was concentrated along the river, with Fourth Street the main thoroughfare. The best known hostelry was the Planters House on Fourth Street between Chestnut and Pine streets. Southern plantation owners and their families came there to spend the winter. It is said that Planter's Punch was the creation of its chief bartender.

But the luxury of the Planters Hotel was not for the young Irish immigrant. Soon he found a job setting type for the St. Louis *Christian Advocate*.[1] The editor and publisher was Dr. David Rice McAnally, who founded the Carondelet Methodist Church in St. Louis. Carondelet is an area in South St. Louis, inhabited then as now, predominantly by German families. Dr. McAnally launched the *Christian Advocate* in 1851, seven years before McCullagh came to St. Louis and he continued to edit it until his death in 1896. He was McCullagh's first mentor in journalism and it is interesting that when McCullagh became managing editor of the St. Louis *Globe-Democrat,* he hired Dr. McAnally's son, David R. McAnally, Jr. The son was a special writer for the *Globe-Democrat* until 1877 when he left to join the faculty of the University of Missouri at Columbia, where he served as head of the English Department from 1877 until 1885.

During this period Professor McAnally initiated and taught the first course in journalism offered at the university.[2] It was described in the university catalog as a "History of Journalism, Lectures in Journalism, with a practical explanation of daily newspaper life." In 1885, McAnally resigned from the faculty and returned to the *Globe-Democrat* as an editorial writer for McCullagh.

Employees of the *Christian Advocate* were expected to attend church and young McCullagh soon began attending a Methodist Sunday School. A pillar of the church was a man named Carlisle who became impressed by McCullagh's diligence and his intense ambition to get ahead. He arranged for an invitation for "the little Irish boy" to join a literary society. Aside from that, there could not have been much time for youthful dalliance. When William T. Harris, then superintendent of public education in St. Louis, started a school to teach shorthand at night, young McCullagh was among the first to enroll. Later, Dr. Harris recalled that "Joe attended regularly and soon he knew more about stenography than I did." [3]

McCullagh explained that he decided to learn stenography in order to be able to report sermons. His interest was to be reflected in the pride he took in the St. Louis *Globe-Democrat* reputation as "The Great Religious Daily." Well into the 1930's, long after McCullagh's death, the *Globe-Democrat* regularly ran reports on four or five sermons every Monday morning.

"Ceaseless diligence," which Captain King had written marked his career, was evident in McCullagh's youth. If there had been any temptation to squander time on less worthy pursuits, there certainly was little opportunity. Through the Carlisles he arranged to board at the home of the librarian of the Polytechnic Institute, the Rev. William E. Babcock, whose collection of books later became the foundation of the St. Louis Public Library.

It was a fortunate arrangement for the boy. The Reverend Mr. Babcock apparently encouraged McCullagh to spend what spare time he had in reading. Moreover, Mr. Babcock contributed a weekly column of book notes to the *Missouri Democrat*, and that association led to McCullagh's first job as a reporter. McCullagh had confided in Mr. Babcock his ambition to become a writer and his hope of becoming a reporter. Mr. Babcock promised to see what he could do. He spoke to Sam Slawson,[4] foreman of the composing room at the *Democrat* and urged him to find a place for "Joe," explaining that the "boy had brains and would make his mark if given a chance."

At that time the foreman of the composing room enjoyed considerably more importance than that position commands today. For many years after McCullagh became an editor, he refused to employ a night editor and insisted that the foreman was competent to handle any late emergencies in making up the paper. Slawson told Mr. Babcock that there were no openings as a printer and all he could offer the boy was a job as a proofreader.

Slawson in recounting his first meeting with McCullagh said later: "Joe came to the office, and after he had proofread one galley, I concluded that he knew more about proofreading than I did and hired him." McCullagh at that time was seventeen years old and when he reported for work at the *Democrat,* was probably the youngest of its employes. He had achieved his first goal—to work for a daily newspaper and he surely knew that the composing room offered the best opportunity to become a reporter. Almost without exception, members of the editorial staff in that period were recruited from the back shop. McCullagh applied himself to making good and waited for the chance to move into the front office.

The opportunity came much sooner than he could have expected. One of the reporters left on a vacation and George W. Fishback, the managing editor, consulted Slawson about a temporary replacement. Slawson suggested McCullagh. Fishback complained that he looked too young but agreed to give him a trial. "The first day on the new job," Slawson reported, "he filled the column and a half allocated to local news on the old blanket sheet. The second day we squeezed in two columns for him. The third day we had to cut down the size of the type to get in his copy. I never saw anyone go at it like that boy."

Such enterprise obviously impressed McKee, for when the regular reporter returned, McKee got him a job in the Water Department at the City Hall and McCullagh was made a permanent member of the staff. Early in his newspaper career, he was demonstrating the ability that prompted Dana's later accolade. Slawson's comment shows why.

Joe not only turned in lots of stuff, but it was bright, spicy and original and it increased the circulation. Before he had worked a week he was knocked down and beaten by a scalper he had written up. These scalpers operated on the levee with one-horse vehicles, offering to transport passengers and baggage to or from steamboats and overcharging those who patronized them. Joe saw one of them slap a poor woman, who had protested against the exorbitant fare demanded, and he everlastingly lambasted him in the paper the next morning. He neither used the scalper's name nor his number, but the description was so graphic that everybody recognized him.

That night when Joe McCullagh came into the office with two black eyes, he declared he would run his assailant out of town. He continued to write him up until the man came around and begged for mercy. But Joe kept his word and the scalper left St. Louis.

In 1859 the old packet boats were still the leading form of transportation and the levee in St. Louis was always crowded with steamboats and roustabouts, passengers arriving or departing, weaving their way through boxes and bales. It was the focal point for much of the life of the city and many of the items gathered by the eager young reporter originated there. It was no place for the timid and young McCullagh did not possess the physical attributes to impress the rough characters who infested the river front. There is no accurate description of him at that time, but those who knew him in adult life recall that he was short, not much more than five feet in height and stockily built. Theodore Dreiser, whom McCullagh hired in 1892, described him as "short, thick, rather pugnacious and Napoleonic, of Irish extraction." [5] One of the correspondents with General John C. Frémont described him as a "bright, belligerent, little fellow who went about cursing like a seven-foot pirate." [6]

Throughout his life McCullagh had few close friends and the reserve that characterized him in later life must have been evident in his youth. But he exhibited early the aggressive persistence that made him an outstanding reporter and there is no evidence that he was ever intimidated in an era of journalism when physical retribution was one of the hazards of a reporter.

Soon young McCullagh was getting good assignments and when the Missouri Legislature convened in Jefferson City in 1859,[7] with talk of secession in the air and the border state bitterly divided, the editor, George W. Fishback, sent him to the state capitol to cover the session. McCullagh believed in the Union cause so strongly and reported the proceedings so vigorously that Charles P. Johnson, a well known St. Louis attorney and member of the Legislature, felt it expedient to go to the *Democrat* office and suggest to Fishback that McCullagh should be recalled to St. Louis for his safety. It was reported at that time that the young reporter did not board the train at Jefferson City for his return to St. Louis, but walked to the next station east to avoid bodily harm. However, in the light of his consistent record of courage under fire, this story seems improbable.

For a reporter still in his teens, McCullagh was demonstrating the ability that later elicited praise from Dana. In 1860, shortly before his eighteenth birthday, he got his next big break. The national political campaign that was to send Abraham Lincoln to the White House, was a heated one and the *Democrat,* as well as all newspapers, were full of it. When Lyman Trumbull, United States Senator from Illinois, came to St. Louis to speak, McCullagh was assigned by Fishback to cover the meeting. Undoubtedly a factor in the editor's decision was McCullagh's shorthand, at which he had studied so assiduously.[8]

Senator Trumbull was so impressed at the accuracy of McCullagh's story as it appeared in the *Democrat,* that he wrote a letter to Fishback to express his appreciation. Later when his campaign schedule took the Senator into Ohio, and he spoke in Cincinnati, he complained to Richard Smith, then editor of the Cincinnati *Gazette,* of the many inaccuracies in the *Gazette*'s report and pointed out that the young reporter in St. Louis had done an excellent job. McCullagh and the Senator were to meet later in Washington when McCullagh was the Washington correspondent of the Cincinnati *Commercial.* Senator Trumbull was one of the few Republicans who refused to vote for the impeachment of President Andrew Johnson.

Senator Trumbull had assured Smith that he felt young McCullagh was "one of the few really good verbatim reporters in the country." William H. Seward, who had served two terms as

Governor of New York and later as the state's United States Senator, was one of the leading figures in the Republican campaign. He planned to come west for an extended speaking tour. Smith wanted McCullagh to cover that campaign swing and wrote to McCullagh, offering him what was for that time the attractive salary of $100 a month to join the staff of the *Gazette*. The *Democrat* was paying McCullagh $16 a week. McCullagh's reply was that he would accept if he could be assured that the job and the salary would be permanent. Smith informed him that he was offering a permanent job, and McCullagh went to the *Gazette*.

However, McCullagh was back in St. Louis in the spring of 1861. Fort Sumter had been fired on, and the Civil War was beginning in the West as well as in Virginia. In Missouri, General John C. Frémont had arrived to take over the command of the Union forces, with his headquarters in St. Louis. The Benton Cadets were being organized in St. Louis to serve as a bodyguard to the general. They took their name from Missouri's noted Senator of that period, Thomas H. Benton, whose daughter General Frémont had married. McCullagh decided to join the Cadets. Again his stenographic training proved helpful. He was given the rank of a second lieutenant, and assigned as stenographer on the general's staff.

Franc B. Wilkie, a war correspondent during the Civil War, gives us a picture of the young lieutenant in *Pen and Powder*. He wrote:[9]

> One day when riding out in the country with some of the Bohemian Brigade, as they were universally termed, we met a young fellow in a federal uniform and mounted on a bony horse of prodigious dimensions. The youth was slender as a rail—in fact he was not much thicker than the long sabre which dangled at his side. His shoulder straps indicated the rank of a second lieutenant, and his youthful beardless face and light hair gave him the appearance of a boy about fifteen. He was blond in complexion, with blue-gray eyes, a large flexible mouth, emaciated features, a face of enormous mobility and an utterance of extreme rapidity.
>
> His form of expression was most emphatic, being interjected at brief moments with colossal oaths, while his tone was intense be-

yond description. As I rode up to the group, I heard him pouring out a savage tirade against Frémont's plans, his dilatory movements, the influence of "Jessie," and the character of the heterogeneous mob which surrounded the commander. When he stopped to catch his breath, I was introduced to him and found that he was a stenographer with the rank of lieutenant on Frémont's staff, the representative of the Cincinnati *Enquirer,* and known as "Mack" in journalism and as "Jo" by his family and intimate friends.

He was a prophet, even in his callow days, when I first saw him on his bony steed. He asserted that the movement of Frémont to Springfield was a farce, and unhesitatingly announced that the expedition would be a humiliating failure. It took less than a fortnight to establish the truth of his predictions.

In his dual role as an aide on General Frémont's staff, and as a correspondent for the Cincinnati *Enquirer,* McCullagh met a number of the best known of the western correspondents. One was Junius Henri Browne, who had worked for the Cincinnati *Gazette* and was at that time the correspondent of the New York *Tribune.* He was later captured by the Confederates and was able to escape from a Southern prison in 1863. Others in the "Bohemian Brigade" included Richard T. Colburn of the New York *World*; George W. Beamen, representing the *Missouri Democrat*; Henri Love, who represented Frank Leslie, and Alexander Simplot, an artist who did the sketches for *Harper's Weekly.*

Wilkie, who was also a member of the "Bohemian Brigade," gives us a description of the staff on which McCullagh served. The staff, he wrote, "was a mixed polyglot, characterized by infinite variety. It was suggestive of the would-be builders of the Tower of Babel, after their speech had become confounded. The language least spoken was English. The hoarse and guttural German, the nasal French, jaw-breaking Magyar from the vicinity of the Ural regions, broken English, Spanish, Italian, Russian, and in fact more tongues than were spoken at the pentecostal gathering, were heard in and about the staff of the commander.

"There was almost as much variety in the dress of the various attachés and in their equipment. There were the regulation cavalry, which an extra supply of yellow trimmings, armed with sabres, pistols, and carbines, and a company of Lancers with hussar hats and legs bandaged to the knees in white cloth, and long poles with lance-heads and pennons, like the Uhlens of the Germans. There were still other forms of uniforms and equipment, all of which gave to the headquarters, when in motion, the appearance of a procession of a brilliant flower-garden."

General Frémont's march from St. Louis to Springfield, Missouri, fulfilled McCullagh's prediction. Long before the army reached Springfield, the enemy had left. As Wilkie put it, the entire expedition, so far as the correspondents were concerned, was without incident. The army "marched from St. Louis to Springfield, and then marched back again." The expedition, however, gave McCullagh his first experience as an editor. One of his duties was to publish a daily newspaper. General Frémont had provided a wagon to transport a press and typecases and four printers were assigned to set the type and run off the paper. It could hardly be described as a newspaper, Wilkie commented, "for it only gave the orders, passes, and the like emanating from headquarters."

The Springfield expedition was the closest McCullagh came to smelling the smoke of battle in Missouri. Back in St. Louis, General Frémont soon managed to incur the anger of President Lincoln. When the General was relieved of his command in St. Louis, McCullagh resigned his commission and returned to Cincinnati and the *Gazette,* with the hope of becoming a war correspondent.

BRILLIANT WAR CORRESPONDENT

2

McCullagh had celebrated his nineteenth birthday only two months before the Cincinnati *Gazette* sent him to Cairo, Illinois in January of 1862. His age was not unusual for a war correspondent in the Civil War. The average age of the men in the field during the Civil War was somewhere in the late twenties. At least a half dozen of those who achieved some fame during the war were nineteen or less in 1861 when the war began. More remarkable is the caliber of the competition. Many of the correspondents were college graduates. Some had had experience abroad. Richard C. McCormick and George F. Williams had been war correspondents in the 1850's, one in the Crimean War and the other in the campaign against the Mormons. Some, like Murat Halstead, later served as correspondents for American newspapers in the Franco-Prussian War. Two were later staff correspondents of the St. Louis *Globe-Democrat*.[1] One of them was Henry M. Stanley, remembered as the man who found Livingstone in Africa. The other was James Redpath, who was to become famous as the founder of the Chatauqua system.

When McCullagh reached Cairo, the city at the confluence of the Ohio and the Mississippi rivers was crowded with correspondents and troops. Earlier dispatches from St. Louis had revealed that Major General Henry W. Halleck, who had taken over as commander of the new Department of Missouri, Illinois, Wisconsin, and the western half of Kentucky, was mobilizing an army of seventy-five thousand men at Cairo to move up the

Tennessee River and strike at the heart of the Confederacy in the West. General Ulysses S. Grant was to command the army and Commodore Andrew H. Foote the thirty-eight river boats that had been assembled at Cairo.

Cairo was recognized as the strategic point and the key to the lower Mississippi Valley, but to the correspondents it had nothing to recommend it. The town was flat and subject to flooding. Its unpaved streets and unhealthy climate were a constant source of complaint. The only hotel worthy even of the name was the St. Charles, a six-story building which swarmed with military officers, civilians, and correspondents.

To oppose the Union forces the Confederates had established a line from Columbus, Kentucky, twenty-six miles below Cairo through Bowling Green to Cumberland Gap, a distance of roughly three hundred miles. The Tennessee River was guarded by Fort Henry and the other water route, the Cumberland River, by Fort Donelson. The two forts were about twelve miles apart just south of the Kentucky-Tennessee line. At the end of January General Grant received his orders from General Halleck to move up the Tennessee River and attack Fort Henry, with support from Commodore Foote, and his gunboats. On February 2, four ironclad and three wooden gunboats and a number of transports left Cairo, the spearhead of the expedition. In contrast to most of the movements of the Northern armies in the Civil War, there was no advance publicity and some of the correspondents were forced to find their own transportation to catch up with the advance units.

Years later McCullagh, writing in the St. Louis *Globe-Democrat,* explained that the secret of success in journalism was the ability to "guess where Hell will break loose next." He demonstrated this knack in the campaign against the two forts. Learning that Commodore Foote suffered from a rheumatic hand, he offered his services as a volunteer private secretary. The offer was promptly accepted and as McCullagh wrote: "Thus I obtained a berth on the flagship of the squadron—the *St. Louis.*"

Louis M. Starn in his "Bohemian Brigade" [2] provides this description of McCullagh during the bombardment of Fort Henry. It is obviously taken from McCullagh's dispatches at that time and it gives a vivid picture of the action. Starn wrote:

In the pilot house of the *St. Louis,* tough little "Mack" McCullagh of the *Gazette* squinted through the Commodore's field glasses as she closed in. Foote, nursing his rheumatism on a cot, ordered McCullagh to keep up a running commentary. The reporter had volunteered as Foote's private secretary, scarcely with this in mind. "We are getting awfully close, I can almost put my hand on the fellows at the guns." "That is right," McCullagh remembered the old man saying. "Put on a little more steam, Pilot, and get as close as you can." Shots were crashing into the *St. Louis* so rapidly that Mack lost his reporting faculty. "Jeesus," he said. Between concussions he heard the old man tut-tutting him. "Don't swear, men, it does no good." McCullagh and the pilot ducked instinctively. Foote tut-tutted again. The next instant the pilot house seemed to disintegrate, a shell crashed through the armour and exploded, smashing the wheel to match timber. The pilot, with a huge splinter protruding from his chest, looked at McCullagh with what seemed to be a wondering, questioning look, sank to the floor and died minutes later. The young reporter turned helplessly to Foote, saw that his leg was shattered, and yelled for the surgeon. Together they carried him down the ladder and along the gun deck to his cabin. The flagship drifted downstream.

McCullagh recounted his experiences in the battle for Fort Donelson in his account in the St. Louis *Globe-Democrat* in 1893 and it was reprinted by the New York *Sun* on March 5 of that year. He wrote:

I called at the Commodore's cabin late on the night of the 13th to ask if my services as an amanuensis were needed. "No," the Commodore said with much cheerfulness, "Everything is ready now. Before I go to bed I will pray for victory, which I think we shall win, or for the next best thing to victory, which is grace to bear defeat."

Everything was in readiness on the morning of February 14, and the Commodore signaled the ships to move in the order previously agreed upon, and to prepare for action. The *St. Louis* being the flagship led the procession. She carried the Commodore's pennant, and this, together with the fact that she was in front, of course made her the principal target for the batteries of the fort. I accompanied the Commodore to the pilot house where we both remained until the battle was over. As we passed along the gun deck, the Commodore, pointing to one of the few among the crew who had seen sea service, said to me, "That old man was with me in the China Seas; he is a typical salt and is full of sailor superstitions. I know he don't like this thing of going into action on Friday." Sure enough: I saw the old man in the hospital that night, nursing a wounded leg, and he insisted it was all because it was Friday. When we reached the pilot house the Commodore said it was one of his "sick headache days," and immediately threw himself on a cot, which filled one of the angles of the small apartment, directing me at the same time to stand at one of the little iron windows and report to him how we were progressing. I had a good field glass which I brought to a focus on the fort. Very soon there was a puff of white smoke from one of the batteries and I cried out, "Here she comes." She did come, too, in the shape of a cannon ball which hissed and whizzed past us in an instant. The pilots began to swear as the first shot was swiftly followed by the second, the third and the fourth. Then there was a slight pause, as if for better aim, for with the renewal of firing the balls began to strike the ship and pound against the pilot house. The pilots swore louder than ever. I thought a thousand damns but uttered none. The Commodore raised himself from his cot in remonstrance. "Tut, tut, tut, men, don't swear, it does no good," said he. Subsequently he rebuked us all for "ducking" in foolish efforts to get out of the way of approaching cannon balls. "You can't escape by ducking; you are more apt to get hit while you are doing that," said he, adding that he had seen men cut in two in the China war by ducking, who would not have been hurt standing up.

He then asked me whether the firing from our ships was damaging the fort. I told him it was doing very well; that the men in the fort were hustling around pretty lively and that our shots were throwing up the mud around the fort in big lots; but I could not tell whether any of the Confederate guns had been dismounted. All this time the *St. Louis* had been moving toward the fort at full speed. "We are getting awfully close, Commodore; through this glass I can almost put my hand on the fellows at the guns in the fort." "That's right," said the Commodore in a voice without the slightest emotion. "Put on a little more steam, Mr. Pilot, and

Joseph B. McCullagh as he appeared at the height of his career. This photograph hangs on the wall of the present editor of the editorial page of the Globe-Democrat. *It is the only photograph of McCullagh that remains. Reproduced with the permission of the* Globe-Democrat.

The birthplace of the Missouri Democrat *at 118 North Third Street in St. Louis. It was in this building that McCullagh began his newspaper career as a reader in 1859. From the files of the* Globe-Democrat.

"The Temple of Truth" at Sixth and Pine Streets as it appeared during McCullagh's later years. McCullagh's office was located on the sixth floor. From the files of the Globe-Democrat, *reproduced by permission.*

Globe-Democrat

St. Louis, March 12 1886

Dear Sir

Your service has been in general so efficient that I do not like to complain of special matters. But you sometimes expend a little too much as in the matter of the Hyde papers, which I have just revised, and the matter of the Dumont Conference which I had to kill on account of its length. Please state facts and avoid elaboration, as much as possible.

Yrs
J B McCullagh

Globe-Democrat

St. Louis, Nov 20 1887

Dear Sir

Just after you left I thought of a good subject for a series of Washington illustrated letters — some of the unpublished features of the Smithsonian Institute. The thing has been written up and pictures of the building are familiar, but I think there is good matter that is new for illustration & description. Then a letter or a series of letters on Oddities of the Patent Office — old & new patents etc. This is only a suggestion.

Yrs
J B McCullagh

Globe-Democrat

St. Louis, Jany 5 1888

Dear Sir

Do not forget Congressional Summary every Tuesday night. I think a thousand words will do.

J B McCullagh

Your work is very good. Sunday Post Dispatch is a great failure.

JBMcC

W B Stevens

These notes in McCullagh's handwriting to his Washington correspondent, Walter B. Stevens, are self-explanatory. The original notes are in the Missouri Historical Society and are reproduced with the society's permission.

Daniel M. Houser, watchdog of the business office of the Globe-Democrat, *who paid the bills for McCullagh's extensive wire coverage. This photograph, now in the Reference Department of the* Globe-Democrat, *is reproduced with the permission of that newspaper.*

get as close as you can." As between the fort and the fleet it was now a mighty hot fight. Shots were striking the vessel and the pilot house at the rate of several a minute. When they struck us squarely on the armored bow, between the two great gun ports, the vessel reeled and trembled from stem to stern; it was like a man struck on the forehead with a heavy fist. From within the pilot house we could hear the great iron balls imbedding themselves in the armor with a thump and a thud, as though knocking for admission and determined soon to gain it. The Commodore, still lying on his cot, unable to see what was going on ahead, as the two little windows were occupied, one by the pilot and the other by myself, as the Commodore's lookout, kept asking for more steam, and was only half satisfied when told from below that the ship could not carry another pound of steam without danger of explosion. "Get right under the fort; that's the way to fight," said the Commodore, with his hand on his forehead, still nursing the headache, but now standing up instead of reclining on his cot as heretofore. We were now within 200 yards of the fort and the air was full of the iron hail of all the guns on both sides. One could almost see the big projectiles as they crossed each other's path going in opposite directions. The men in the fort were being rapidly driven from their guns; but they had good refuge in bomb-proof embankments and they rallied easily and speedily. What had been long feared and expected came at last. A shell from the best and largest rifled gun in the fort—a gun that had been trained on our pilot house since the opening of the battle—struck our armor plating at right angles, and came crashing through the iron and oak as though a piece of pasteboard. It must have exploded either on coming through or immediately on entering the pilot house; at any rate we picked up a whole bushel of iron fragments from the floor of the pilot house that night. The pilot who was at the wheel at the time, a brave fellow named Reilly from Cincinnati, was struck on the thigh and bled to death in an hour. The Commodore was badly and painfully wounded on the leg, and went on crutches during the remainder of his life; three others were hurt in various ways. I was the only one of the six who entirely escaped. The steering wheel was battered into match timber and all the apparatus for controlling the vessel was utterly destroyed. Everything was in chaos inside our shattered citadel, but the Commodore, sorely wounded though he was, had sufficient presence of mind to order the steam shut off, as the vessel was still moving toward the fort without pilot or rudder, and the fort was playing upon her with terrible effect. What saved us all from death or capture was the fact that we were fighting upstream, and when disabled we soon drifted out of range. The other vessels of the fleet were all badly damaged but none so badly as the *St. Louis*. The Commodore lost neither courage nor temper on account of his wound. I summoned the surgeon to his aid but he would receive no assistance until the others had been served. We carried him down the ladder and along the gun deck to his cabin; but he was cool, watchful, courageous and observant, and did not retire until he knew that his injured vessel was safely moored to the shore beyond the reach of the Confederate guns. "God's will be done; it is only a temporary setback," said he, as we laid him on his cabin lounge. And so ended the gunboat battle of Fort Donelson after an hour and a half of terrible cannonading, with a loss of 25 per cent of those engaged in it on the Union side. At the wardroom mess table on the *St. Louis*—of which I had been courteously made a guest—consisting of commissioned officers below the rank of captain, there were ten for breakfast on the morning of the 14th and only six for supper that night. The fight received little attention at that time because it was overshadowed by General Grant's victory and Buckner's surrender two days later. And if I had a chance to choose for a future experience between two hours on the hottest battlefield of the war and ten minutes in that pilot house, I would pick the battlefield for comfort.

After fighting furiously for more than an hour, the river fleet withdrew. Most of the gunboats were seriously crippled. The *St. Louis* bore the scars of fifty-seven hits and the pilot wheel had been shot away. The army then took over and by February 15 Fort Donelson surrendered with some fifteen-thousand troops, forty pieces of artillery and a substantial quantity of military stores. It was an important victory at a time when the war was going badly in the East. Joe McCullagh had had a ringside seat and had begun to establish his reputation as one of the great correspondents of the Civil War.

The morning after the surrender the gunboat *Carondelet*, the first of Commodore Foote's boats to reach Cairo, brought news of the victory. Cairo was the nearest telegraph office to Fort Donelson and that morning the news began ticking off the wires. In the office of the Cincinnati *Gazette*, and in other newspaper offices in the Middle West, arrangements were hastily made to send more correspondents to General Grant's army. Whitelaw Reid was told to take the first train to Cairo. He was ordered to take charge of the paper's correspondents and assign them their duties. The March 15 issue of the *Gazette* reported that the newspaper had five correspondents in and around Nashville, three with General Don Carlos Buell's divisions and two at large. One of them was McCullagh.

Reid was undoubtedly one of the best known correspondents of the war. In June of 1862 the *Gazette* sent him to Washington as its capital correspondent. The St. Louis *Democrat* offered him the editorship at a salary considerably higher than his salary for the *Gazette*. Richard Smith, owner of the *Gazette*, met the offer with a one-twelfth interest in the paper, which could be paid for from dividends from the stock. Reid agreed to stay and supplemented his income by serving as a Washington correspondent for a group of papers, including the Chicago *Tribune,* the New York *Times,* the *Missouri Democrat* and the Cleveland *Leader*.

McCullagh's association with Reid on the *Gazette* lasted less than two months. Both men were with Grant at Pittsburg Landing, about nine miles south of Savannah, Tennessee when General Albert Sidney Johnston led his Confederate army in an attack on Grant on the morning of April 6. The battle that followed, referred to by the South as the Battle of Pittsburg Landing and by the North as the Battle of Shiloh, was a bloody fight, and it evoked as much controversy as any engagement of the war. The conflicting accounts of the correspondents contributed to the subsequent debate. Some of the self-styled eyewitness reports came from correspondents who never got any closer to the fighting than Cairo. The phrase "Cairo war correspondent" current at the time had an obvious unflattering connotation.

One result of the controversy was a new job for McCullagh. The story is told by Walter B. Stevens in his series of articles on McCullagh in the *Missouri Historical Review* in January 1931. McCullagh was shocked with what he had seen of some of the Northern officers. He wrote a letter to the *Gazette,* setting out his observation of drunkenness and mismanagement. Before sending it, he showed the letter to one of his colleagues on the *Gazette,* who informed him that the *Gazette* would never print the letter as it stood. McCullagh replied that if the letter was not printed he would resign—and he carried out his threat.

William P. Fishback, who had been associated with his brother, George W. Fishback on the *Missouri Democrat* before moving to Indianapolis, Indiana where he was dean of the Indianapolis University Law School at the time of McCullagh's death, offered a different version of McCullagh's falling out with the *Gazette.* As quoted in the Chicago *Tribune*'s full-page obituary of McCullagh (Jan. 1, 1897), he explained it this way:

> Whitelaw Reid, under the name of Agate, was the war correspondent of the *Gazette,* and McCullagh as a subordinate correspondent was directed to report to Reid. All that McCullagh wrote came under Reid's hand and was published over the name of Agate, and thus Reid got the credit of whatever McCullagh did. Joe was the only war correspondent who had the sand to go upon a gunboat during the attack on Fort Donelson. The enemy's missiles tore through the gunboats and the fight was a terrific one. Joe was in the thickest of it, and when he came ashore he did not try to find Reid, but wrote his own account and signing it "Mack" sent it to the *Gazette*. Reid was furious and told Richard Smith of the *Gazette* that it had been understood that his subordinate was to report to him. Thereupon McCullagh wrote to Murat Halstead of the Cincinnati *Commercial,* asking him if he wanted a war correspondent. Halstead, recognizing Mack's enterprise and ability, immediately engaged him for the *Commercial.*

Since Reid did not go to Cairo until after the capture of Fort Donelson, Fishback's version must be discounted, although it may be assumed that relations between Reid and McCullagh at that time were not too cordial. Later, when the *Commercial* sent McCullagh to Washington, the two men were again rivals.

McCullagh's independence, however, got him a raise in salary. No sooner had Murat Halstead, editor of the Cincinnati

BRILLIANT WAR CORRESPONDENT

Commercial, heard of McCullagh's resignation, than he offered to double the *Gazette*'s salary, if McCullagh would join the *Commercial*'s staff. Moreover, Halstead stipulated that McCullagh would be free to write what he chose as long as he worked for the *Commercial.*

One story, which appeared in the *Commercial* on May 16, 1862 showed McCullagh's ingenuity. While attempting to pass through General Buell's lines near Corinth, Mississippi, he was halted by a sentry, who was obviously a recent recruit. McCullagh was carrying a pass signed by General Grant, but he was fully aware that it would not be recognized by the irascible General Buell. He was quick to see a way out of his predicament when the sentry asked if he was a commissioned officer. "Don't you know that none but commissioned officers are allowed to ride gray horses?" he demanded. When the awed sentry admitted he was not aware of that fact, McCullagh rode on without protest.

If General Buell's opinion of the correspondents was not flattering, they in turn were not impressed by the General. Later in a dispatch to the *Commercial,* McCullagh described him this way:

> His dress was that of a Brigadier instead of a Major General. He wore a shabby straw hat, dusty coat and had neither belt, sash or sword about him. A majority of the field officers, behind and before him, looked more consequential and dignified than he. Though accompanied by his staff, he was not engaged in conversation with any of them, but rode silently and slowly along, noticing nothing that transpired around him . . . Buell is certainly the most reserved, distant and unsociable of all the Generals in the army. He never has a word of cheer for his men or his officers; and in turn his subordinates care little for him save to obey his orders, as machinery works in response to the bidding of the mechanic. There is in McClellan and Frémont an unaccountable something that keeps this machinery constantly oiled and easy-running; but Buell's unsympathetic nature makes it "squeak" like the drag wheels of a wagon.

One of the problems of correspondents in the Civil War was that they had no official status and were frequently considered to be combatants if captured. McCullagh was faced with this problem in late August, 1862 while still covering General Buell's forces. Near the little town of Richmond, Kentucky, Confederate General E. Kirby Smith, with twelve-thousand men encountered two brigades of inexperienced Northern troops and put them to rout. Among the prisoners caught in the Confederate pursuit were McCullagh and a correspondent for the *Gazette,* who wrote under the name of Telmah. As reported later in the *Gazette,* the two men were riding on an artillery wagon with the retreating Union column when they heard the order, "Cavalry to the front." McCullagh sensed the order should also have included "all others to the rear." The two reporters decided discretion was the better part of valor, leaped from the wagon and began running across a field. The only place of concealment was several large haystacks and the correspondents took refuge behind them.

When the Confederates approached, they heard some one say, "Take down that fence and fire a few rounds into that haystack." Several shots thudded into the haystack and the two correspondents came out from behind it and surrendered. Three cavalrymen rode up and ordered the two men to accompany them. McCullagh asked if it was their habit to arrest noncombatants. The reply was, "We'll arrest everyone we catch with this god damn crowd." With several Union soldiers who had also been captured, the correspondents were marched at the double back toward Richmond. Told they would camp there for the night, one of the soldiers asked McCullagh if he had a watch. McCullagh pulled out his watch and replied that it was half past five. But that was not what his interrogator had in mind. "Give me the watch," he ordered.

McCullagh, who always seemed remarkably brash in dealing with bullies, replied: "It ain't in arms against the Confederacy, what do you want it for?"

"To keep—what the hell do you think? You are a prisoner and we will take every damn thing you've got."

"Why I thought you were a soldier when I surrendered," was McCullagh's retort.

"What the devil do I look like?" the man replied.

"I only meant I thought I surrendered to a soldier, and not

to a highwayman," McCullagh said with more courage than prudence. He was saved from any possible violence as just then an officer rode up and asked what was going on. When McCullagh explained, the officer denounced the guard as an "infernal thief" and the watch was restored to McCullagh.

The following day the two correspondents were taken to General Smith's headquarters and told they would be released if they would be willing to be paroled as prisoners of war. Protests by McCullagh that they were unarmed and therefore could not be treated as prisoners of war, were to no avail. The officer interviewing them replied that they were "more than in arms against the South and in fact were continually publishing news that gave aid and comfort to the North." The correspondents, realizing that they had no choice, signed their paroles and started out on foot for the eighty-mile walk to Cincinnati.

A few weeks later McCullagh was back in the field for the *Commercial*. If it was true that the North received "aid and comfort" from the correspondents, the same complaint was frequently lodged against them by Northern generals. Fishback told the Chicago *Tribune*: "At that time the rebels were getting Northern newspapers and from these papers they learned much of the movements of our armies. Mack stood in with the generals and his accounts of what was going on frequently made very interesting reading to the Confederates. On one occasion a council of war was held, presided over by General Sherman. Mack, who had posted himself outside the tent in which the council was held, gave the result of his eavesdropping in his next letter. Sherman was exceedingly angry and for a time hesitated as to whether he would put Mack in the trenches or have him shot."

However, with a few exceptions McCullagh seemed to maintain friendly relations with most of the Northern generals. Only once did he receive a rebuke from General Grant. That rebuke was recalled later by McCullagh in the *Globe-Democrat*.[3] It came shortly after the capture of Holly Springs by the South. He wrote:

The only rebuke I ever received from General Grant for matters written by me from his army—covering the year and a half from

Donelson to the surrender of Vicksburg—was on account of the Holly Springs episode. A week or ten days after the Van Dorn raid I was in Memphis, and there met Colonel Murphy who had surrendered the post. Out of a long conversation with him at the Gayoso House I made a letter to the *Commercial,* showing from his official reports that a very large percentage of his men were unavailable for defense because detailed under orders from his superiors for duty in hauling and guarding cotton. Murphy contended that he could have successfully resisted Van Dorn if his little army had not been depleted by the exigencies of cotton speculating. I published the official figures showing the number of men composing the garrison and the number of those that were on cotton duty. The ratio of the latter to the former was very large. I attempted no justification of Murphy's surrender, but thought he was entitled to the publication of his side of the case. The name of General Grant's father appeared prominently in the list of cotton speculators for whose service the soldiers had been used. The old gentleman dearly loved a dollar and had allowed some business men of Cincinnati, for a consideration in the form of a commission or percentage, to make use of his name for the purpose of obtaining special permits and privileges for buying cotton within the lines. General Grant was incensed at the contents of my letter, and when I saw him, six or eight weeks later, he asked me if I was the author of it. I replied in the affirmative, and he asked where I got my information. I answered that all the information as to the disposition of the troops on the day of the battle—the number of soldiers who were hauling cotton, for whom they were hauling it, and by whose order they were thus assigned —were from Colonel Murphy's official reports. "Didn't you know that Murphy was a traitor—that he had proved a traitor at Iuka?" said the General. My answer was very respectful, but to the effect that I did not suppose a man who had proved himself a traitor to a former trust would have been selected as commander of a post like Holly Springs. Murphy had evacuated Iuka on the approach of a much superior force under General Sterling Price and had been censured by General Rosecrans for so doing. In his "Memoirs," General Grant treats briefly of the matter and concludes by saying that Murphy was either a traitor or a coward. The chances are that he was neither, but that he was simply incompetent—a man unfitted to command and born only to obey. The whole matter of cotton speculation at Holly Springs was afterward reviewed in a law suit over some of the profits before Judge Bellamy Storer of Cincinnati, and that eminent jurist, in rendering his opinion, stated facts and made strictures, which, if attempted by me, would have sent me to the Dry Tortugas. It is proper to state that the cotton permits to the General's father and others were issued by division commanders without the knowledge of Grant, who promptly put a stop to the whole business when he heard of it. The famous order expelling the Jews from the army lines after the Holly Springs raid, on account of the inducements which their cotton accumulations had offered to Van Dorn, was undoubtedly dictated from Washington, although it was afterwards very promptly revoked from the same place.

Holly Springs, with a large store of supplies, fell shortly before Christmas, 1862. It was a setback for General Grant, but McCullagh called it "a smile for Grant behind the frown of fortune," for it showed Grant the right way to get to Vicksburg.[4] McCullagh wrote:

On the part of the Confederates it was one of the most successful movements of the kind in the whole rebellion, eclipsing the most daring deeds of Forrest who had been considered the master of that branch of warfare. The capture and parole of that garrison of more than 1,500 men, under Col. Murphy, of the 8th Wisconsin, was a small part of the achievement, compared with the destruction of many millions' worth of military and medical supplies stored there for the use of the Federal army, and the bonfire of all the cotton that had been gathering there for months, awaiting shipment to the North. Holly Springs was the secondary base for Grant's army, the primary base being Memphis from which it was distant forty-five miles by railroad. The smile of fortune came to Grant in the demonstration that he was on the wrong road to Vicksburg, for which point he had started from Jackson, Tenn., on November 2. In gaining a victory for himself, Van Dorn taught a lesson to his adversary which vastly more than compensated for the injury he inflicted. Up to this time, Grant, as is apparent from his "Memoirs", had been conducting a campaign under orders from Washington which directed him to move through the interior of Mississippi to Jackson. He was then at Oxford, and had 150 miles of movement ahead of him, and sixty miles behind him to Memphis. The Holly Springs raid convinced him that he could not maintain a railroad line 210 miles long—from Memphis to Jackson, Miss.—without depleting his army to such an extent that when he got to Jackson he would have no fighting force worthy of the name. At Washington about that time they concluded to take down the fingerboard with which they had been directing military operations 1,000 miles distant, and to let Grant make his own way to victory in the Southwest. The result was the new departure which stamped Grant as a really great commander.

Much is said by adverse critics about Grant as a man of luck rather than of genius as though luck and genius, as applied to war, were both convertible terms, and both mere synonyms of success. It is undoubtedly true that Grant's military pathway was brightened and lightened by a great many streaks of good fortune; but it may be doubted if any of them equalled the Holly Springs raid, which, however, was a piece of luck only when supplemented by Grant's good sense to turn misfortune into instruction.

McCullagh's adventure in the role of a spy had no connection with Holly Springs, except that it came shortly thereafter. General Hatch had obtained a leave of absence and started from Oxford, Mississippi, to go to Memphis with a small cavalry escort. McCullagh recalled it this way:[5]

I concluded to make one of this party and was on hand at the start. Among the civilians with us I well remember the venerable ex-Governor Wood, of Quincy, Ill. He had been doing a little cotton trading—had, I think, been one of the victims of Van Dorn's bonfires, and was anxious to get home. We started bright and early one fine morning, with a ride of sixty miles before us. Reports of headquarters said there was no enemy on the road between Oxford and Memphis. This proved to be almost true but not quite. Before we had gone many miles we could see mounted men crossing the road ahead of us, and sometimes behind us in twos and threes. They would dash out of the woods on one side of the road and disappear in the woods on the other side. They showed no disposition to fight or in any way to challenge our progress. And yet their movements looked ominous and made some of our party quite nervous. They might, for aught we knew, be fragments of a considerable force concealed somewhere in the vicinity, and liable to entertain us at some chosen point with an ambuscade or an open attack. As I was quite as unwilling as any of the others in the party to be killed or captured that day, I asked General Hatch what he proposed to do about it. The general was not much alarmed, yet I could see that he would be gratified by a little definite information as to the strength and intentions of the enemy. After a while I asked him how it would do for me to pass myself off, at some farm house at which we would stop for dinner, as a Confederate prisoner, and while so doing see if I could not find out from the family how many of these troopers were on the road and what they were going to do. The suggestion was at once approved, and I proceeded to enforce it by unbuckling from my saddle bow a Confederate jacket which I had captured on the Tupelo expedition. As we rode along, I removed my coat and donned the article of apparel. It was a small size, so was I— "Not an eagle's talon in the waist." It fitted me well and gave me an appearance well suited to the character I was to assume—that of a youth suspected of being a guerrilla, and on his way to Memphis to be tried for his life for violating the laws of war. My plea, on the other hand, was to be that I was in the regular service of the Confederacy when captured, and was entitled to treatment as a prisoner of war. It was necessary for me to be accused of a capital offense in order to account for my removal to Memphis for trial.

A splendid farm house loomed up in the near distance just as General Hatch, ex-Gov. Wood and myself had arranged a few preliminary details. The escort halted on the roadside and prepared to give themselves and their horses the rations they carried, while four or five officers and citizens of our company dismounted and walked through a fine lawn to the door of the mansion. A lady of middle age and of fine appearance responded to their call. General Hatch acted as spokesman. He said they had been riding since early morning, and would like a dinner, for which they would pay liberally "in good Yankee money." The response was a very courteous smile and invitation to walk in; she would get dinner ready in about half an hour; she had nothing very fine to offer but she would do the best she could. As we entered the parlor I stood in front of General Hatch—careful to be within hearing distance of the landlady—and said, having first given the regulation army salute. "General can I have the parole of the grounds while we are here?" pointing to the fences which surrounded the house. "Yes," he said, "you can go as far as the fences, but not beyond them, and you must be ready to start at a moment's notice after dinner. By the way, I suppose I will have to pay for your dinner too, although I am only allowed so much a mile for taking you to Memphis as a prisoner." The hostess drank in every word of this information, and as it proceeded, her eyes turned toward me with an expression that was full of kindness and favor. A moment later she left her guests in the front parlor and retired to the back parlor, and as she closed the door between the two, she beckoned me to come to her, which I promptly did. "Oh," said she, "I'd know you were not one of those horrid Yankees, even if you didn't have that uniform on. They needn't give themselves any trouble about paying for your dinner. You'll take dinner with the family right here—myself and my two little girls; my husband and my three boys—well they're where every Southern man should be until the Yankees are whipped." She called one of her daughters into the room and asked her to play on the piano for the little Confederate, and in an instant the "Bonnie Blue Flag" was in process of very creditable elucidation. Then she inquired as to my nativity and the details of my capture. My story was a short one—that I was a native of South Carolina, had enlisted in a Missouri regiment, and had been captured while on scouting service near Corinth. My reason for belonging to a Missouri regiment was that I knew the names of several of the Camp Jackson boys with whom I attended Centenary Sunday School just before the war, and this knowledge might come handy on cross-examination. My hostess went into raptures over my South Carolina birth, because it was an honor I shared with herself.

Time was passing, and I had made no progress on the work of my mission, which was to ascertain the chances of our little band being captured by the enemy. "Madam," I said in a whisper, "How many of our men are there on the road between here and Memphis?" "About twenty in all," said she. "They are scattered along the road. I fed ten of them this morning, and I expect to get supper for ten of them this evening." I accompanied the good

BRILLIANT WAR CORRESPONDENT 27

lady, at her request, to what were the negro quarters before the Yankees, as she alleged, carried off all her negroes. The quarters were fitted up like garrison rooms. In the center of each room was a neat table, and the shelves all around were filled with dining were in tin under the highest state of polish. "This is where my boarders come for their meals," said the madam smiling. While engaged in this survey, a little girl about thirteen rang the dinner bell and four of us—the landlady, her two daughters and myself —were soon seated at an excellent family dinner. The "Yankees" in the outer room had first been served with a meal from which the trimmings, which graced our table were entirely missing. The hostess and myself talked freely while we dined. She repeated that there were about twenty of "the boys" as she called them— meaning the Confederate cavalry—between her house and Memphis; they were widely scattered though. As to their armament, she said in answer to a question, that it was not good—some had rifles strapped on their shoulders and others had pistols which were not very effective. "What kind of guns have these Yankees got?" she said alluding to the troopers who were resting on the roadside. I assured her they were splendidly armed with the best of carbines and pistols, and were picked men and picked horses. "Well," she said, "it doesn't make any difference. Our boys are not going to attack them; it would be too risky, and there wouldn't be anything gained even if they defeated them. Besides, it would take a whole day to get them together, and on the way to Memphis you won't see more than three or four of them in a bunch." In a few moments I was let into the secret of the whole matter. "The boys" as the lady affectionately termed the Confederate cavalrymen, were on the lookout for provision trains for Grant's army, which had to be hauled from Memphis to Oxford by wagons in consequence of the destruction of the railroad at Holly Springs. They had information that a big wagon train would start from Memphis tomorrow night, and they were going to make a dash for the capture at some point to be agreed upon. While we were discussing this topic a knock at the door of our dining room reminded me that time was up, and that my excellent friend and I must part. She accompanied me to the door and, facing General Hatch, asked him very tenderly if he really intended to hang me. The General couldn't tell exactly what would happen; that I would certainly be hanged if proved to be a guerrilla. As I said "Goodby," the kind-hearted hostess gave me a motherly embrace and almost cried as she said: "Well, if you have to die, die like a South Carolinian."

There was one part of my experience as a spy that I did not relate to General Hatch because I feared he would interfere to prevent its execution. I told him exactly what I had heard at the dinner table, that our party was perfectly safe, but that to-morrow night's wagon train was doomed. He said he would fool "the boys" by asking for a double guard for the wagon train as soon as he got to Memphis. I was anxious to see the Confederate scheme foiled by an increased guard, but it did not seem right to allow the sons and friends of my informant to be sacrificed by death or capture in consequence of my betrayal of a secret confided in me. If the handful of Confederates scattered along the road from Memphis to Oxford should attack a heavily guarded train, supposing it to be lightly guarded, they would surely get the worst of it. So I concluded to send them advice to let the train alone. This was not easily done, but it was done. Among other secrets revealed to me at the farm house was the address of a family in Memphis, between whom and my hostess constant communication was kept up. It was from this source that the information about the wagon train had been derived. I concluded to call on these people, make up a plausible story for excuse, and send word to "the boys" not to meddle with the train. I got one of the troopers of our company to go with me to the door of the house so as to enable me to continue the appearance of a prisoner. The bell was answered by a middle-aged lady of fine appearance, with whom I was soon on terms of conversational intimacy. I told her I was a prisoner captured near Oxford, and that I had obtained permission to visit her house under guard to call on a family friend. She was quite as well posted as I expected her to be on the subject of the wagon trains; she had a friend at headquarters through whom she learned everything that was going on, and she sent all important information to "the boys" by relays of couriers over unfrequented bridle-paths. "Well," said I, "I have come to tell you something that the boys should know. On my way to Memphis today I overheard the Yankee officers say that they had sent word to increase the train guard very much, to put three or four trains into one, and to send fifty or sixty cavalry and a hundred infantry with it. If that is done the boys along the road will have no hope to make anything by attack, and the chances are they all will be killed or captured if they try it on. So I think you had better send word to them to keep out of the way and let the train pass unmolested." My advice was immediately acted upon. A horse was soon saddled and mounted and word was sent to the first station of the boys (distant about five miles from Memphis) whence it was taken from place to place along the line, to let the wagon train go on its way. While I remained in Memphis, I heard of its unvexed arrival at Oxford.

Memphis had fallen to General Grant's forces in June 1862, leaving only two barriers to the control of the Mississippi River, Port Hudson, Louisiana, and Vicksburg, Mississippi, which the newspapers referred to as the "Gibraltar of the West."

In February 1863 McCullagh, and two other correspondents, Finley Anderson of the New York *Herald* and Albert H. Bodman of the Chicago *Tribune*, boarded the gunboat-ram, *Queen of the West*.[6] Admiral David D. Porter, who had been ordered to command the Navy's new Mississippi Squadron, decided to attempt to run some of his boats past the Vicksburg batteries. The *Queen of the West* was to proceed them up the Red River to see what was there. The *Queen of the West* was a small vessel, armoured only at the prow and carried a crew of about thirty men. For a full hour the boat twisted its way through a heavy bombardment from the Confederate batteries on shore and then sighted a Confederate gunboat lying in the river. The *Queen of the West* rammed it with such force that the *Queen* for a time was unable to withdraw and threatened to capsize. Then it backed away and soon was out of range of the shore batteries. The boat had been hit twelve times, but no one was wounded. The *Queen*, escorted by the tender *De Soto* then continued on its way downstream, past Natchez and up the Red River.

Late on February 14 when about seventy miles from the mouth of the Red River, the *Queen* was approaching Gordon's Landing when a Confederate battery was sighted. Before the battery could be engaged, the *Queen* ran aground and was unable to back off. Unable to bring its broadside guns to bear on the little fort, some five hundred yards distant, the boat was soon put out of commission when a shell penetrated the boiler and filled the boat with scalding steam. McCullagh leaped into the river, landed on a bale of cotton and reached the *De Soto*. With the Confederate gunboat *Webb* in hot pursuit, the survivors of the expedition fled back down the river on the river packet *Era,* which had been captured on the way upstream. Shortly after entering the Mississippi the Federal gunboat *Indianola* put the *Webb* to flight and McCullagh continued up the river on the *Era* to land safely on the west bank of the Mississippi at Vicksburg on February 22. In March, 1863 General Grant in an attempt to gain a beachhead on the east bank of the Mississippi, ordered his men to dig a canal across the peninsula formed by a bend in the river just west of Vicksburg.

McCullagh reported to the *Commercial* in the typical news style of that period: a combination of fact and personal interpretation, as follows:

The Vicksburg canal seems to afford an inexhaustible theme for newspaper letter writers. And there is this singular fact connected with it, that the farther north you go, the more favorable is its condition and prospect. For instance, down here the impression is that it is a decided failure (and I claim at least the credit of having been consistent in pronouncing it a failure from the first, and adhering to that opinion ever since); at Memphis it is always progressing slowly but surely; at Cairo the sensation men usually have it "doing well when last heard from"; but at Chicago and St. Louis there is no middle ground—it is always a splendid success.

McCullagh's prediction was right. Six weeks after the canal was started the river rose and swept away the dam and the project was abandoned. Grant then decided to move south and capture Port Hudson before renewing the attempt to take Vicksburg. Learning that Confederate General Joe Johnston was on his way to Jackson, Mississippi to take charge of the defense of Vicksburg, Grant swung his army northeast and routed the enemy at Raymond and then pushed on to Jackson on May 15. McCullagh reported both actions and two weeks later, his account of the battle at Champion Hill is described in J. Cutler

Andrews' "The North Reports the Civil War," [7] as "one of the best accounts" of that battle.

McCullagh wrote:

> We (the Mule and I) were traveling toward the left, in the immediate rear of Hovey's division, then fighting desperately for the ground on which it stood. Pretty soon Hovey had to fall back. I tried to indicate to my long-eared steed that I wished to do the same, but he evidenced a stubborn disposition to advance instead of retreat. I pulled one rein and then the other, but the mule wouldn't stir. I spurred the animal, but it only made him kick, and I was obliged to desist in prospect of being left on the roadside. The rebels were advancing—were already within rifle range—and the bullets were whistling in pursuit of our men, not of me, I thought, for they surely would not hit a non-combatant. And still the mule wouldn't turn back . . . if I had had a rat tail file, I should have spiked and abandoned him. He then commenced an unearthly bawl, which I interpreted as my funeral dirge, which would undoubtedly have proven so had I not dismounted and led him to the rear, arriving there just in time to save myself. I have studiously avoided mules ever since, and intend to do so for three years, or during the war.

This sample from his dispatch, which appeared in the *Commercial* on June 1, is indicative of the first person reporting of the war. If McCullagh seemed to be dramatizing himself, he was only following the generally accepted practice of the time. In World War II Ernie Pyle revived this intimate style with great success. Summing up the coverage of the siege of Vicksburg, Mr. Andrews observed: "Probably the best reporting was done by men like Wilkie (Franc B. Wilkie of the New York *Times*) and McCullagh, who had won distinction in earlier campaigns and continued to turn out superior writing."

In September McCullagh was on his way to Chattanooga, Tennessee. By this time he had made an arrangement with the New York *Tribune* to contribute letters to that newspaper at $5.00 a column, in addition to his work for the *Commercial*.[8] Following the Northern defeat at Chickamauga, northern newspapers sent more men to cover the Army of the Cumberland,

and McCullagh was among the first to reach the headquarters at Chattanooga. He told of his experiences enroute in a series of letters to the *Commercial,* which appeared in that paper on October 5 and 7. At Nashville, he wrote, no one seemed to have a clear idea of what was happening and after two days he boarded a Nashville and Chattanooga train, which took him to Stevenson. From there he wangled a ride with a wagon train with some members of the United States Christian Commission, a welfare group. He was forced to travel the last thirty miles on foot over the mountains, arriving in Chattanooga exhausted, on the morning of September 30. He found a distinct atmosphere of hostility from the military. There was the feeling that the correspondents had misrepresented the facts in reporting the battle at Chickamauga. For a time telegraphic communication from the city was intermittent, and when it was restored, military priorities prevented its use by correspondents. With little to report, correspondents tried to interview deserters from the Southern forces but rarely were permitted to talk to them. Digests of articles in Confederate newspapers smuggled through the lines could be the basis of a story. McCullagh in one of his occasional letters to the New York *Tribune,* published on October 29, told of one of his own experiences in attempting to obtain a rebel paper. He worked his way close to the Southern picket line and was waving a copy of the *Commercial* to attract attention when a Confederate officer stepped from behind a tree some three hundred yards away and demanded to know whether McCullagh was waving a newspaper or a flag of truce. When McCullagh explained it was a newspaper and he would like to exchange it for a Southern paper, the officer replied: "We don't want your damned papers. They're a pack of lies and if you don't get back I'll shoot." McCullagh admitted that he beat a hasty retreat.

McCullagh became one of the victims of the Army's crackdown on correspondents, who were charged with revealing the movement of reinforcements for the Army of the Cumberland. He was ordered banished to Nashville the last week of October after a dispatch published in the *Commercial* on October 16 had reported the arrival of General Joseph Hooker's troops at Bridgeport. The dispatch speculated that the reinforcements might be used in a flanking movement to force the evacuation of Lookout

Mountain. In a story in the *Commercial* on November 4, he wrote that "if there was a man, North or South, who had not known of Hooker's arrival two weeks before I published it, he is in great danger of voting for General Jackson for next President."

McCullagh's banishment from the Army of the Cumberland marked the end of his career as a war correspondent. In a little less than two years with the Union forces in the West, he made the byline "Mack" nationally known. He had won the respect, and sometimes the ire, of the military. George P. Upton, who had been a friendly competitor at Cairo and who had worked with him in the battles in the spring of 1862, when they frequently shared a room, was a member of the editorial staff of the Chicago *Tribune* at the time of McCullagh's death.

In an interview which was included in the obituary of McCullagh in the *Tribune*,[9] he said:

Mr. McCullagh was one of the best correspondents developed by the war. He was alert, active, and had a marvellously thorough knowledge of military maneuvers. He was a genial character, a great joker, and a good storyteller. He was a thorough Bohemian, but an instinctive newspaperman long before his training in the profession. Among all the war correspondents—and I know a great many of them—I never knew one who could so quickly grasp a military situation. He had the whole thing in his head all the time and could draw a diagram of the situation at any time.

In the fall of 1863 McCullagh returned to Cincinnati and was promptly assigned to Washington as the *Commercial's* correspondent in the nation's capital. However, some of McCullagh's best writing about the war did not appear until twenty years later in his recollections published in the St. Louis *Globe-Democrat*.

Of General Grant during the siege of Vicksburg, he wrote:[10]

When the battle involved only a subdivision of his army, he left everything to one of his corps commanders, and only when all his corps commanders—of whom there were three at Vicksburg—were engaged, did he take full control. Thus in his Memoirs he speaks of being "with Sherman" at a certain battle on one day, "with

McPherson" at another battle on another day, and so on. But when it comes to an engagement in which all his troops participated, he makes it plain that everything was under his personal control and direction. The two assaults on the Confederate works at Vicksburg were two occasions of this kind. The second of these assaults took place on the 22nd of May, when the whole army, with scaling ladders, forlorn hopes and all the ingredients of the terrible thunder of battle, made a desperate but unsuccessful effort to capture the Confederate stronghold. As the bearer of an unimportant message from a division commander, I had an opportunity of seeing the great soldier in one of the most eventful hours of his eventful life. I had been told to look for him "somewhere near the center and well to the front," and I found him very well to the front and almost exactly in the center of the line extending from the Yazoo river on the right to the southern limit of Vicksburg on the left. He was the least military-looking member of the small group, consisting in addition to himself, of staff officers and orderlies—six or eight in all. He wore a soft hat surrounded by a cord, on which there were traces of gold cord, and a blouse without shoulder-straps, a garment of which a second lieutenant would have felt proud. But while careless of his own garments he had imitated Caligula by conferring rank upon his horse, whose saddle cloth wore the glittering double stars of a Major General. Only his left leg was in a stirrup; the right was drawn up, and seemed to be twisted around the pommel of the saddle. In his left hand the General held a pine stick, which he was whittling with a big knife grasped in the right. In his mouth was a big cigar which he was smoking violently. I delivered my message, to which an approving nod was all the answer required or given. The General continued to whittle and smoke without betraying the slightest emotion. It was about noon and the battle had been raging since ten o'clock, every man in the whole army engaged. The staff officers and orderlies in the group around the General were discussing the situation in all forms and degrees of agitation, but the General said nothing unless asked a question, and then said very little. He was watching with his ears rather than with his eyes, because the range of vision was short owing to the trees and the fortifications. He listened to the firing as the noise advanced or receded and told him that his troops were gaining or losing ground. Suddenly a shell from a Confederate battery plowed into the ground near where our party stood. The General, without moving a muscle except of his legs, straightened himself up in the saddle, and, in a tone of voice not stronger than he would use to call for a glass of water, said to one of his staff officers: "That battery ought to have been silenced an hour ago. See why it has not been silenced." The staff officer went off on a gallop and the General renewed his attack on the pine stick, which had by this time been whittled to the dimensions of a lead pencil. I mustered courage enough to approach him and ask how the battle was going. He answered in a very pleasant voice that he thought everything looked well, but that there was a great deal to be done yet before Vicksburg was taken. What he meant was that there was much heavy fighting over trenches and earthworks and against almost impregnable mud-forts, between where the army was then and actual possession of the stronghold. I am satisfied now that when the General answered my question he made up his mind that the assault was a failure, and that Vicksburg could not be taken in that way; but there was nothing in his manner or voice to indicate such a conclusion. There probably would not have been the slightest noticeable change in his manner or voice if, instead of defeat, he had felt assured of victory. His imperturbable self-possession could not have been wrested from him by any change of fate or fortune. If his army had been annihilated he might have smoked two cigars at a time instead of one, but that is as far as his emotions would have carried him, at least in their outward manifestations. I started back whence I had come with my message, and learned in a short time that the troops were coming back, leaving Vicksburg still in Confederate hands. That night I heard General Grant say: "We'll have to dig our way in," and so it happened. In the *Memoirs* the attack of the 22nd is not treated as a disaster, but rather as an unsuccessful experiment, which it undoubtedly was. The siege began immediately; and at the end of six weeks General Grant took dinner in Vicksburg.

During his two years with the Northern armies, McCullagh demonstrated convincingly his own courage under fire. Looking back on his experiences, his recollections offered his conclusions about courage. He pointed out that there seemed to be a popular misconception of the physical courage of the average soldier.[11] He added:

In all armies under fire cowardice is the exception, and the rule is all the way from slight nervousness which borders on fear, to a dauntlessness which is on the lookout to blossom into real heroism. The fear of battle is like the fear of death, of which it is perhaps a part—it vanishes as the actual fact approaches. An officer who had been under fire more than fifty times, once told me that he entered every battle with the same sensation of nervousness, but in each case he had braced up after a couple of rounds had been fired. It was a little "buck fever" or stage fright paralleled in minor form in the case of one of the best known public speakers of his country, who once said that although he had been making fifty speeches a year for twenty years, he was not able to face an audience without showing and feeling considerable tremulousness for the first five minutes. But in the army a dozen sentiments appeal to a man to keep him from giving way to an exhibition of cowardice should he feel like making one. The effect of comradeship and association is to dissipate all sensations of fear. The reputation which a man in or out of the army most dreads is that of a coward, and every soldier in battle knows that the eyes of all his comrades are upon him. But the fact is that none of these inducements are necessary to give a man courage enough to do a soldier's duty—that is to say, to shoot and be shot at. Macaulay, in one of his essays, speaks of the "vulgar courage of a soldier," using the word "vulgar" in its proper signification, as a synonym for "common," and not in its perverted meaning of "low" or "indecent." But to my mind, very strong evidence that every man has the courage of a soldier is found in the fact that we never hear of the test of courage in the recruiting office of any nation in the world. They put the heart, the lungs and the limbs to trial, but never think of trying, before accepting a recruit, how he will act in time of peril. Even Frederick William, who was a connoisseur in soldier-giants and hunted the continent of Europe for tall recruits, paying as high as $6,500 for an Irishman who measured 6 feet, 7 inches, never thought of asking in advance if his high-priced men would stand in front of hostile guns. He took it for granted that his costly grenadiers would fight. If it be true that no two men are exactly alike by nature, it is more true that no two men will act exactly alike in a given emergency. Hence, upon the battlefield, among men equally fearless of danger, we have a variety of actions, according to the temperament of each individual.

McCullagh thought there were many kinds of courage. He cited the "Christian" courage of Commodore Foote, the "imperturbable" bravery of General Grant, and the "impetuous" courage of General Logan. The most heroic example, he said, was probably General George H. Thomas "urging his men to stand pat at Chickamauga after his superiors and equals had fled to Chattanooga, but I prefer to confine myself to matters coming under my own observation, and I was not at Chickamauga."

General Logan, he wrote, was "the radiant incarnation of war." He added:

Military critics have said that Logan lacked the contemplative disposition to make him a planner of campaigns; that he was nothing of a strategist; and that he would have failed as the supreme officer of independent command. This may be all true, although it is a half-answer to it all that he never was tried in that capacity. But as the Commander of any number of troops in action he certainly had no superior. He was at his best when leading a command to action, or better still, in action. He never said "go," but always "come." He was both an example and an inspiration. With Logan on the front of the line, carrying his hat on the point of his sword, determined to route the enemy by swearing, if not by firing, it was hard for any of his men to be less than good soldiers. He seemed at times to be drunk with enthusiasm, which was the only form of inebriety possible to him in the army, as he was during his military service very temperate, if not totally abstinent as to ordinary intoxicants. The air of a battle seemed to mount to his brain like the fumes of wine, and with nearly the same outward effect. But he never lost control of himself in the wildest delirium of war. He kept his command under absolute control always, and seemed gifted with the power of omnipresence while his troops were in action. He rode his lines constantly, and always in front. Once he thought he saw a little faltering of a small portion of his troops under a heavy fire, and he called to one of his staff officers to "stick a flagstaff in the ground, with a flag on it, and see if the boys wouldn't rally round it." He would stop in the intervals of battle to talk to boys of his old regiment—the 31st Illinois—and to tell them they had been doing so well that he would write home and tell their mothers what good soldiers they were.

General Logan provided the spark for one of McCullagh's many verbal tilts with General Sherman.[12] The general in his memoirs had criticized Logan for leaving the army after the battle of Atlanta, disregarding his duty to the country on the field. McCullagh took issue. "This was all wrong," he wrote. "I took occasion to point it out. I happened to know that Mr. Lincoln ordered Logan north to service on the stump in the Presidential campaign."

McCullagh was critical of much of the writing about the war after its close.

"The great want of our literature," he insisted, "unquestionably is a full accurate and satisfactory history of the War of the Rebellion" . . . "Take Sherman's *Memoirs* for instance. There is not a reliable page between their covers, and yet we do not know of any source of information to which the candid chronicler would be more apt to turn. Accepting their statements as true, he would be deceived as to nearly every important movement in the West and South, from Shiloh to Savannah. Indeed, it is impossible to accept these *Memoirs* at their face value without acknowledging that the world has misunderstood and wrongly estimated Baron Munchausen. Other specimens of 'Official' war literature are almost equal to Sherman's in their want of veracity, though they have the negative merit of not seeking, as Sherman does, to exalt their authors by disparagement of worthier and better men."

General Sherman was one of McCullagh's favorite targets in the postwar years. Certainly Sherman's low opinion of the correspondents was well known. One of the stories about him was the occasion when he was informed that several correspondents had been killed. His reply, according to the story, was "Splendid, now they will have company in hell." During McCullagh's years after the war as a Washington correspondent for the *Com-*

mercial, Sherman remarked in his presence at a public reception that he had never heard of a war correspondent being killed in action. McCullagh's retort was: "Well, General, there were as many of us as of you killed."

After McCullagh had become editor of the *Globe-Democrat,* Sherman returned to St. Louis and became a shining target for McCullagh's biting paragraphs and in spite of the antagonism between the two men apparently was a willing subject for interviews. McCullagh's interest in the feud is obvious in this interview in the *Globe-Democrat:*[13]

> General Sherman, on being asked a few days ago if there was any truth in the report that he had recently joined the Catholic church, replied: "No sir, it is a d——d lie." It is evident from this that while Tecumseh may not have joined any particular church, his mind has been taking a religious turn of late.
>
> General Sherman says he doesn't want "four years of hell" and, therefore, he will not be a candidate for President. The country doesn't want "four years of hell" either, and, therefore, it will not elect General Sherman.
>
> Gen. Logan's forthcoming book will make it appear that there were at least two men engaged in the late war. Gen. Sherman's *Memoirs* leave the impression that there was only one.
>
> General Sherman says, in an interview in the *Republican,* that he "would rather have written Mr. Lincoln's first inaugural than to have won a victory." Which leads us to inquire when and upon what occasion did General Sherman experience the sensation incident to winning a victory? It must have been before the battle of Shiloh and since the surrender of the Confederate army.
>
> The official order for the transfer of army headquarters to Washington has been issued. It is perhaps good for the country that it should be so. But speaking for the *Globe-Democrat,* we cannot help regretting the loss of such an excellent interviewee as General Sherman. We have used him to good advantage in that capacity, but now that he goes East, he will fall into the hands of the shoemakers of the *Herald* and the sentimentalists of the *Tribune,* and between the two he will appear badly in print. Farewell, Tecumseh, and if forever, still forever, fare thee well!
>
> General Sherman, who shuns notoriety with a degree of horror

equaled only by that with which a kitten shuns new milk, consents to announce everyday in the week the exact day upon which he will retire from the command of the army and turn it over to his predecessor. Public thirst for the information is insatiable, and hence the General's reluctant departure from the rule of modest seclusion which usually governs his conduct. The oft-repeated news is of absorbing interest to the comparatively few of our citizens who know we have an army of sufficient importance to be commanded. The last fixed date is November 1, and on the morning of that day the American people will be expected to rise en masse and salute Tecumseh as he vacates the headquarters in which he has drawn much pay for little work for many years agone.

That is all gammon about Sherman driving me out of the army (Mr. McCullagh once said when the tradition was mentioned by a newspaper man.)[14] I had my credentials from Grant to go or stay, as I pleased. When Sherman was located in Raleigh I left Washington for North Carolina in the interest of a newspaper. I carried a letter of introduction to Gen. Sherman from his brother, John, for whom I had acted as private secretary. Gen. Sherman issued orders every day forbidding the correspondents to come within the lines. As a news gatherer I couldn't afford to pay any attention to them and I didn't. Sherman's discourtesy to the press was mere affectation. He liked nothing better than being talked about by the newspapers, especially in the way of flattery.

HE SCOOPED THE NATION

3

McCullagh had barely attained legal voting age when he arrived in Washington in November 1863 to take over as the Washington correspondent of the *Commercial*. Perhaps his two years as a war correspondent in competition with reporters with many more years of age and experience, gave him confidence, but surely it must have been tempered by some misgivings when he considered the responsibilities of his new assignment and the high caliber of his competition. Whitelaw Reid, his former superior on the *Gazette,* had preceded him to Washington. It was Reid's distinguished reports of the fall of Richmond and the assassination of Lincoln, which prompted Horace Greeley to hire him as managing editor of the New York *Tribune* in 1868. There were others whose reputations might well strike awe in the mind of a young reporter.[1]

But if he had qualms, he must have kept them to himself, and he quickly set to work with the same zeal and dedication which had served him so well. During the four years he served the *Commercial* in Washington, he established the national reputation which led to the executive positions in Cincinnati, Chicago, and finally St. Louis for the remainder of his life. The New York *Times* in its front page obituary of McCullagh on January 1, 1897 gave credit to his Washington years as the cornerstone of his career. The *Times* said:

Joseph Burbridge McCullagh, "Mack" was, by birth Scotch-Irish, by destiny a keen, shrewd, thorough journalist of the type that at will plods or soars. His correspondence in Washington founded his reputation. His letters were terse, incisive and sparse of adjectives, but they revealed him as a man of ripe judgment, who could not only think quickly but soundly and grasp political situations so as to foretell their outcome.

Undoubtedly it was his Washington experience that spurred his deep-seated interest in politics and his lifelong adherence to the Republican Party, to be reflected so vigorously later in the columns of the St. Louis *Globe-Democrat*.

It was his proficiency in shorthand, acquired in St. Louis that helped open the door to the contacts which made possible his early success in the nation's capital. He wangled a position for a time as a stenographer on the floor of the Senate, which brought him into close relationships with the members of that august body. By the spring of 1865 he was serving as secretary to Senator John Sherman of Ohio.[2]

One of the by-products of historical research is to trace how fate, fortune, or if you will, the long arm of coincidence, fits the pieces of a jigsaw together. It can be argued that the outcome might have been the same, given another set of events, but the speculation persists. The first in the series of happenings that led to McCullagh's famous interview with President Andrew Johnson occurred on the eve of President Lincoln's second inauguration on March 3, 1865.[3] The war was not yet over, though the end was plainly in sight, and perhaps the foreboding of assassination to come a few weeks later, hung over the city. In any event, extraordinary safety precautions were ordered. Admission to the Capitol the next day was to be by ticket only.

McCullagh, through his service as Senator Sherman's secretary was well aware of the measures being taken. To make certain he would be able to witness the inaugural ceremonies, he decided to remain inside the Capitol all night. As he recalled it later, he and John W. Forney, a Philadelphia reporter, were sitting in one of the Senate committee rooms the morning of March 4, waiting for the time to go to the Senate Chamber. One of the windows in the room afforded a clear view of an outside entrance to the Senate wing of the Capitol. Two men came to the door and found it locked. Though rain was falling heavily at the time, Forney recognized one of the men as Andrew Johnson. Forney went to the window, rapped on it to attract attention and then opened it. The Vice-President-elect and his physician climbed through the window, wet, cold, and shivering. The physician immediately asked if there was any whiskey available. Forney went to a closet, obtained a black bottle and set it with a glass on the mantel.

McCullagh recalled that the Vice-President-elect poured a generous half tumbler of whiskey and swallowed it in a gulp. He sat down by the fire for a time and then took a second drink as generous as the first. As the spirits and the heat of the fire took effect; he grew talkative. Later, when the oath of office was being administered to him, his mumbled response was so noticeable that the reporters in describing the ceremonies mentioned his condition. That incident began the relationship which gave McCullagh access to the man who was soon to become the seventeenth President of the United States.

During Johnson's occupancy of the White House, much was written about his personal habits. McCullagh, however, defended him. Of Johnson he wrote:[4]

A great part of the public still believe he was a drunkard. This is far from being the truth. He said to me one night it was strange that he could not take a glass of whiskey and water without being denounced as a drunkard, while others could get blind drunk and be indorsed by the temperance societies. During his life in the White House, Johnson rarely used wine or liquor. He was supposed to be drunk when he made his famous 22nd of February speech in which he denounced Forney as a "dead duck"; but he had not tasted liquor that day. He could get drunk on his own talk quicker than the oldest toper can get drunk on whiskey. He was a good talker, with a rather limited vocabulary, but with plenty of ability to express his ideas, and a disposition to use curse words in great profusion. Both in public and private, in speaking on topics of men or measures that excited his denunciation, he was apt to work himself into a ferment, which, to those unacquainted with him, might pass for the result of overindulgence although he might not have touched liquor for a week. He was liable to become intoxicated with the fumes of his own indignation.

He was not a teetotaler, I believe, but I dare say he was not an habitual drinker during his Presidential incumbency.''

While it was the formal interview with Johnson that is recognized as a notable "first" in American journalism, it should be noted that even before that interview appeared, McCullagh had achieved another "first" in American journalism. He was the first newsman to establish the kind of relationship with the White House which has been capitalized on by others in recent years.[5] It was the confidential relationship which Arthur Krock, during his years as head of the Washington Bureau of the New York *Times* used effectively and which is now enjoyed by his successor James Reston.

The relationship between the two men, viewed from the perspective of a century later, seems even more remarkable in the light of the difference in their ages. The President was fifty-seven, had been in public life for nearly forty years and had served as Governor of Tennessee, as Senator from that state, and as a brigadier general in the war. McCullagh was twenty-three and had been a reporter for less than six years. The discrepancy in itself is indicative of the ability and integrity of the youthful correspondent of the *Commercial*.

As the President's feud with Congress deepened, the relationship between the two men grew closer. McCullagh's instructions from the *Commercial* were to "do the fair thing to both sides." There is no evidence that McCullagh ever violated his orders, but as he frankly said later, he was inclined to favor the President, not because of the justice of his cause, but because he felt the President was the underdog.

"Both political parties were against him," was McCullagh's shrewd observation.[6] "The Democrats, though making a show of support, were secretly in league with the Republicans who were bitterly fighting him; they hated him for the past, and they were unable to use him for the present and they feared him for the future. The blood of the Republican martyr might become the seed of the Democratic church, and scatter to the winds the hopes of a whole score of Democratic candidates, chief among them Hendricks and Pendleton who had just erected Presidential lightning rods over their heads.''

McCullagh explained that it was an incident from Missouri politics which began his close relationship with the President. McCullagh was sitting in the press gallery in the Senate one day when a page brought a message informing him that the President would like to see him that night.

"I was considerably astonished," he wrote,[7] "when Mr. Johnson revealed the purpose of his invitation and still more astonished at the manner in which he made the revelation. As I afterwards learned, he was given to very strong language in private conversation. Indeed, he swore like our army in Flanders when excited on topics of personal concern. But it was a harmless sort of profanity, a sort of conversational heat lightning that lit up the sky of his tete-a-tete without intentionally injuring anybody's person or character. With him, as with many others, damns and hells were made to supply the deficiencies of a vocabulary picked up without the aid of schools or books. He swore for the same reason that uneducated people as a class, and women as a sex, underscore most of what they write. He italicized his conversation.

I was scarcely seated when he asked me if I had not recently written a letter to the *Commercial* about Senator Drake. He had seen it or heard of it and he wanted to get a copy of it to have it republished in the *National Intelligencer*. The letter referred to was a review of Mr. Drake's early career as a pro-slavery Democrat in Missouri, provoked by a rebuke which, as a Republican Senator, he had, very soon after his admission to the Senate, administered to Wilson, Fessenden and others for their "timidity and conservatism." Johnson's personal interest in the matter arose from the fact that Mr. Drake had introduced a resolution censuring him (Johnson) for one of his reconstruction messages. "I would like to have that letter printed in the *Intelligencer* on the same day that Drake makes his speech in support of his resolution against me, D——n him! I want the people to see the kind of men who are calling me a traitor and a renegade."

McCullagh agreed to provide a copy of his letter. The term "letter" was widely used at that time as synonymous with dispatch. It was reprinted in the *Intelligencer* and McCullagh reported:[8]

It made Drake very mad and brought him into the Senate one morning with a hatful of manuscript by way of personal explanation, but the facts were against him and he never after that shook his finger at the old Republican Senators to tell them they were timid.

The routing of Senator Drake encouraged the President to rely on McCullagh.[9] There were frequent invitations to visit the White House. The President not only agreed to interviews but in some instances encouraged them. In fact, the first meeting produced an interview. After the request for the Drake letter, the President continued the conversation for an hour or more. McCullagh recorded that conversation:

The elections of the previous fall—1866—had gone largely against him, and his Philadelphia convention had proved a great failure, but he attributed a great deal of this to the treachery of the Democratic Party, whose leaders, he said, were afraid he wanted to be a Democratic candidate for 1868, whereas, according to his own declaration, nothing was further from his purpose. "Six months in this position," said he, "would disgust anybody. You hear nothing from morning to night but the cry of Office—Office—Office. It is the old cry of Beef—Beef—Beef that Patrick Henry talked about in Revolutionary times."

As I rose to leave, I asked him if I might use the substance of his talk for a letter to the *Commercial,* and he replied with a careless cheerfulness, in the affirmative, "that is," he said, "if you put me down right; but the d——n newspapers are as bad as the politicians in misrepresenting me. I don't want you to take my side," said he. "I can fight these fellows singlehanded; but put me down correctly." I assured him that I would do so, and I afterwards got his word for it that the promise was kept. He was greatly pleased, and soon—in less than two weeks—I think—he sent for me again. "I want to give these fellows"—this was always the term he used in speaking of Congress, pointing in the direction of the Capitol, as he spoke—"hell," said he, "and I think I can do it better through your paper than through a message, because the people read the papers more than they do messages." In truth, however, he wanted to let off a little steam of personality which would not have looked well in a message. He wanted to have it known why Ashley, Logan, and a host of others had first deserted him and then opposed him—because he would not grant their requests, which varied from the appointment of a crossroad postmaster to the approval of a gigantic war claim.

In December of 1867 the President's feud with Congress boiled over into talk of impeachment, and a resolution calling for such action had been introduced in the House. No attempt was made at that time to bring it to a vote, but as McCullagh wrote later, the President seemed to know what was ahead. "He talked freely and bitterly," McCullagh recalled, "against his enemies whom he denounced as usurpers and rebels and traitors —all in league to subvert the Constitution."

To understand McCullagh's part in what followed, it is helpful to review a little of Johnson's background. He was born in a shack on a back street of Raleigh, North Carolina, of parents who could neither read nor write. Johnson himself never attended school and did not learn to write until after his marriage. At the age of fourteen he had been apprenticed to a tailor, had run away from his master and found his way to eastern Tennessee where eventually he built a prosperous tailor's trade.

In many respects his story had much in common with that of Lincoln. But the hardships that gave Lincoln compassion and understanding seem only to have embittered Johnson. In contrast to others who had preceded him to the White House he was always carefully tailored and barbered. One biographer even added that he was one of the few public men of his era who took a daily bath. His one fall from grace was what Lincoln described as "a bad step": his intoxication during the inaugural ceremonies. When he succeeded Lincoln as President the radicals of the North assumed that he was with them. More than once during the war he had referred to the Southern planters as "traitors." When they were speedily disillusioned, they turned against him.

In March 1867 Congress in the so-called First Reconstruction Act, passed over the President's veto, organized the South into five military districts, each under a general appointed by Congress. In the same month Congress passed the Office of Tenure Act, which stripped the President of the power to remove any

Federal officer without the Senate's consent. In the Command of the Army Act, the President was forbidden to give the army any orders except through General Grant.

When Mr. Johnson, in defiance of the Tenure Act, sought to remove Secretary of War Stanton, the stage was set for the adoption of the impeachment resolution. McCullagh again takes up the story:[10]

General Grant had been appointed Secretary of War in Stanton's place during the preceding summer, under personal promise, as Johnson more than once very forcibly asserted, that he would hold it at the pleasure of the President and surrender it to him, but never to Stanton. When, very early in 1868, General Grant, after the Senate had refused to sanction the surrender of Stanton, resigned the position into the hands of Mr. Stanton, there was no measure to the denunciation of Grant by Johnson. I had heard him abuse Thad. Stevens, Sumner, and all the rest of the Republican leaders, but his language concerning them was mild and decorous compared with what he said of what he called Grant's treachery. He told me once of a Cabinet meeting in which he confronted General Grant with the question of veracity, and, said he, "I pinned him down to it, and he looked as if the floor would open under him and let him through."

The quarrel thus begun lasted while both men lived, and it furnished the occasion for the violation of a precedent as old as the country. The custom had always been for the outgoing and incoming Presidents to ride to the Capitol in the same carriage on inauguration day, as joint participators in the quadrennial ceremonies. On the 4th of March 1869, it took two carriages to do what one had always done before. The next day I met Mr. Johnson on Pennsylvania avenue and spoke to him of the matter. "Well," he said, "I did my part of the business. I sent him an invitation and he didn't accept it." This, it is proper to say, is an expurgated report of the ex-President's observations. It must not be supposed that General Grant was behind Johnson in the matter of personal denunciation. He kept his end of the line up in a less demonstrative but quite as effective way. What his curses lacked in loudness they made up in depth, and if he was not willing to speak himself, there were hundreds of willing ones to do the damning for an incoming President—for Grant was therefore ordained candidate of the Republicans even before his quarrel with Johnson. It is curious to reflect how the leaders of those times swung back from the extreme of denouncing the one-man power of Andy Johnson to the other extreme of fostering and fawning upon the one-man power in his destined successor. The incense of flattery which was burned under the nostrils of General Grant just then must have been anything but sweet to a man of his discernment and good sense; and it is pleasant to know that some who were most active in the work were disappointed in their expectations of substantial reward."

McCullagh's interview, which was hailed at the time as an outstanding journalistic feat, is generally recognized today as the first formal newspaper interview in history.[11] The interview appeared in the *Commercial* on February 13, 1868, eleven days before the House of Representatives voted its resolution of impeachment.

The full text of the interview as it appeared in the *Commercial,* is given in the appendix. It was written in the style of that period, which was more chronological than news stories are today. The first five paragraphs set the stage and even explained what McCullagh had anticipated finding when he called at the White House. It was written in the first person. The lead paragraphs indicate the tone of the interview. It read:

WASHINGTON, D.C., Feb. 10, 1868—I called on the President last evening and had an interview with him of about an hour's duration. From the revival of the impeachment project and the recent correspondence between him and Gen. Grant, which I had been informed, on the authority of several eminently loyal newspapers, was literally "crushing" to A. J., I expected to find His Excellency in a prostrate and enfeebled condition, or perhaps "writhing in the agonies of despair," as Forney's two dailies would express it. But he was not prostrate, and he didn't writhe any. Quite the contrary, I never saw him more cheerful or in better health and spirits.

"They're after you again, Mr. President, with an impeachment," said I. "So I hear," he said, "but I can't get at the point they're trying to make against me this time; though for that matter I haven't taken much trouble to find out."

With the liberal use of direct quotations, the interview gave the President's views on his dealings with General Grant, his opinion of Grant's veracity, the reconstruction problems in the South and the next Presidential election. In type the interview ran to more than two columns.

The length of that interview suggests that among McCullagh's attributes as a reporter was a photographic memory. Envious competitors in Washington speculated that he had used his knowledge of shorthand to take notes on his shirt cuffs. McCullagh denied it. He wrote later of his first interview with Johnson:

I had not introduced pen, pencil or paper, and did not attempt to write a line of it until the next morning, when I devoted about two hours to the first interview with Andrew Johnson, or so far as I was concerned, with anybody else. Nor did I submit the manuscript to Mr. Johnson for revision on that or any other occasion.

No aspiring journalist ever awaited more anxiously the result of a first effort in a new branch of work than I awaited the arrival in Washington, and at the White House of my first attempt at interviewing, although the art had not then been christened. I thought I had "struck a good lead," but I could not tell until I had heard from the President. The mails were slower then, and I think it was five days from the writing of the letter until one afternoon at the Capitol, the White House secretary greeted me with "the sweet assurance of a smile" and told me the President had read my production and had said that I had "got him down to a dot." "From the way he talks," said the secretary, "I think he would like to see you again."

I am satisfied thaat the introduction of pen, pencil or paper would have spoiled the whole business so far as President Johnson was concerned. It would have frozen the irrascible current of his soul, when he came to freeing his mind about his wicked adversaries at the other end of the avenue, to have seen a man taking it all down on cold paper. He would have hesitated, stopped, asked the reporter to read his notes to him, and otherwise shown signs of concern which would have hindered the flow of his conversation and abated his interest. The only way was to get him started, and let him alone until he had run down, then wind him up with a new question.

The art of the interview has been developed and refined by many able practitioners since McCullagh invented it, but the principles he laid down remain sound. He pointed out that if a stenographic interview is punctured by questions it becomes a catechism, and if the questions are omitted it is a stump speech.

McCullagh explained what he regarded as a poor interview in an editorial paragraph:[12]

We print today from the Cincinnati *Enquirer* an interview with Mr. George W. Curtis, mother superior of the Mugwumps, concerning current politics and politicians. The work of the interviewer is crudely and badly done. Although Mr. Curtis is made to speak in the first person, there is scarcely a sentence worthy of Curtis in the whole article.

The interview for which I contend, he wrote, requires on the part of the interviewer a gift of condensation as distinguished from amputation, with which it is often confounded—of compression as distinguished from excision—a good memory, a familiarity with the subject to be discussed, and the faculty of leading a conversation while seeming to follow it. This latter is a nice distinction which those who have anything to do with interviewing will appreciate. A little dramatic power will help too—the power that is, to personate in writing out the interview, the man or woman interviewed. This holds, of course, only as to persons of strong individuality and well recognized modes of thought and expression—and none others are really worth interviewing. Andrew Johnson and Benjamin F. Wade were two noted illustrations of this class in my interviewing days. Half a dozen descriptive words thrown into a paragraph in a column interview will bring a man like either of these two to the reader's eye and mind as clearly as a Rembrandt picture. One thing the interviewer should never forget is to keep his hold on the conversational helm, and confine the talk and the talker to the channel marked out in the first place.

The third, and not the first person, should as a rule be used when an interview is written from memory. Nothing is more absurd in all journalism than an hour's interview pretended to be given in a column and written in the first person. The words spoken would occupy seven or eight columns and the chances are that the reporter in writing the article uses his own language entirely and not that of the party interviewed. The third person is always safer than the first, for the strong reason that it commits a man only to certain opinions, and does not pretend to give his exact language or to commit him to specific expressions. Nine-tenths of the disavowals of published interviews would be avoided if the pretense were not made of repeating the identical words used. The right idea in the wrong words is a fruitful source of grief to those who are accustomed to be put into print by the interviewer. The use of the first person in an interview written from memory is commendable only for the purpose of catching and holding a remarkable or an unusually strong sentence. A man with half a memory can store up a goodly number of such phrases and make them serve as ornaments to relieve the typographical monotony of an article.

One of McCullagh's contemporaries suggested [13] that the personality of the interviewer had much to do with his success. McCullagh, he wrote, "was one of the few correspondents who could invade the sleeping room of a political leader, a member of Congress, or a Cabinet Minister, without being treated as an intruder. If occasion required he would go to the bedroom of a noted soldier or statesman, explain that the interests of the man to be interviewed demanded that something be said, would present the urgency of the affair from the standpoint of the individual himself and the public, would turn up the light, and ask the victim to make himself as comfortable as possible, and to dictate the speech he would make the next day, or his views on some question that was to come up for discussion the next day. The man interviewed was the more ready to do this because he was sure of having the next morning a clean copy of the speech he wanted to make. 'Mack' succeeded where others failed because he was aggressively courteous and because he made himself a convenience to the men he served. Several of the most noted interviews ever published were obtained by him this way.

Mr. McCullagh's work on the Cincinnati *Commercial* made him a reputation that carried him into newspaper management."

Although McCullagh's letter on Alexander Stephens, the former vice president of the Confederacy, is generally regarded as one of his best interviews, McCullagh insisted it was not an interview, but merely a report to his newspaper of the visit he paid to Stephens' home in Atlanta, Georgia, early in 1867. The letter described the Stephens home and included some of his comments on the Civil War. The comments on Jefferson Davis and other Southern leaders, which in McCullagh's opinion would have made it an interview, were omitted at Stephens' request.

McCullagh in describing the visit later[14] in his reminiscences in the St. Louis *Globe-Democrat,* wrote:

I had a letter to Mr. Stephens and was very cordially received by him. He insisted on my becoming his guest at "Liberty Hall," as he called his home. I remained with him three days, spending most of the time in riding about his farm in his company, visiting the negro quarters where his slaves lived—people whom he said he "owned" because he could not give them away with an assurance they would be well treated. We kept up a pretty lively conversation all the time, and renewed it each night on the porch of Liberty Hall for about two hours before retiring. On the night before my departure I told Mr. Stephens that I intended to make use of such points in our conversation as would be of public interest, provided he would give his consent to the publication. "I would like to print what you have said about Mr. Jefferson Davis," said I. "No, no, no. Young man, that wouldn't look well in print from me just now. You drew me out on Mr. Davis farther than I intended to go. Everybody knows that he and I did not agree very well, but now that he is in defeat and misfortune, I do not wish to attack him."

Thus vanished from my youthful mind what I had conjured up as a rattling good article by itself alone. We had devoted many hours to the discussion of the character and capacity of Mr. Davis, whom Mr. Stephens blamed for all the misfortunes of the Confederacy. Mr. Stephens contended that Mr. Davis believed himself to be a great soldier, when he was not, and that he allowed his personal prejudices to control him in the selection of officers to such an extent as to ruin the army. I had names and dates and specifications all in my memory, but at the emphatic denial of Mr. Stephens (if I may paraphrase Gibbon for such an occasion), I sighed as a reporter but obeyed as a guest. I assured Mr. Stephens that his wishes were law as to all that had passed between us, and asked him how about his declaration that the Northern Democrats were regarded by the Confederates as their friends all through the War, and that it was believed by the Confederates that the election of McClellan in 1864 would have stopped the war and restored the Union with slavery. He gave permission to print this and I did so, but he would not allow me to print his assertion that the Democratic platform of 1864 was written in Richmond and sent from there to Chicago, where it was reported by Mr. Vallandingham. He said with a smile, "I would rather you would not use that statement." And behind that smile I can now see enough to convince me that Mr. Stephens himself was the author of that platform. With these two exceptions Mr. Stephens interposed no objection to the reproduction of his rambling talks as I repeated them from memory.

I carried the matter in my head to my next stopping place, which was either Macon, or Augusta. Then I wrote them out in a letter of considerable length, which attracted some attention. Strange to say, the only statement questioned by the Southern press was that Mr. Stephens had told me that he considered Jefferson's first and Lincoln's second inaugural the two greatest state papers in the annals of America. I wrote Mr. Stephens calling his attention to the declaration in a Georgia paper that he could not have favorably compared anything emanating from Lincoln with any production of Jefferson's, and he replied in a very graceful note saying that he had probably said it, because he had believed it ever since he had read Mr. Lincoln's address of 1865. Mr. Stephens was a great admirer of Mr. Lincoln. He said to me in speaking of Jefferson Davis, "If you had had a Davis, and we a Lincoln, the war might not have ended as it did."

On March 2 and 3, 1868, the House of Representatives voted eleven articles of impeachment against the President. On March

5 the Senate, with Chief Justice Salmon P. Chase presiding, was organized as a court to hear the charges. McCullagh wrote,

There was an appearance of grim reality when the formal presentation was made at the bar of the Senate.[15]

I immediately availed myself of Mr. Johnson's general invitation to call upon him at any time, always assured of a hearing, or rather of a talking for my role in his presence was that of auditor, and not orator. If I talked at all, it was after the manner of a person who pours a pint of water down a country pump in order to get a bucket full out of it. My greeting on this first evening after the "articles" had been presented, was as cordial as ever, and a shade more profane. Mr. Johnson was anxious to know, so far as I could tell him what was the general impression as to the result. I told him the Impeachers thought they had a sure thing on conviction, and that men were already being promised positions under Ben Wade as the new President; but that he still had a big chance for acquittal in the personal hostility of Senators Fessenden, Grimes and Trumbull toward Wade. In fact, it was not so much the trial of Andrew Johnson as the election of Benjamin F. Wade, and I thought there were Republicans enough to bolt to secure Wade's defeat. This may seem like an extremely unjudicial view to take of so grave a matter, but observation in Washington makes a man acquainted with strange ideas of statesmanship. The Juliet we fall in love with through an opera-glass from the dress circle is not always so adorable when we go behind the scenes and confront the paint, powder and gewgaws which enter so largely into the make-up; and some of our best statesmen at Washington are liable to the same criticism. At any rate, as between their prejudices and their principles, they will always incline in favor of the former. If the succession to Andrew Johnson had devolved upon some man entirely unmixed with the personal wrangles of the United States Senate in 1868, conviction would have been almost certain. Mr. Johnson was at first unwilling to believe this; he thought every Republican Senator hated him worse than he hated anybody else. But the sequel showed his mistake. That night Mr. Johnson spoke very freely about the pending trial. I gathered from his manner and tone that so far from being afraid of conviction, he rather courted the martyrdom of it. He said that if they convicted him he would start out through the country with a view to convicting them before the people. In his most troublous hours he never lost faith in his own ability to show the people that he was the sole defender of the Constitution, and I have always thought that nothing would have suited him better than to have walked out of the White House on a warrant of conviction, and entered upon another swing of the circle, more elaborate than the first.

McCullagh, in looking back on his relations with Mr. Johnson, felt that "one of the most memorable of my interviews took place about the first of May when the vote was supposed to be at hand, although it was two weeks off, owing to postponements."

Mr. Johnson, he wrote,[16] had requested me to call every night and "tell him how things were going." It was known that the vote would be very close—it was finally 35 to 19, while 36 to 18, or a change of a single vote would have convicted, and there were rumors every day of changes from one side to the other. On the night in question I opened the conversation by saying, "It looks rather bad, Mr. President. They are betting 100 to 80 on conviction in New York." "The hell they are," said Mr. Johnson, pounding the table with his fist. "So they have called the gamblers in to help them against me, have they? I wonder what they will do next. Well," he continued, "I shouldn't be surprised from what I hear of them if they carried their point." He went on to say that, so far as the office of President was concerned, he didn't care a cent—perhaps he said he didn't care a d——n for it—but he would hate to be put out by "a lot of usurpers like those fellows at the other end of the avenue." If removed he would quietly take his hat and leave, but, as sure as there was a God in heaven, he would make "those fellows" hear from him. He would go on the stump all over the country and impeach them as traitors and rebels and let the people decide between him and them. He brought his tirade to a sudden close, looked at me rather sharply and said, "How many men were there in the court that beheaded Charles I?" This unexpected query rather dazed me, but I answered to the best of my recollection of history, there were about sixty members of that court. "How many of these fellows are there up yonder?" said he, pointing to the capitol. The answer was an easy one—

fifty-four. "I believe the murderers of the English king are called the Regicides," was the next observation of Mr. Johnson. "Now," he continued, "what became of those Regicides? According to my recollection a good many of them died outside of their beds." I helped Mr. Johnson, to the best of my ability, in solving this and kindred problems, but suggested that the best way to get at the truth of the matter would be to consult the *History of the Regicides* which could, undoubtedly, be found in the Congressional Library. He asked me to do that and write a letter showing what became of the men who beheaded King Charles, how many of them, after the Restoration, were compelled to leave their country, how many were convicted of crimes, and if the bodies of some of them who had died were not exhumed and hung in irons. "That will make a good letter just now," said I. "Yes," said he, "but don't send it to the Cincinnati *Commercial*. The crisis may come before it gets back, and it may be too late to do any good. I want these fellows at the other end of the avenue to know what their fate may be if they keep on. Write that letter and send it to a New York paper so that it will get back here in a day or two. And have a copy of it sent to every member of that High Court of Impeachment, as they call themselves." This, and a promise on my part to have a letter about the Regicides printed in a New York paper, closed the interview for the evening. Two days later the letter was duly forthcoming but its effect on the final vote of the Senate is still an unknown quantity.

I find by consulting the *History of the Regicides* that fifty-nine persons signed the death warrant of Charles. Of these several died before the Restoration. Of the survivors twenty-nine were tried, and of these thirteen were put to death and the rest were imprisoned. Twenty were declared incapable of holding civil office. The rest absconded and died in exile—three in America.

It was about this time that Mr. Johnson again appealed to McCullagh for help. A messenger in a hack, McCullagh recalled, came in search of him one night, urging him to go to the White House at once.[17]

I found Mr. Johnson pacing the room and swearing as he paced. "Well," said he, "I don't know what these d——d scoundrels (meaning the impeachers) will do next. They can't beat me any other way, and they are trying to get the jury drunk." Then he turned to me and asked if I knew Senator ———. "Oh, yes," I replied, "he boards at the Seaton house, and I see him nearly every day at meal time, except when he is on a bender, which happens quite frequently." "That's the very point I am coming to," said the President. "I am told, on the best authority, that these fellows (meaning the Impeachers) hired a man the other day to go to his room and represent himself as the agent of New York wine and liquor importers anxious to get some change in the tariff on these articles; but in fact his mission was to get him (Senator ———) to accept some samples of brandy and whiskey, so as to start him on a spree, get him to appear on the floor of the Senate while drunk, and then expel him and take a vote on impeachment before his successor could take his seat." After denouncing this "infamous scheme" in unmeasured terms, the President asked me if I thought I could do anything with Senator ———, if I came across him while he was on one of his sprees. I reminded the President that there was already pending in the Senate a resolution for the expulsion of Senator ———, which had been offered by Mr. Sumner, and which was only held in abeyance on promise of reformation. It was liable to be called up on any occasion created by the Senator's conduct. "The best thing to do," said I, "is to have somebody instructed to let me know the moment Senator ——— appears at the Capitol under the influence of liquor. I think I can get him home easily because he is always very docile with me when he is tipsy. He is the finest of gentlemen when he is sober, but when drunk he makes a break for the nearest dive and wants to "wallow a nigger." But when I meet him on the street and ask him to come home, he always comes." The President promised to attend to the matter, and again fell to denouncing the "villainous conspiracy" which he detected behind the Senator's drunks. I left the White House after promising to do my best to see that Senator ——— was present when the vote on impeachment was taken.

"But I had no idea that the worst fears of the President would so soon come near to realization. The Senator got furiously drunk on the day rendered memorable in the history of the trial by the anti-impeachment speeches of Fessenden, Trumbull, and other Republicans. It was a secret session of the Senate. I was walking the corridors of the House, when Mr. Christy, one of the Senate doorkeepers, rushed up to me and said, "Senator ——— is blind drunk and trying to get the floor and make a speech. If you can't get him out pretty quick, Sumner will call up his resolution and expel him." I rushed to the Senate door, sent my card to Senator ——— and out he came, hitting both sides of the door in his exit. The ruse I adopted to get him home was to remind him that he had invited me to dine with him that day, and that it was about time for dinner. Arm-in-arm we marched to the steps of the Capitol when he suddenly stopped and said he must postpone that invitation as he felt it to be his duty to go back to the Senate and "answer those d——d Abolitionists." A Kentucky Senator came along just then, and, easily taking in the situation, took my side on the controversy. We were soon at the Seaton house where Senator ——— was helped to his room by a couple of stout porters who put him to bed. The vote was expected the next day, and, as it was important to have the Senator present, a consultation was held as to the best and quickest means of sobering him off. Somebody suggested a big fright as a good thing under the circumstances. There was a Babcock fire extinguisher in the hall, which was immediately transferred to the bedside of the Senator. He rose on his haunches to ask what the infernal thing was for, and the agonizing manner in which he begged for mercy when told it was a stomach pump, and that it would be applied to him if he were not duly sober by 5 in the morning, was not soon forgotten by the few who witnessed it. That night I went to the White House and told what had happened. The Senator thereafter was under a guard of two stout Irishmen, who took him to the Capitol in a hack every morning, waited for him and brought him home in the afternoon. When the roll was called on impeachment he voted "Not Guilty."

There was a sequel to this. The President's friends resolved to retaliate in kind for this conspiracy. They set a wine baited trap for one of the leading Impeachers and the record will show that the "High Court" adjourned from day to day several days on account of the "illness" of a gentleman on that side of the question.

A favorite expression of the President during the trial, McCullagh said, was "I don't care how much the papers abuse me if they will only give me a chance to be heard."

These words, McCullagh added, reveal what may be called either the strength or the weakness of Mr. Johnson throughout his whole career in the White House—according to the point of view from which that career is viewed—whether Mr. Johnson really had great faith in the people as the governing power, or whether he allowed himself to believe that the people were strongly behind him in all his acts and words. My own idea always was that he carried to the White House such vivid recollections of his early success in Tennessee that he allowed them to tinge the whole of the higher life to which the death of Mr. Lincoln called him. To his mind the whole country was an enlarged Tennessee and the President was its Governor. He never seemed to realize that there was a New York and a Pennsylvania and a New England, differing in many respects from the State which had lifted him, as the friend of the people and the enemy of the aristocracy, from Alderman to Governor and Senator. His public speeches always smacked of the mountains of Tennessee, and his ideal gathering was an audience of Tennessee mountaineers. His early life had made him a "demagogue" using the word in its higher sense and meaning, and not in the lower sense and general acceptation. He was by nature and experience a leader of the masses.

The President, McCullagh said,[18] was concerned with only one charge. That he had used his position to make money out of it, gave Mr. Johnson "serious annoyance."

One night I waked him up to an unexpected degree by telling that Ben Butler's Impeachment committee was going to examine his bank account next day—which was a fact I had learned from the best authority. "Do they think they can prove me a thief too?" he exclaimed, and added that if he had much money in the bank he would want to have the committee searched after the examination. Ben Butler's committee summoned one of the clerks of Jay Cooke's bank and put him through a very close examination as to Johnson's money matters; but without discovering anything at all tending to substantiate the charge of personal corruption. One night the President got very much excited on this subject, and, drawing forth a little memorandum book, proceeded to figure up what he had before the war, what he had received since from all sources, and what he then considered himself worth. He made himself a loser by a considerable sum. Then he began to figure on what he supposed Grant was worth. "Let us see," said he, "he wasn't worth a d——n in 1861. He got so much, naming a figure, in Philadelphia, and so much, naming another figure, in New York. He must be worth nearly a quarter of a million." Then he named a number of Republican Senators who had entered public life very poor and had become very rich. "Now," said he, "if they could make me out richer today than I once was, they'd say I stole it; but these saints at the other end of the Avenue all came honestly by theirs, of course." In this connection he referred to the fact that he had declined a present of a carriage and a pair of horses very early in his administration; he said that since the commencement of the Impeachment trial a gentleman in New York had sent him a check for $10,000 to help him out of his troubles, but he had returned it immediately; for, said he, "Of course, if a man gives me ten thousand dollars it's because he thinks I have something worth more than ten thousand dollars to give him; and although I suppose I make a great many foolish appointments, I don't want to have it said that I make any corrupt ones."

Commenting on the rumors prevalent at the time that acquittal was bought with money, McCullagh refuted them this way:[19]

I will state what I think I know to be a fact: that Mr. Johnson not only never consented to the use of money, but often said in my hearing that if he could be acquitted for five dollars he would not pay that sum, nor let anybody else pay it for him. I am borne out in this assertion by the fact that he allowed Jere Black to withdraw from his defense rather than give official sanction to a corrupt land trade in which Black was interested. He told Black that he would rather be convicted ten times over than purchase not only defense, but even acquittal at such a price. Black evidently believed he had Johnson in his power, and it looked like a bad piece of business for such a man to withdraw from a case on the eve of a trial, but Johnson was not the kind of man to be intimidated, and besides, as I have already said, he did not look upon conviction as an unmixed evil to him. Undoubtedly money was used in a variety of ways to defeat the scheme of conviction, and, what is more, there was a good deal more money ready to be used in case of necessity. There were votes cast for conviction that could have been persuaded in the other direction, in case of an emergency. The great consideration of the anti-Impeachers was to make sure of nineteen votes, and they were cautious to get a few "alternates" as they do in conventions.

The assertion may be received with incredulity, and yet I make it from well-grounded knowledge, that Johnson got some of his most efficient help from the society ladies of Washington—not the resident rebels or Democrats of the Capital, but the wives and daughters of some of the most ardent Impeachers in Congress. There was a womanly sympathy for Johnson from the beginning of his troubles. He was not "a lady's man" by any means, but there was something about himself, and his quiet, unostentatious family which served to win the women, and they helped him by furnishing information to his friends, and in a variety of ways quite creditable to the ingenuity of the sex. Take it for all in all—it was a strange proceeding—that Impeachment business. The most active workers are dead. I do not mean Senators or Representatives, but the men who prompted Senators and Representatives from the outside and furnished the sinews of war to conduct the campaign. Johnson was less concerned all the time than the least of these. It seems to me to have been impossible to live in Washington just then, and not either want an office under the new regime, or be strongly opposed to the Impeachment proposal. It was hard to listen to men like Chandler of Michigan, Conness of California, and other leaders of the Republican party, without thinking that Impeachment was nothing more than a scheme to get the ins out and the outs in.

It was not surprising that McCullagh's interviews resulted in a subpoena to testify as a witness for the defense. McCullagh described his appearance before the Senate.[20]

Attorney-General Stanberry sent for me one day and questioned me as to the declarations of Mr. Johnson respecting his intention in removing Secretary Stanton. In letters to the *Commercial* I had stated that the President had asserted his right to test the validity of an act which he considered to be unconstitutional—such as the tenure-of-office law—in order to get the judgment of the Supreme Court on it, and that it was for the purpose of making this test that he had suspended Secretary Stanton. The Impeachers, on the other hand, concluded that it was the duty of the President to obey and execute every law until the Supreme Court had decided it unconstitutional. This was one of the issues of the great trial. After a short conversation, Mr. Stanberry said he would call me as a witness to the defense. I was never put upon the stand, however, because by a general ruling of the court, it was decided that declarations of intention by Mr. Johnson made to other parties should not be received as evidence. Until my fate was thus decided I waited several hours each day subject to the call of the sergeant-at-arms. What I most dreaded was the cross-examining torture of Gen. Benjamin F. Butler, to which I had seen many witnesses exposed. To make matters worse, it had come to my knowledge that Gen. Butler had declared to one of my newspaper friends that he would have some fun with "Mack" when he got him on the stand. It was easy enough to think of things to say in response to Butler's keen-edged wit, but I knew that the august presence of the Senate chamber would have a paralyzing effect upon my tongue in attempting to say them. So I concluded, after careful reflection, to use an "argument" which would cost me no effort of speech and would be quite as effective as the best of uttered wit in turning the laugh from myself to Mr. Butler. I borrowed from the Seaton House, where I boarded, the largest silver soup spoon in the house, and, tying a pocket handkerchief around the middle of the handle, put it inside my breast pocket, where I carried it every day during court hours until discharged as a witness. There was at that time a special and ludicrous correlation of ideas between Butler and spoons which time has largely dissipated. It was my intention, should the cross-examination by the General proceed too far and become too funny at my expense, to draw the spoon from my pocket and lay it on the table adjoining the witness chair, without saying a word, as if I had simply drawn my pocket handkerchief without knowing of the spoon attachment. I had friends in the galleries who were posted on the subject and ready to start the laugh, which would probably have become contagious. Before fully resolving on the spoon act, I broached the subject delicately to Chief Justice Chase, the presiding officer of the High Court of Impeachment, with whom, as a reporter, I had a very good talking acquaintance, knowing that he cordially detested Butler and his methods of conducting the prosecution of the President. I put the case to him hypothetically—suppose a man had been subpoenaed and was in mortal dread of Gen Butler's cross-examination, would it be contempt of court to pull out a spoon for the purpose of turning the laugh. The Chief Justice gave a large smile, and said, "Of course I would advise against any such thing, but if anybody should attempt it, I don't see how it could be called contempt of court. It would be for Mr. Butler to object, and (with a very big laugh), I don't think he would care to say anything about it." The opportunity for introducing the spoon never occurred, and as soon as I was dismissed and paid off as a witness I returned that useful article to its rightful owner."

McCullagh's apprehension of the "torture" of General Butler proved to be unfounded. But it is interesting to note that Butler, the inquisitor, was not able to avoid "Mack" the interviewer. It happened a number of years later when Butler visited St. Louis.[21] McCullagh was then the editor of the *Globe-Democrat*. Like some other great editors he never ceased to be a reporter and he frequently turned over to his city editor news items written in his own handwriting and in the brisk, terse style for which he was noted. Occasionally he did an interview. Butler was among his victims. Butler had arrived in St. Louis to confer with James Campbell, a fur dealer and broker, about a business matter. McCullagh went to the brokerage office, and without revealing his identity began to talk with Butler. Soon he turned the conversation to the impeachment trial. No doubt Butler must have wondered how his questioner came to be so well informed on the subject, but he talked freely and provided the grist for another McCullagh interview.

By May 26th the impeachment trial was over. By the narrow margin of 35 to 19, one short of the required two-thirds, Johnson emerged victorious.

There is no way to evaluate McCullagh's influence on the verdict. Certainly he did more than any other Washington correspondent in presenting the President in a favorable light. His letters to the *Commercial* marked the highlight of his four years in the nation's capital and virtually the end of his career as a Washington correspondent. Soon he was to return to Cincinnati and to his first executive position.

They had been busy years. In addition to his work for the *Commercial* and his employment in Congress, he also served for most of the time as the Senate correspondent for the old New York Associated Press. Apparently his work left little time for social life in Washington. It was the period in his life when one might expect a young man to turn to thoughts of romance. Of his private life, McCullagh was always reticent.

MANAGING EDITOR

4

Shortly after the excitement of the impeachment trial died away, the *Commercial* called McCullagh back to Cincinnati. His work in Washington, and especially the Johnson interview, had attracted national attention, including that of the *Commercial*'s rival, the Cincinnati *Enquirer*. Washington McLean, publisher of the *Enquirer,* offered McCullagh the position of managing editor, and he accepted it. The *Enquirer* was recognized as one of the leading Democratic papers in Ohio. In 1841 two brothers, John and Charles Brough had purchased the Cincinnati *Advertiser* and renamed it the *Enquirer*. In 1848 the paper was sold to James J. Faran, who had been mayor of Cincinnati and a member of Congress. Washington McLean became a partner in 1852. Both men were prominent in politics and they had developed what they claimed to be the largest job printing business in the world.

The *Enquirer,* however, had not fared as well. When McCullagh took over as managing editor, the circulation was little more than sixteen thousand and the reason was evident in its mediocre news and editorial pages.[1] It offered a challenge to its new managing editor. One of the interesting coincidences of that period of McCullagh's career is that among the reporters he hired was a young man who was destined to become his strongest rival later in St. Louis. The young reporter was John A. Cockerill, who had started his newspaper career at the age of fourteen on the weekly *West Union Scion of Temperance* in

Adams County, Ohio. Cockerill was a drummer boy with the Twenty-fourth Ohio Volunteer Infantry at the battle of Shiloh, which McCullagh reported for the *Gazette*. After the war Cockerill had published for a time the Hamilton, Ohio *True Telegraph*. His work there was spotted by McCullagh while reading the exchanges and McCullagh wrote to him, offering him the job as the *Enquirer*'s correspondent in Hamilton.

In 1869 Cockerill was invited to come to Cincinnati as a full-time reporter for the *Enquirer*. While McCullagh, who was three years older than Cockerill, left the *Enquirer* a few months after the new reporter arrived, his influence must have been considerable. Homer W. King, Cockerill's biographer, noted that influence.[2] "Cockerill," he wrote, "was forever finding himself in association with men ranging in flavor from the eccentric to the brilliant. In the latter category was Joseph Burbridge McCullagh . . . McCullagh's passion for editorial independence could not have escaped young Cockerill's attention."

In the fall of 1870 McCullagh was approached by some Chicago men who wanted him to take charge of the Chicago *Republican*. The *Republican* had been launched in January 1865, with an authorized capital stock of $500,000. The owners purchased the Chicago *Morning Post,* which had begun publication five years before, largely to obtain the *Post*'s Associated Press franchise.[3] Charles A. Dana was hired as the editor of the *Republican* at a salary of $10,000 a year, a high figure for that period. The first issue under Dana's direction appeared on May 30, 1865, but from the outset there were serious differences between the editor and the business department. On May 22, 1866, the stockholders met and voted to discharge Dana. He was replaced by V. B. Denslow, who moved over from the editorial staff of the Chicago *Tribune*.

Denslow's tenure was also brief. By the end of that year, he had resigned and was replaced by James F. Ballantyne and later Ballantyne was succeeded by John G. Nicolay, who had been President Lincoln's private secretary. Perhaps it was the lack of any strong continuous direction, but the paper failed to prosper and by the early fall of 1870 the owners were ready to sell. Three Chicagoans were interested in acquiring it. One was John R. Walsh, then president of the Western News Company and later president of the Chicago National Bank. The other two were business men, Homer N. Hilbard and William H. Schuyler. They invited McCullagh to join them and offered him a share in the ownership.[4]

They had heard of his work with the *Enquirer* and wanted a strong man to take over the editorial direction of the paper. McCullagh must have been tempted by the opportunity of acquiring a share in the ownership as well as the challenge of building a successful paper in Chicago. He accepted the offer and persuaded his brother, John W. McCullagh to join him. John McCullagh, who was born in 1838, had been apprenticed as a printer in Dublin at the age of thirteen, had come to the United States in 1861. He had a small reputation for his humorous writing.

One of the first acts of McCullagh after he became the managing editor of the *Republican,* was to reduce its page size and the price. It sold for three cents. Soon the *Republican* was beginning to attract attention—and circulation. But building a newspaper and acquiring readers takes time, and unfortunately, time ran out for McCullagh in Chicago before he could accomplish his objectives. The great Chicago fire in October 1871 destroyed the offices and plant of the *Republican,* and with it McCullagh's private library. McCullagh and his brother lost all they had invested, in the flames that swept through the business district and the south and west side residential sections of the city.

Melville E. Stone, general manager of the Associated Press, summed up McCullagh's year in Chicago when he told the Chicago *Tribune*[5] at the time of McCullagh's death that: "When Charles A. Dana made a failure of the paper, Mr. McCullagh was sent for, came here, and made a success of it. He continued as the responsible editor until the time of the Chicago fire. That destroyed everything and he found it impracticable to restore the paper. This was not surprising when it is remembered that it was a serious question even with Mr. Storey whether the *Times* should resume publication." The *Times* in 1871 was the leading newspaper in Chicago.

McCullagh's comment was more laconic. Asked a number of years later about it he replied,[6] "I have lived here (St. Louis) since I was burned out in Chicago. Previous to that Divine dispensation, I had lived here in 1859 and 60."

Divine dispensation may not have been an idle phrase. The fire might even be said to be a blessing in disguise, for it led to the offer for McCullagh to return to the *Missouri Democrat*. The *Republican* did continue a token publication until the following March in order to retain its Associated Press franchise. Its goodwill and subscription list were then sold and it became the Chicago *Inter-Ocean*.[7]

In St. Louis the *Democrat* had prospered since the war. Six years earlier the paper had moved to a new building at Fourth and Pine streets and had installed a new four-cylinder Hoe press. The owners, George W. Fishback, William McKee and Daniel M. Houser, had begun to expand their news coverage and were spending money for telegraph tolls. In 1867 they had hired Henry Stanley, whom McCullagh had known as a war correspondent, to cover Northwestern Missouri, Kansas, and Nebraska. He won distinction that year for his reports on the Indian wars. Advertising rates had been increased and by 1870 McKee, who held a one-half interest in the paper, was netting $25,000 a year. Fishback owned a third interest and Houser one-sixth.[8]

But differences over policies and politics were beginning to develop. Colonel William M. Grosvenor, who had been named editor in 1866 after having edited two papers in New Haven, Connecticut, had fallen out with McKee over politics. On January 24, 1871 readers of the *Democrat* were notified in its columns that Grosvenor was "no longer connected" with the *Democrat*. By the time of the Chicago fire, the owners had not found the replacement they wanted and the news that McCullagh might be available gave them their opportunity. They offered him the position as managing editor, and as a bonus, a small share in the ownership. McCullagh came back to St. Louis late that fall.

Had McCullagh been able to foresee what the next twelve months would bring, he might have hesitated to accept the offer. He had scarcely settled down in his job when the *Democrat* was sold on March 22, 1872. Certainly before that time he must have become aware of the disagreement between Fishback and the other two partners. One cause may have been political differences among the partners. Support for this assumption came later when Fishback hired Grosvenor as editor of the *Democrat*. There probably were also differences of opinion on the amount of money being spent for news gathering; Fishback was not an enthusiastic believer in this policy as were the other two. It can also be assumed that Fishback wanted a larger share of the profits and was jealous of McKee's financial position.

In any event the dispute came to a head in March. Fishback announced he would either buy out his partners, or sell his interest to them.[9] Finally, when Fishback saw he was getting nowhere with his offer, he went to court and sought an order for the sale of the *Democrat*. The public sale was conducted on March 22 in the law office of Irwin L. Smith, one of the lawyers for McKee and Houser. Fishback opened the bidding at $100,000. McKee countered with a bid of $150,000. When the bidding was over Fishback had topped McKee and Houser's final bid of $456,000 by $100.

It meant that Fishback would have to pay $304,066.64 for McKee's half interest and Houser's sixth interest. A previous stipulation provided that whoever bought the paper would protect McCullagh's interest. The price was surprisingly high for that time, as the *Missouri Republican,* the *Democrat's* leading rival, commented the following day:

"The actual material in the Democratic establishment would be valued at a comparatively small proportion of the price which the journal has just sold for, but this material comprises only a small proportion of the real value of the establishment. The attributes of age, established character, political views, advertising patronage, public influence and subscription lists, all constitute the substantial elements of value in an established journal. The *Democrat* has its share of the value elements, and they repersent a large proportion of the handsome price for which the paper sold."

On March 25, Fishback announced to the readers that the *Democrat* would continue to be a Republican paper and would strive to be "a full and complete newspaper—a faithful record of the world's history from day to day, and a complete chronicle of all the interests of all the people in their relations to each other as social and moral beings." Presumably it would be McCullagh's task to fulfill that promise. To complicate his problem, the *Democrat* was soon to face new competition from the former part owners of the *Democrat*. On July 18, McKee and Houser published the first issue of the St. Louis *Globe*. They had leased a building at 118 North Third Street and had designed a new format. The *Globe*'s name plate was set in Old English type, just as is the *Globe-Democrat* today. The new format was in "quarto form" with eight pages of six columns each, twenty-three inches long. The format was an innovation, but in the following four years, three other St. Louis dailies, the *Dispatch,* the *Republican* and the *Times* followed the *Globe*'s example. The *Democrat* continued to appear in what was the usual blanket format of the times, with four pages thirty inches long and ten columns on each page. The *Democrat* charged $14.00 for a year's subscription and thirty cents a week delivered by carrier. The *Globe*'s annual subscription was $12.00 or twenty-five cents a week by carrier. The reduction obviously indicated the concern of the *Globe*'s owners, who recognized they were adding to the competition in a crowded field. The newcomer was the tenth daily in St. Louis, including the four German language papers.

McCullagh's counterpart on the new paper was Charles R. Davis, who had been on the staff of the *Democrat* for sixteen years. On July 26 the *Globe* launched the *Weekly Globe,* published on Fridays and the *Semi-Weekly Globe,* issued on Tuesdays and Fridays. McKee and Houser also lowered the advertising rates. The *Democrat* charged fifteen cents an agate line for one publication and ten cents for the second and third insertion. The *Globe* cut the price to twelve cents and eight cents respectively.

It was inevitable that the rivalry between the two papers should spill over onto the editorial page. McCullagh referred to the *Globe* office as the "Robbers' Roost," a reference to his charge that the *Globe* was reprinting news items from the Western Associated Press, culled from other papers. He also hinted that McKee's activities smelled of graft.

It was an era when sniping on the editorial page was accepted by the readers, and no doubt, relished. If personalities were bruised, the recipients of the paragraph block-busters seemed to bear up remarkably well and usually retaliated with vigorous gusto. Politicians in that day apparently were equally thick-skinned. Long before President Truman summed up the proper posture for a politician in his pointed axiom, "If you can't stand the heat, get out of the kitchen," editors and politicians had learned to be philosophical.

However, McCullagh soon found that his Irish inheritance could not accept another kind of infighting. Shortly after Fishback took over the sole ownership of the *Democrat,* he was joined by his brother, William P. Fishback, more familiarly known as "Pink." The brother had been living in Indianapolis, Indiana, and later returned to that city to become dean of the Indianapolis University Law School. He brought with him a number of Indianapolis newspaper men and the *Democrat* proudly announced the newcomers were prepared to give St. Louis a "real newspaper." [10]

Included in the important talent was Newton Crane, a young man from the east who boasted of a college education. Apparently he possessed considerable charm and a patina of good manners, for he promptly began to be received by the social elite of the city and to pay court to the daughter of one of the wealthier citizens of St. Louis. He also impressed George W. Fishback. In October, just six months after the withdrawal of McKee and Houser from the *Democrat,* Fishback sent for McCullagh to inform him that he had decided to name Crane as the managing editor. McCullagh, Fishback said, could remain in the employ of the *Democrat* as the city editor.

McCullagh's reply was characterized and no doubt inspired by his experience as a war correspondent. "A general," he told Fishback, "does not take orders from a corporal." [11] Rather than step down, he added, he would resign, and he did. One can only speculate as to whether McCullagh had any premonition of Fishback's action and had sounded out McKee and Houser, but no sooner had his resignation become known than the owners of the *Globe* sent for him and offered him the managing editorship of the paper. McCullagh in later years dismissed his departure from the *Democrat* with this brief comment: "I became managing editor of the *Globe* in the fall of 1873, having previously been discharged from the St. Louis *Democrat* by its proprietor."

The transfer of jobs, and the loyalties, was made with a singular absence of fanfare. It is interesting to note that in September the *Globe* carried a paragraph on the editorial page which said: "An item in yesterday's *Times* stated that Mr. McCullagh will assume an editorial position on the *Globe*. There is no foundation for the statement." The denial suggests, not only that rumors of the breach between Fishback and his managing editor were being circulated, but also that the owners of the *Globe* were aware of them and perhaps had sounded McCullagh out on a possible shift to the *Globe*.

There was no formal announcement of his appointment at the *Globe,* but surely the paper's readers must have soon become aware of a new fighting spirit in the editorial shafts directed at the Democrat and its owner. On July 21, Charles R. Davis, who had been the chief editorial writer, died, so McCullagh was the logical man to take over. He accepted the challenge of the editorial sniping of the *Democrat* with all of an Irishman's delight in a lively scrap. The *Democrat* attacked its former editor with the charge that McCullagh had slandered Dr. Stuart Robinson in that paper, and then had gone over to the *Globe*. McCullagh promptly fired back with this blast:[12]

> Does it occur to the editor of the *Democrat* that none but dirty birds ever befoul their own nests? And doesn't that individual know that in publishing the Old School Presbyterian's attack upon a person once in the *Democrat*'s employ, and at present an involuntary stockholder in it, he commits the very offense? The subject matter of the assault is an article in relation to Dr. Stuart Robinson, and the individual assailed is one who was supposed to be managing editor of the *Democrat* at the time of publication. If Geo. W. Fishback was not holding that position at the time referred to, he must have sworn falsely in the partnership then pending. For the first time in American journalism, a newspaper opens its columns to the venom of an exasperated ass directed against itself, and then pats the author on the back. This is impersonal journalism with a vengeance.

McCullagh was referring in his editorial to the fact that he still held sixteen shares of *Democrat* stock, and Fishback had stubbornly refused any compensation for the shares. A little later he admonished his rival with this paragraph: "The *Democrat* ought not be severe on Dana as the editor of Appleton's *Cyclopedia*. He contributes most of the leaders that adorn the columns of that journal."

In another editorial paragraph, he pointed out that the *Democrat* was paying $50.00 a week to the Associated Press for its wire news. The *Globe,* he wrote, pays $50.00 a day in telegraph tolls to keep its readers abreast of the news. Moreover, he charged, the *Democrat* was stealing the *Globe*'s dispatches and reprinting them the following day. By December McCullagh in another editorial salvo claimed that the *Globe* was printing three thousand more copies every day than the *Democrat*. By January the *Globe* was running an open challenge in italics at the top of its editorial page, challenging the *Democrat* to an impartial audit of circulation. "The *Globe*," he wrote, "is willing to open its books to an audit. If the *Democrat* could show its circulation to be greater, the *Globe* would donate $200 to charity. If its daily circulation was larger, another $200, if the circulation of the *Weekly Globe* was not three times greater than the *Democrat,* and $100 if the *Globe* did not have a bigger Sunday circulation."

Apparently McCullagh was confident of the accuracy of his figures. He had a personal interest in the *Globe*'s circulation, aside from professional pride. His agreement with McKee and Houser stipulated that he would continue to serve as managing editor as long as the circulation of the *Globe* continued to grow.

One reason why the *Globe* was paying much more for telegraph news than the *Democrat* was that the *Globe* did not own a Western Associated Press membership. Under the rules of that cooperative association, the unanimous consent of the members in St. Louis was necessary to obtain a franchise. The *Globe* had made several attempts to secure a membership, and as might have been expected, each time Fishback voted against the *Globe*'s application. However, early in January 1874, McKee and Houser solved the problem. The German language paper, the *Missouri Staats-Zeitung* had failed and on January 6 was purchased by Joseph Pulitzer at a foreclosure sale. Pulitzer, a shrewd businessman, recognized that the paper had one important asset—its

Associated Press membership. The same day Pulitzer negotiated the sale of the paper to McKee and Houser for slightly more than $40,000.[13] It was this nest egg that Pulitzer used later to buy the St. Louis *Dispatch* in 1878.

To meet the legal requirements, the *Globe* changed the name of the publishing company to the Missouri Staats-Zeitung Company. On January 8 the masthead stated that the Missouri Staats-Zeitung Company was the publisher of the *Globe*. The same day, in an editorial paragraph, McCullagh announced that the *Globe* was now a member of the Associated Press. There was also this comment: "The *Democrat* reportial end is afflicted with a rumor that the *Globe* will be printed in German. For all the influence it has, the *Democrat* might as well be printed in Scandinavian."

Other papers in St. Louis found this verbal dueling amusing and there was considerable speculation among local observers as to whether the *Globe* would outlast the *Democrat,* or visa versa. On January 11, McCullagh answered not only the *Democrat,* but the other papers when he wrote: "Men who pay $40,-000 in cash for the privilege of special advantages with their rivals are not to be easily distracted . . . If they do not wake up, the consolidation of the *Republican* and the *Democrat* will be seriously talked of before the consolidation of the *Globe* and the *Staats-Zeitung* has ceased to be laughed at."

Five days later, McCullagh leveled another round at the *Democrat*. He wrote: "Those who are particularly interested in reading the *Democrat* editorials, can read most of them in advance by perusing the *Anzeiger,* and competent translators tell us they read much better in the original."

Fishback did not take the *Globe*'s success in obtaining a franchise quietly. He demanded a meeting be called of the St. Louis members of the Associated Press to discuss whether a German language paper could be turned into an English paper. As members in good standing McKee and Houser attended the meeting and defended their position. The St. Louis *Dispatch* in reporting the meeting summed it up this way: "It was finally ended by recognizing the right of the English proprietors of a 'Dutch' newspaper to change its language at their own sweet will, with all the members of the Association except the *Democrat,* voting 'aye.' "

Fishback did not lose that round gracefully. The *Democrat*'s editorial comment this next morning was:

> The *Globe* concluded, after mature reflection, that it was better to buy the dispatches of the Associated Press than to steal them, and as our columns show, its proprietors have purchased the *Staats-Zeitung* and have changed it to an English morning paper under the name of the St. Louis *Globe*. This, it is claimed, gives the *Globe* the right to receive the dispatches heretofore delivered to its German predecessor as will be seen in the proceedings of the local Board of the Associated Press. The *Democrat* voted "No" on the proposition to admit the *Globe* to the Association. We have a prejudice to the effect that a man who steals his neighbor's property is a thief; and by our negative vote we testified to our opinion that men who confess themselves to be thieves are undesirable associates.

On January 16 the *Democrat* took the fight to court by filing an injunction suit to restrain the *Globe* from using the Associated Press. The petition alleged the *Democrat* had suffered "irreparable damages" and claimed that the only way the *Globe* could obtain a franchise was as a new member. The following morning McCullagh's comment was that "The *Democrat* has made another exhibition of its own weakness and sadly shows its sores to the public." On January 18 there were seven separate paragraphs in similar vein inveighing the *Democrat* and its resort to the courts. Then on January 18, McCullagh reprinted an editorial comment from the Cincinnati *Enquirer* and speculated that it must have been written by Cockerill. McCullagh pointed out: "When a newspaper steps into court and puts on the public record that it has been 'irreparably damaged' in the short space of ten days, it must not expect to receive a large amount of sympathy from the journals of the country." But he felt the *Enquirer* had been "a little too rough, even for the poor *Democrat*." Referring to the *Enquirer*'s comment, he added: "Don't say the *Democrat* wants any paper to be as stupid as itself. Whatever its disposition may be, it knows that is impossible." Frequently in this period the *Globe* inserted a one-line comment between its editorials: "And the actual damage is irreparable."

While McCullagh concentrated his heaviest editorial barrages against the *Democrat,* he did not neglect his other morning rival, the *Missouri Republican.* It was the *Republican*'s boast that it was the oldest paper in St. Louis. "The *Republican*," wrote McCullagh on November 3, 1873, "flaunts its antiquity as proof of its sagacity, but age and experience are not always guarantees of merit." He suggested that the *Republican* add the letters, B.C. to the 1808, the year it was founded, because "the Psalms of David were published in it as original matter and it had the letter list when the Apostles were writing to each other."

To keep his hand in, there were comments on the other papers as well. On February 5, 1874 McCullagh noted: "The *Dispatch* wants the State to build an asylum for the partially insane. We think the State has quite enough to do without taking care of the editorial staff of the *Dispatch.*" Later when the *Dispatch* accused the *Globe* of sensationalism in its news coverage, McCullagh fired back with a lecture on what the *Globe* considered sensational journalism.

This sort of editorial skirmishing, in which McCullagh obviously delighted, did not distract his attention from the news pages of the *Globe.* While the readers of the *Globe* seemed to enjoy his barbed comments, he knew that the way to increase circulation was to print more news than his competitors. The acquisition of Associated Press service provided the opportunity, and in addition, the owners seemed willing to spend money for special correspondents and telegraph tolls. The expanded news coverage quickly became apparent. There was much less reprinted material culled from the exchanges and more special dispatches. Local coverage increased and much of it was spicy by today's standards. For example, there was a column story with the enticing one-column head: "Galled Jades." It was an interview with the mayor on conditions at the city's Social Evil Hospital, which treated the "Jades" of easy virtue.

Even before McCullagh took over, the *Globe* had been printing reports of one or more Sunday sermons each Monday. McCullagh expanded this feature under the eye-catching head: "Sanctuary Drippings."

On April 25 McCullagh reminded his readers in an editorial paragraph that "Tomorrow's *Globe* will be the best newspaper in St. Louis, as usual. It will contain more choice reading than can be found within the covers of any two books that can be bought for three dollars." In the issue of May 2 he scored a clean beat and made local journalistic history by devoting the entire front page, with a runover on page 2, to printing the complete text of the eulogy of Senator Carl Schurz of Missouri in the Senate, to Charles Sumner, the distinguished Senator from Massachusetts, who had died a few days earlier. On the editorial page McCullagh explained that the text of the address had reached the *Globe* office at 11 o'clock the previous night and was immediately put into type. He added that "the makeup of today's *Globe* is somewhat changed by the pressure upon the first page," but assured his readers that other news had not been neglected and could be found on the other pages. The unusual treatment of the speech inspired considerable comment by rival papers, not all of it laudatory.

On May 3 another editorial paragraph informed *Globe* readers that "a special correspondent of the *Globe* is on his way by boat to New Orleans to report the facts on the great overflow." A week later he noted that "the situation in Little Rock is well told today by our special correspondent in Little Rock." The reference was to a hot fight in the Arkansas Legislature.

The *Globe* at this time was printing eight pages daily and twelve or more on Sundays as compared to the *Democrat*'s four pages with thirty inch columns. Advertising however, had declined for all newspapers. On September 24, 1873, a day long remembered as "Black Friday," Jay Gould's devious scheme to corner the gold market was thwarted by President Grant's order to the Treasury to sell, and the collapse of Gould's banking house in New York set off a mild panic across the nation. As unemployment rose advertisers reduced their expenditures. January 21, 1874 was a typical day for the months that followed the bursting of the gold bubble. The day the *Globe* carried no advertising on the first four pages, only two columns of ads on page 5, none on page 6 and five columns on page 7, including a one-column house ad. There was a scant half column of classified advertising on page 8.

Circulation however was increasing steadily. By February 1, 1874, McCullagh claimed the *Globe* was printing five thousand more copies every day than the *Democrat*. In another paragraph he wrote: "The Genteel Chief of the *Democrat,* accompanied by the vulgar partners, will attend the session of the Circuit Court tomorrow. They will swear to the fact that the *Democrat* has been 'irreparably damaged' by the *Globe* and it will probably be the first time in their lives that they ever told the truth."

The hearing on the *Democrat*'s injunction suit was postponed, and by this time it was increasingly evident that the *Democrat* was in serious financial trouble. Crane, who had supplanted McCullagh as managing editor, left and had been replaced by Grosvenor, whom McCullagh referred to as "Bummer Bill." Crane married and went to England, where he practiced law. McCullagh noted his departure in this paragraph: " 'Journalism is the grave of genius,' says one of the eastern college graduates this year. If he wanted to make a first class axiom, he should have said that college graduates are the grave-diggers of journalism." [14]

Early in the summer of 1874 Fishback was ready to sell out. The *Democrat* was deeply in debt and he was faced with the necessity of purchasing new presses if he continued to publish. He sent his lawyer, Henry T. Blow to McKee's office. McCullagh later described what happened:[15]

Early in the summer of 1874, Henry T. Blow called at the *Globe* office as an authorized agent of George W. Fishback, to negotiate the sale of the *Democrat.* The price named was within a few thousand dollars of that subsequently paid. Mr. McKee was absent from the city and the conference was held with Mr. Houser. Mr. Blow stated that Mr. Fishback was tired of the controversy which seemed inevitable so long as the two papers existed, and I edited one of them. He had recently employed Grosvenor to edit the *Democrat,* but with no other perceptible effect than to develop that remarkable person's power to reduce circulation, and his only hope of solvency was to make a sale to McKee and Houser. After a while McKee came home and gave the matter some attention. I expressed to him the opinion that extinction was cheaper than purchase, and that the *Democrat* could be sunk for half the money named as its price; that so long as it was edited and managed as it was at that time it was no rival of the *Globe*; and that the *Globe*'s only source of danger was in the possibility of the *Demo-*

crat passing into the hands of men of some newspaper ability and experience, which would give us a lively competition for the supremacy we then held. The *Democrat* was then shouting itself hoarse for Gentry, and although it had the entire Republican party of the state at its back, while the *Globe* was indulging in the luxury of a guerrilla war against both tickets and all candidates, the *Democrat,* as the books will show, went steadily down, while the *Globe* went steadily up in circulation and business.

There is no indication as to whether McCullagh's advice was a decisive factor, but in any event the offer was rejected and the feud continued. When the *Democrat* accused the *Globe* of being responsible for a disturbance in a ward meeting, McCullagh minced no words:[16] "When the editor of the *Democrat* says the *Globe* was directly or indirectly concerned with the disturbance of the Seventh Ward meeting, he is a willful and malignant liar."

Advertising began to pick up and the *Globe* was again running advertisements on the front page. Readers were lured by such heads on local stories as "A Horrible Outrage," which related the details of the rape of a servant girl; "Senile Lechery," and "Fearful Accident." The *Globe* began a new feature on the editorial page listing at the top of the first column directly under the masthead, a daily report of the proceedings in Congress. The Sunday edition carried a column of letters to the editor under the enticing head: "The Sunday Growler." McCullagh's editorial paragraphs covered a wide range of subjects. On April 28, for example, he wrote as follows: "The following note was received at the *Globe* yesterday: 'Dear Mack: John C. Priest will be recommended to the Circuit Court for appraiser in Forest Park business. Please pull him through.' We take it as insulting to suppose the *Globe* requires a reminder. The *Globe*'s towline is always at the service of Mr. Priest. We shall pull him through though the heavens fall."

The Rev. Henry Ward Beecher, pastor of the Plymouth Congregational Church of Brooklyn, popular lecturer and editor of the *Christian Union,* was in the news in the summer of 1874 as the result of the law suit brought against him by a member of his congregation charging adultery. McCullagh played the story to the hilt, usually putting it on the front page. The *Democrat* chided him for what it asserted as poor taste and sensationalism. In one of his few longer editorials, McCullagh vigorously defended the *Globe*'s handling of the story. The editorial was appropriately entitled "Mad Dogs and Editors."

McCullagh was understandably irked at the refusal of Fishback to pay him for the sixteen shares of stock he still held in the *Democrat*. On July 20 he wrote: "The *Democrat*'s boast that it has a policy can hardly refer to its internal policy for the treatment of small shareholders. That certainly is not a thing to be proud of." On August 4 McCullagh answered an attack by the *Democrat* this way: "Mr. George W. Fishback, the willful and malignant liar of the *Democrat* alluded to the editor of the *Globe* as having disgraced his former journalistic alliance, apparently unmindful of the fact that with full knowledge of the previous history of the editor of the *Globe,* he employed him to edit the *Democrat*. What disgusted Mr. Fishback was the fact that the managing editor of the *Democrat* had no more money to be swindled out of."

There was always a waspish humor in McCullagh editorial infighting. The day after calling Fishback a "willful and malignant liar," McCullagh, probably with tongue in cheek, was writing: "There is still painful evidence of personal journalism in the *Dispatch* and the *Republican*. We sincerely regret this, as the *Globe* has for a long time been setting a good example to its neighbors, by rigid abstinence from unfavorable epithets. We have often appealed to our brother editors to speak kindly of each other, or else observe a dignified and respectful silence. Let us have peace."

As the summer wore on, there began to be talk of the consolidation of the *Globe* and the *Democrat*. On September 8, McCullagh took notice of the rumors in this editorial paragraph:

> There has been some talk in the papers and among the people about a consolidation of the *Globe* and the *Democrat*—a double-barreled newspaper to be called the *Globe-Democrat*. All we have to say, so far as the Globe is concerned, is that the statement is not justified by the shadow of fact. The *Democrat* may be for sale for aught we know, but as the *Globe* is quite enough of a paper for one set of men to manage and own, we are not interested as a pur-

chaser. We are consolidating the subscription lists of the two journals very rapidly and it is not costing us a cent beyond the making of a first class paper. The statement that the *Globe* is for sale is true. The price is five cents a copy or twenty-five cents a week delivered by carrier.

As McCullagh had pointed out to McKee and Houser earlier, it was apparent that he was at the heart of the controversy between the two papers, and it is a reasonable assumption that one of Fishback's obsessions was to eliminate McCullagh from the newspaper scene in St. Louis. McCullagh in turn was just beginning to fight. Much later he recalled that period:[17] "I was then an unwilling stockholder in the *Democrat* and had sent several lawyers in pursuit of a bad investment, but all to no purpose. I thought I would begin the new year (1875) with a new row, and I was in a fair way to make things lively in the bowels of the *Democrat*."

He opened fire on January 5 with a paragraph which noted that "the annual meeting of the stockholders of the *Democrat* is called for next Wednesday. Five pallbearers are to be selected. It is getting to be a very sad business." On January 17, he wrote: "The Genteel Chief of the *Democrat* has a new way to punish his enemies. He compels them to own stock in the *Democrat*." A few days later he wrote: "The actual damage is irreparable, and not only that, Mack has threatened to ruin the company. This makes it doubly sad."

By this time the end of the feud was in sight. The *Democrat* was continuing to lose circulation and McCullagh was boasting on the *Globe*'s editorial page that the Sunday *Globe* would reach twenty-five thousand by June. On May 11, McKee and Houser made their move. They called on Fishback and offered to purchase the controlling interest in the *Democrat,* held by Fishback and Otto A. Hasselman, for $325,000. The figure was $131,000 less than Fishback had paid in 1872. McCullagh later commented: "The price named at the start was precisely that given at the end, $325,000. The *Globe* had distanced the *Democrat* out of sight, but there was still the dangerous possibility of combing Grosvenor out of the latter journal and making it a rival to the former. This greatly enhanced the value of the *Democrat* to the proprietors of the *Globe*."

The reason cited by McCullagh undoubtedly was a consideration weighed by McKee and Houser, but it probably was not the decisive factor. By that time the partners had learned of McKee's connection with the Whiskey Ring and probably feared the *Democrat* would exploit it. The sale was announced in both newspapers on May 12. The *Globe* reported that it was the "merging of the two papers." The *Democrat* said that arrangements had been made under which the "two papers would be published by McKee and Houser."

The sale, which was formally consummated on May 18, included a provision to retain for McCullagh the stock he held in the *Democrat,* valued at $16,000. McCullagh was also given some additional stock in the consolidated paper.[18] Fishback agreed not to enter the newspaper business in St. Louis for a "term of years."

Bitter as the personal feud between McCullagh and Fishback had been, it is interesting to note that McCullagh did not hold a grudge against his adversary. A number of years later, Fishback was a candidate for a lucrative federal appointment in St. Louis. His friends, remembering the feud, worried whether the *Globe-Democrat* and its editor would oppose him. When one of Fishback's supporters asked the *Globe-Democrat*'s Washington correspondent what the paper would do, McCullagh wired to the correspondent:[19] "I know of no rule of diplomacy which makes a case of persona non grata against a man for having a d——d fool for a brother. Fishback is the best suggestion yet made."

The first issue of the consolidated paper appeared on May 20, 1875, using the *Democrat*'s blanket format. The equipment of the *Globe* was moved to the *Democrat* building and on June 5, with the *Globe*'s press installed, the paper appeared in the *Globe*'s format and the pages were widened to seven columns. In the first issue McCullagh pointed out that neither the paper nor the owners were new, and the paper was more of a marriage than a birth. He assured the reader's that the *Globe-Democrat* would remain Republican in politics and would remain "true to the party, always supposing that the party will be true to the principles that gave it birth." He added that it was his aim to make the *Globe-Democrat* "as near perfect as liberal means, large outlay and large experience could make it."

On October 3, some four months later, he wrote that "The *Globe-Democrat* is everywhere regarded as a model newspaper, and has more readers than any paper in the West."

In retrospect, it can be said that the merger of the *Globe* and the *Democrat* was a significant milestone in McCullagh's career. It was as the editorial genius of the *Globe-Democrat* that he was to make his greatest imprint on journalism. The contract he made with McKee and Houser for his services as managing editor was never put in writing. It was an understanding that he was free to run the editorial and news departments of the paper "as long as he kept up the circulation." One of his first acts was to make it clear that there was to be no censorship of the "upstairs," the news and editorial departments, from "downstairs," the business department.

After the merger, the *Globe-Democrat* Printing Company was incorporated with a paid-up capital of $500,000. In the new corporation McCullagh held stock worth $20,000. Houser owned $166,000; Henry McKee $10,000; Simeon Ray $10,000; and William McKee approximately $300,000.

THE NEW JOURNALISM

5

Journalism's historians agree that marked changes took place in American newspapers in the last three decades of the nineteenth century. It was a period when new ideas in news coverage and presentation were developing, new concepts of makeup and headlines were evolving, and an infusion of new vitality was given to editorial pages. It was also a period when advertising expanded and newspaper promotion began to appear. It is ironic that the two men who were the real pioneers in the new journalism are almost entirely ignored today. One of them was Daniel M. Houser, business manager of the St. Louis *Globe* and later of the St. Louis *Globe-Democrat*. The architect of the new journalism was McCullagh, but his achievement would not have been possible without the solid backing of Houser.

It is only fair to say that some of the precepts on which McCullagh built the *Globe-Democrat* into one of the outstanding newspapers of the period had been started by Houser before McCullagh moved over from the *Democrat*. It is interesting to speculate what might have been the outcome of the *Globe*'s duel with the *Democrat*, had Fishback been willing to give McCullagh the free hand he enjoyed on the *Globe* after taking over the editorial direction of that paper. Houser spent money for news on a lavish scale far beyond anything St. Louis had known up to that time. As Eugene Field noted in his poetic tribute to McCullagh:

> No matter what the item is, if there's an item in it,
> You bet your life he's on to it, and nips it in a minute!

> From multifarious nations, countries, monarchies and lands,
> From Afric's sunny fountains and India's coral strands,
> From Greenland's icy mountains and Siloam's shady rills,
> He gathers in the telegrams and Houser pays the bills.

Both men had the vision to recognize that American readers were changing. The readers wanted more than local items, police news, and politics. It was McCullagh who blazed the trail in expanding the news coverage and disregarding tradition.

The two men who are usually credited with having made the greatest contribution to the new journalism are the first Joseph Pulitzer and William Randolph Hearst. There were others who perhaps should be mentioned: men like Melville E. Stone and Victor F. Lawson in Chicago, Henry Watterson in Louisville and William R. Nelson in Kansas City. Certainly McCullagh must be included in this list. He was the innovator of many of the ideas and politics which the others adopted so successfully. He is credited with inventing the interview.[1] He set an example in comprehensive news coverage, both local and national. He was a vigorous campaigner against malfeasance and misfeasance in public office. He was among the first, if not the first, to introduce newspaper promotion. He was sensationalizing the news before either Pulitzer or Hearst were in the field.

Frank Luther Mott in his *American Journalism* broke Pulitzer's "new" formula into six parts: an aggressive news policy both for local and national news; crusades and stunts; a vigorous, outspoken editorial page; physical size of the paper in number of pages; liberal use of illustrations, and a continuous promotion policy for the paper. With the exception of newspaper stunts, such as the New York *World*'s raising funds for the base for the Statue of Liberty, and Nelly Bly's trip around the world, McCullagh was doing all of the things Pulitzer used, before Pulitzer became a publisher.

Why then has McCullagh been so completely ignored? One reason is obvious. All who knew him agree that he was extremely reticent. He had few close friends and seemed deliberately to shroud himself in anonymity. Another reason undoubtedly was his death at fifty-four in 1896 before the full impact of the new journalism became apparent. A third factor was that he was content to remain in St. Louis instead of going to New York where Pulitzer and Hearst attracted national attention. Still another explanation is that the two men who receive the credit for the new journalism were publishers. McCullagh was first and always an editor and after his experience in Chicago apparently had no interest in becoming a publisher.

Certainly none of those mentioned faced a greater challenge than the situation that confronted McCullagh after the consolidation of the *Globe* and the *Democrat*. St. Louis in 1875 had seven morning dailies, including the four German language papers. The *Missouri Republican* was his foremost rival. Until McCullagh began to challenge its leadership, it was admittedly the most influential paper in St. Louis, and perhaps in Missouri. The *Republican* was the voice of the Democratic Party. Its conservative policy endeared it to the businessmen of the city. While its circulation was not much more than fifteen-thousand, it could boast of wide readership of its weekly edition throughout rural Missouri. McCullagh was well aware of the nature of his competition as is shown by his editorial attacks on the *Republican* after the consolidation of the *Globe* and the *Democrat*.

One of the theories advanced by critics of the press is that in every community the newspapers are a mirror of the community itself. They argue that such factors as the ethnic heritage of the citizenry, the cultural standards of the community, and its industry and commerce, determine the character of its newspapers. While a valid case can be made to the contrary by those who insist that the newspaper can and should be a leader in educating its readers, the influence of the community cannot be discounted. What then, was St. Louis like in 1875?

It was a sprawling city of some 330,000 inhabitants. It stretched then, as now, for nearly twenty miles along the Mississippi River. It had made a remarkable recovery from the disruptions and the division of its sympathies in the Civil War. It was still the gateway to the rapidly growing west and southwest. Industry was expanding and the city was the distribution center for the Mississippi Valley. St. Louis in 1875 was the largest flour milling center of the nation. Its first brewery was established in 1810 and by 1875 it was beginning to make good on the familiar description of "first in booze, first in shoes, and last in the American League." The last in the list was not always accurate, for the old St. Louis Browns, owned by Chris von der Ahe, brought the city its first baseball championship in 1885. By 1875 the shoe industry was well established and St. Louis had a number of neighborhood breweries. The *Missouri Republican* had reported as early as 1860 that the average beer consumption per capita in St. Louis was 658 glasses annually.

    The packetboats were still lining the levee but their era was running out. On July 4, 1874 St. Louis held a special celebration in honor of the day. The occasion was the formal opening of the Eads Bridge, one of the engineering marvels of the time. It was named for the man who built it, James Buchanan Eads, and it was the first bridge of its kind in America. More important, it enabled St. Louis to compete with Chicago as the railroad center of the nation. By 1874 there were nine railroads with terminals on the east side of the river, but until the bridge was opened, both passengers and freight had to be transported across the river by ferry.

    By 1875 the city was beginning to move west. Fourth and Fifth Streets were where the best shops were located. The Merchants' Exchange was located on Fourth Street and was one of the principal buildings. It was big enough to accommodate a national political convention in 1876 and it was the scene of many of the city's social and civic gatherings. Fifth Street was later to become St. Louis' Broadway and beyond it was the impressive, but as yet unfinished Post Office and the old Four Courts Building, which housed the courts, the municipal jail, and the Police Department. Out on Twelfth Street, now a major thoroughfare of the city, was a large farmers' market. McCullagh in 1875 was living at 610 Walnut Street, about five blocks from the *Globe-Democrat* office.

    The notable structures in the older section of the central district were the Old Cathedral at Third and Walnut, built in 1834, and the Courthouse, which occupied the block bounded by Market, Chestnut, Fifth, and Fourth Streets. It was in this building the famous Dred Scott case was filed and before the Civil War slaves were auctioned off from the east steps. The two historic structures have been retained and restored as part of the Jefferson Riverfront Memorial in St. Louis.

Much of the older section from Third Street to the levee was given over to cheap rooming houses, bagnios, and saloons. West of Twelfth Street, the middle class citizens still clung to Lucas Place and Lafayette Park. St. Louis, like its sister cities of the Middle West, was a gas-lit, horse-drawn city, with as much but certainly no more than its share of misery and vice. It could boast that it was the fifth largest city in the nation.

In one important respect, however, St. Louis was different. If its rivals sneered at it as being stodgy, it had a charm all its own, compounded of the ethnic groups that mingled on the bank of the river, and its location, where north met south. The French, who came first gave to St. Louis the names for many of its streets: Gravois, DeBalivere, Bellefontaine, and a spirit of gaiety. The Irish, who arrived in droves during the first half of the nineteenth century settled in "Kerry Patch" just north of the business district, built St. Patrick's Church at Sixth and Biddle in 1845, and enlivened the city with their violence and their brawling zest for life. The Germans also arrived in the early decades of the nineteenth century and settled in both north and south St. Louis. By 1875 about 150,000, roughly one-third of the population either had been born in Germany or were the children of parents who came from there.

The Germans, like the Irish, tended to isolate themselves and the very fact that there were four German language newspapers indicated how they clung to their Old World customs and affections. Their homes were invariably neat and clean; the custom of frowning on anyone who neglects to scrub the front porch steps every Saturday, persists to this day in south St. Louis. They were hard working and ambitious and they contributed to the city's growing importance as an industrial and trade center. They also brought to St. Louis the Old World's convivial atmosphere with open air summer beer gardens such as Schneider's and entertainment spots like Uhrig's Cave. They formed Liederkranz societies and intellectual discussion groups. They loved good food, and older St. Louisans still sigh for the gourmet delights of such restaurants as Tony Faust's and Papa Koerner's.

The city's location on the border line between north and south and east and west, gave it an atmosphere and a flavor all its own.

It was an urban city, sophisticated and serene before Chicago was more than a small hamlet. If it was conservative and even a little smug, it was also tolerant and friendly. Theodore Dreiser joined the staff of the *Globe-Democrat* in 1892 and noted [2] that "Contrasted to Chicago, it was not a metropolis at all. While rich and successful, it was a creature of another mood." St. Louis was not a city in a hurry. Its citizens were convinced it had already arrived; hence there was no reason for bustle and frenzy, nor for rudeness and ruthlessness. These traits remain distinctive of St. Louis today.

St. Louisans in 1875 took their newspapers seriously and felt a personal relationship to the owners and editors. McCullagh discovered this relationship soon after he came to St. Louis from Chicago. Reminiscing later, he said:[3]

> In general I may say, after I came down here, as I remarked to a friend, there was a large part of the population that would not allow their wives to have a baby without coming to see Mr. McKee as to the name of the baby. Or I can state more accurately that I have never known a man to run for office, whether for marketmaster or President, who did not first want to come and see Mr. McKee—I mean on our side—and Mr. McKee always took more interest in that man than if he were running himself. I told him on one occasion since I went into the *Globe* office there was getting to be a little too much of this. People would ask to see the editor when they could not see Mr. McKee, and I had to tell them that there must be a divorce between the editorial department and the counting room, because I could not afford the time to everybody that wanted to see Mr. McKee, and run the paper at the same time.

McCullagh not only believed there should be a sharp line of demarcation between the editorial department and the business office, but he discouraged callers. One reason was the obvious consideration that they wasted his time, but he also felt he should insulate himself from pressures of every kind. When he took over as the managing editor of the *Globe-Democrat,* he chose for himself the smallest room in the editorial department upstairs in the building at Fourth and Pine Streets. It was sparsely furnished with a large desk and two chairs, leaving little vacant space. McCullagh occupied the chair facing the desk. The other chair was at his right against the wall, and it was usually piled high with newspapers.

Typical of his reception of guests is the account of a call upon the editor by Congressman Jehu Baker of Illinois.[4] "He asked me to sit down," the Congressman reported. "I looked about me. There was no place to sit down." His experience was typical. McCullagh's invitation to sit down was only a superficial gesture of courtesy. He knew that if the visitor remained uncomfortably on his feet, his business would be quickly transacted and he would leave. The few occasions when McCullagh would rise and remove the papers indicated his concession to a visitor he wanted to see. McCullagh frankly admitted that it was a premeditated strategy. He told a friend that he was constantly annoyed by well-meaning but tiresome citizens who came in almost every afternoon, sat an hour or more and told him how to run the *Globe-Democrat*. He loaded the chair with exchanges deliberately, he said, and shortened the calls by providing standing room only.

McCullagh recognized, as did Houser, that the *Globe-Democrat* could not rely on the old Western Associated Press if it was to be an outstanding newspaper. He also saw that there was a fertile field in which to expand the paper's circulation far beyond the city's immediate trade territory, particularly in the Southwest and West. He began to build his own news service and to train the hundreds of correspondents he hired himself. For their guidance he laid down forty-eight specific rules—and he sternly enforced them.[5]

The first rule emphasized his passion for exclusive news. It read: "Correspondents of the *Globe-Democrat* must not act as correspondents of any other morning paper published in St. Louis." Knowing that correspondents far from the home office were tempted to exaggerate and even to draw on their imagination, the second rule reminded them: "Matter sent this paper must be strictly accurate as to fact. Bogus items, manufactured sensations and highly colored articles lacking in solid basis of fact are not wanted." Other rules were equally explicit:

Rule 3. Correspondents who send matter by wire in contravention of the rules of this circular may expect to have their dispatches returned for the collection of tolls. No reason exists why any correspondent should willfully or carelessly put a newspaper to the expense of paying for matter which cannot be used.

Rule 4. Do not use the mail for sending news. The mail is irregular, liable to delay in collection, forwarding and delivery. The post office is not responsible for accidents. News that is worth printing in the *Globe-Democrat* is worth paying telegraph tolls on.

Rule 5. Good news is often scarce. This journal desires no other kind. When there is nothing to send, send nothing.

Other rules gave detailed instructions for the preparation of copy and how stories should be filed. Illustrations of the right and wrong way to file specials were given.

Make a separate special of each item, McCullagh emphasized. No rule is so frequently disregarded as this. Correspondents have a great fancy for sending several distinct items lumped together between one date line and one signature. Put the filing time of each special immediately after the date. This gives a check on the operator who is compelled to transmit the filing time as written.

File your matter as early as possible, McCullagh urged. Nothing causes more trouble in a newspaper office than the bad habit which many correspondents have of filing matter unnecessarily late. Reports of today's happenings should be filed not later than 7 P.M.

Let your matter be free from comment. Don't use the first person. Don't lug in "your correspondent" when it is possible to avoid doing so.

All items must be clean cut, and give names of persons and places and date on which the event occurred. Indefinite items, lacking in these particulars, are not wanted.

From time to time the managing editor issues special circulars requesting particular classes of news. The circulars are to be, under all circumstances, regarded as confidential. We do not prompt our correspondents for the benefit of other papers.

Never say "A prominent citizen says" so and so. If his name cannot be used, leave out his statement. The "prominent citizen" never materializes when a libel suit is on trial.

Correspondents in Texas are prohibited from sending us items worded like those which they send to any of the Texas papers.

Other rules dealt with instructions for specific kinds of news. Some of them laid down the *Globe-Democrat*'s policy in reporting news of crime. In a period when criminal news was usually played up in sensational fashion, the *Globe-Democrat*'s was conservative. Instructions were liberally interspersed with "dont's."

The statements of prosecuting witnesses and prosecuting officers, McCullagh reminded his correspondents, are to be received with caution and never given as absolute fact. Every man accused of crime is entitled to a fair and truthful presentation of his case. Be particularly careful about cases regarding the use of other people's money. A man may have used his employer's money and be guilty neither of larceny nor embezzlement. A misappropriation of money which should form the basis of a civil suit for restitution does not always admit of a criminal charge being preferred.

In murders give the facts fully, but don't write against space, and don't stop to moralize. If possible send histories of the murdered man and his slayer. Don't hint at mysterious causes of crime. Do not send daily reports of testimony in murder trials without orders. In such cases, ask for instructions.

Seductions, rapes, cases of incest, and other unnatural relations are not wanted beyond the briefest possible mention in decent language. If lynching follows the commission of any of these crimes, send the lynching in full and then recite the original crime. When a lynching appears imminent, a correspondent should be on the lookout and have arrangements made for the instant use of the wire. All occasions in which a mob spirit finds full exhibition should be reported.

The following crimes are not wanted at all: horse stealings, larcenies, and burglaries, unless a large sum of money, not less than $1,000 is involved, or the burglar kills someone, or is killed or wounded himself; cutting scrapes and assaults which are not fatal. In a general way avoid trivial criminalities of all kinds.

When it is finally assured that a man is to hang, send by mail at least seven days before execution, a history of the crime for which he dies. This history should not exceed over 500 to 700 words. On day of execution send 300 to 500 words by wire of scenes of execution.''

Politics dominated much of the news in that period and partisanship was shared by both readers and editors. McCullagh gave special instructions for handling political news. He told his correspondents:

When a big political event is near at hand, notify this office and ask for instructions. In "off years" when there is no national campaign, trim political matter to the smallest possible number of words.

In an era when political slanting of the news was an accepted practice, McCullagh's insistence on fair and impartial reporting was unusual. On the editorial page he showed no mercy to the opposition, but he made it clear that he would not tolerate any unfair tactics in the news columns of the *Globe-Democrat*. It must be remembered that newspapers made no pretense of political independence as they do today and practised the old adage that "all's fair in love, war, and politics." McCullagh believed he could carry the torch for the Republican Party with his editorials and it can be argued that the readers' respect for the integrity of the *Globe-Democrat* benefited from his policy.

Some of his other instructions are interesting:

Obituary literature should at all times be as condensed as possible. Funerals need not be noticed.

In civil court proceedings report only cases involving large amounts or values. Do not advertise the counsel in a case.

Don't send a weather report every very hot, or very cold or very wet day.

Send all interesting elopements. Remember that the fact of a man and woman going to a train and failing to show up for a day or two does not necessarily constitute an elopement.

Send by wire only high society weddings. Make the report brief and do not use stereotyped phrases. Toilets and lists of presents are not wanted.

In strikes and lockouts send only facts. State the case from the employers' as well as from the employee's side. Report all cases of violence by strikers. The communistic utterances of labor agitators are not wanted.

Keep the office notified of important religious gatherings. In a general way report what is done at church assemblies rather than what is said. It is only the great leaders of the flock whose utterances should be reported by wire. A church controversy or any individual squabble is always in order.

Make reports of teachers' institutes and commencement proceedings as brief as possible. Full programmes are not wanted, but the more important and deserving features might be briefly noticed. Puffery of teachers and graduates will not be tolerated.

These rules of nearly a century ago are now almost universally accepted. They were not intended as precepts for all newspapers, but rather for the guidance of one man's staff of correspondents. It was not until the late Walter Williams, founder and first dean of the University of Missouri School of Journalism, wrote "The Journalist's Creed" in the 1890's that there was any widely disseminated code of ethics for the press. It was nearly fifty years after McCullagh that the American Society of Newspaper Editors adopted its code of ethics in April 1923. The language of both codes is more eloquent, but the basic principles are essentially the precepts set out by McCullagh.

McCullagh was not above pointing out the slips from grace of other papers, whose correspondents were not as thoroughly instructed. In an editorial paragraph he noted:[6]

The *Globe-Democrat* as a newspaper professing and intending always to keep up its record of current events, is grieved to confess that it has been distanced in a matter of purely local interest by two "foreign" journals, to wit: The Cincinnati *Enquirer* and the Chicago *Tribune*. The matter is the hanging of Sam Orr at Mount Vernon, Lawrence County, Illinois, on Thursday last, which is fully and graphically portrayed by our Cincinnati and Chicago contemporaries. They both assure us that Mr. Orr "died game." We dispatched a reporter to Mount Vernon, and instructed him to send us details of the execution by telegraph. He attempted to excuse his apparent dereliction by the allegation that Mr. Orr, so far from having "died game," did not die at all, the supreme court having granted him a stay of execution until the 18th. This trifling circumstance, however, was not allowed to interfere with the overwhelming desire of the *Tribune* and the *Enquirer* for "news."

McCullagh's success in building his staff of correspondents was due in part to his insistence that they be paid promptly and in full. The correspondents were required to keep a record of what they sent and what was printed. McCullagh gave specific details of his policy:[7]

Correspondents are paid either a stated salary or so much per special, or by space.

Correspondents paid by space are paid at the rate of $6 per column, solid nonpareil, not including headlines or special lines, and will be required to furnish a pasted "string" at the end of each month. Such correspondents should send a "string" and not a collection of separate clippings.

Correspondents paid by the special will be paid 50 cents for each special of 100 to 150 words. Large items will be paid at the regular space rates. A correspondent who is paid by the special should see that his dispatches average at least 100 words to each 50 cents. Where a long string of specials averages only from 30 to 50 words each, they will only be valued and paid for at the rate of 25 cents each.

No correspondent receives the *Globe-Democrat* free.

The value of news depends upon quality and good news brings more than poor news. For exclusive good news an extra rate will be paid, according to quality. This office will cheerfully pay extra expenses incurred in getting valuable exclusive news.

In that period, before the electronic media took away the opportunity for newspaper "beat," McCullagh was aware of the competitive advantages of exclusive stories, and as his instructions emphasized, he was willing to pay for them. He wanted to be first with the important news, not only in St. Louis, but throughout a vast area which he regarded as *Globe-Democrat* territory. This area extended north into Southern Iowa, Illinois, and Indiana to the point where the *Globe-Democrat* encountered the competition of the Chicago papers. Eastward it stretched to the Wabash River, which was the dividing line for the Cincinnati papers. To the west it reached to the Rocky Mountains, to the Southwest into most of Texas, and then South as far as New Orleans.

Throughout this far-flung area McCullagh hired local correspondents and if there was the promise of a big story he did not hesitate to dispatch reporters to the scene from St. Louis. It is interesting to note that the correspondents were selected for their reporting ability and reliability, rather than their political leanings. While no breakdown along political lines exists, it was estimated that more than half were Democrats and a sizeable number owned or worked for Democratic weekly papers.

In retrospect, it is easy to wonder whether such an exclusive news service was justified. The West was increasing rapidly in population and papers were springing up in the towns in Kansas, Colorado, Texas, and other points on the frontier. The Associated Press was expanding its services. Few business managers of newspapers had the vision, or the nerve of Daniel Houser, and without his unwavering support such a news service would not have been possible. With the possible exception of one or two of the New York newspapers, it was unprecedented anywhere, not only for its size but for its general excellence.

After the huge staff of correspondents had been hired and trained, and not before that, McCullagh commented on his achievement. By 1884 he noted at the top of the editorial column in impressive type:

> The *Globe-Democrat* is now paying more money for the collection and transmission of telegraphic news from all parts of the world than is paid by any other newspaper in any city of the world, New York and London excepted.

It was not an idle boast and McCullagh reminded the readers at regular intervals of the *Globe-Democrat*'s coverage. On November 16, 1877, for example, he wrote:

> The *Globe-Democrat* of yesterday contained four times as many words of special telegrams as were contained in all the other newspapers in the city—English, German, morning and evening. And we intend that the good work shall go on. We aim to make the publication of newspapers as expensive as possible.

On the previous day an editorial paragraph called attention to a front page exclusive: "Our special dispatch from Chicago gives an interesting account of the circumstances attending the suicide of Mr. Coolbaugh, the noted banker." On the front page that day the banker's unfortunate demise was reported at length, In addition to some Associated Press news, the page included a special dispatch from Washington, D.C. on the work of Congress, a special from Carthage, Missouri, reporting a double elopement, and specials from Springfield, Illinois, Stamfordville, Kentucky, Wheeling, West Virginia, Independence, Missouri and Brownsville, Texas. The front page also carried two columns of advertisements. Page 2 was made up largely of material reprinted from other papers, including one item from London. Page 3, with one column of advertisements, devoted a column for railroad news, twenty special dispatches and suburban notes from Alton and Belleville, Illinois. Page 4 was the editorial page. Page 5 with three columns of advertisements offered ten specials, including a fairly long report of a spectacular Chicago fire and a special from Pittsburgh, Pennsylvania recounting the mysterious disappearance of a wealthy citizen. Page 6 was devoted entirely to financial and market news, including a number of specials from various parts of the country. Pages 7 and 8 were devoted to local news, including a column of personals under the intriguing head, "St. Louis Splinters." Page 8 also carried four columns of want ads. On that day, as McCullagh did frequently, there was a column of telegraph briefs under the heading "Electric Flashes."

As his rules for correspondents indicated, McCullagh collected society news from a wide area by wire. The Sunday edition always carried one or more pages of social notes. An unusual feature on January 1, 1878 was two full pages listing the names and addresses of St. Louis "ladies" who would be at home to receive callers on New Year's Day.

The success of such social coverage was noted by McCullagh a few years later. On June 3, 1883 this paragraph appeared on the editorial page: "The *Globe-Democrat*'s 'Society Elsewhere' department is booming. In today's issue we print society news from fifty-six cities and towns outside of St. Louis. The *Globe-Democrat* inaugurated this feature of Sunday journalism several years ago, and it is now in vogue in most of the large cities. But no newspaper covers anything like the extent of territory or the number of towns covered by the great religious daily."

While much of the intensive news coverage provided by the *Globe-Democrat*'s literally hundreds of correspondents was centered on reports of government and politics, McCullagh, like Pulitzer and Hearst, realized the readers' fascination with crime and sex. Under his direction the paper was circumspect as to wording, but few of the spicy details were blue-penciled and the headlines were lurid enough to attract attention. The top deck on a special from Quincy, Illinois reporting the arrest of an abortionist read: "The Devil's Den." Other typical headlines: "Lured by a Libertine," "Baptised in Blood," "Bloodshed in a Brothel," "Bathed in Blood." "Danglers," with a second deck "Five Necks stretched at Fort Smith."

McCullagh's rules, and particularly his precepts for covering criminal trials, were put to the test shortly after the merger of the *Globe* and the *Democrat,* when the rumors of a whiskey ring fraud which had been smouldering for several years began to appear in print. Stories of the fraud filled the St. Louis papers for nearly a year and to complicate McCullagh's problem, William McKee, the principal owner of the *Globe-Democrat,* was cast as one of the villains. In fact, it was suggested that it was Fishback's threat of exposure that was a decisive factor in the purchase of the *Democrat.*[8]

To understand the background of the story, it is necessary to go back several years.[9] There had been a whiskey ring scandal in 1869 and McKee had been critical of President Grant and his appointments to federal posts in St. Louis. McKee believed the appointments were against the best interests of the city, and of the Republican Party, and he resented particularly the naming of C. W. Ford as director of the Internal Revenue Service. In 1870 McKee was one of those who helped form the Liberal Republican Party in Missouri. Ford, as the head of the Internal Revenue Service, had control over the reopening of the distilleries closed as a result of the earlier scandal. McKee was one of a number of St. Louisans who urged the naming of General John McDonald as the district supervisor in St. Louis and the President appointed him to the position on February 14, 1870.

The General said later that in his talks with McKee to smooth over the latter's opposition to the President, McKee suggested the possibility of a ring of revenue officials in St. Louis to obtain money from illicit distilling of whiskey to raise money for political purposes. Whether the original suggestion was made by McKee or General McDonald is a matter of conjecture, but McDonald had learned that Ford and his deputy, John H. Concannon, were already receiving profits from illicit distilleries. When McKee was informed of their activity he agreed to participate in forming a ring in St. Louis. McDonald explained later that there was an understanding with the President, Ford, and John A. Joyce, McDonald's private secretary, that the proceeds would be used to support the President's interests. Also included in the ring, according to McDonald, were E. O. Babcock, Grant's private secretary, and several men in the Treasury Department in Washington. One of the objectives of the ring was obviously to assure the Democrat's support for the President in 1872.

The scheme was successful. The profits poured in and the *Democrat* softened its opposition to the President. Then on October 23, 1873, Ford died, and there were rumors that it was a suicide. He was succeeded by Constantine Maguire, who was McKee's original choice for the position. More significant, McKee and Houser had sold their interest in the *Democrat* to Fishback and had launched the *Globe,* some charged with money received from the ring. There does not seem to be any basis for the charge since McKee was independently wealthy, but there was no doubt the ring was a highly profitable venture, The ring collected the tax of seventy cents a gallon on the illicit whiskey and divided the money with the distillers. The half that went to the ring was split five ways, Concannon testified later in McKee's trial. Two shares were delivered to McKee, who to pass one on to someone else who was never named. In fourteen months each of the five shareholders, Concannon estimated, received between $45,000 and $60,000.

While it was clearly established that the tip upon which criminal prosecution was based came from Fishback and the first news stories of rumors of a whiskey ring in St. Louis appeared in the *Democrat* on May 6, 1875, both the *Globe* and the *Democrat* on May 11 reported the seizure of the illicit distilleries, which took place the previous day. It was the same day that Fishback's negotiations for the sale of his paper began with McKee and Houser.

McKee left St. Louis early that year to spend the summer at his New York farm, as he was accustomed to do. Apparently, he believed, as did others, the affair would die down and nothing would happen. But during his absence indictments were returned in which McKee was charged with conspiring to defraud the government. Others named in the true bills included distillers, gaugers, Joyce, and W. O. Avery, an employe of the Treasury Department in Washington. As might be expected, McKee's newspaper rivals had a field day. The St. Louis *Evening Journal*, which had urged his indictment, predicted the *Globe-Democrat* would be forced out of business. Grosvenor, who had been discharged when the *Democrat* was purchased, had gone to New York, and wrote a series of stories about the St. Louis graft ring.

McKee and several of the other defendants went on trial in the United States District Court in St. Louis on January 22, 1876. The trial lasted eleven days and the courtroom was jammed each day. On at least one occasion the police had to be summoned to restrain the crowds attempting to gain entrance. On the editorial page of the *Globe-Democrat* the day after the trial opened, McCullagh called attention to it in two editorial paragraphs. The first one read: "A full page of yesterday's evidence in Mr. McKee's case will be found on the 6th page." The second paragraph made clear the paper's handling of the story. It stated:

> Since the accusation and indictment of Mr. McKee by the United States Grand Jury, the columns of this newspaper have not been used for the purpose of his defense. We did not care to argue before a hundred thousand readers a question which ultimately must be decided by twelve men; and so we contented ourselves with the general statement made on the day after the indictment, that, at the proper time and in the proper manner, Mr. McKee would furnish his own vindication in court.

Reading the *Globe-Democrat*'s reports of the trial nearly a century later compels admiration for McCullagh's impartial handling of the case. The paper published the proceedings in full.

As the trial neared its climax, McCullagh was devoting more than a full page to the story. On January 28, there were five columns on page 1, with the remaining columns allocated to advertisements, and nearly eight columns on page 3. The next day in addition to five columns on the front page, all of page 3 and a column on page 6 were devoted to the story. On January 31 after the trial ended all of page 3 and five columns on page 7 were given to the wind-up of the case.

In contrast to the *Globe-Democrat,* its rivals, the *Republican,* the *Times,* and the *Dispatch* summarized much of the testimony and omitted some parts entirely. There was less restraint on the editorial pages of the other papers. The *Dispatch* and the *Times* remained reasonably neutral, but the *Republican* pulled out all the stops in its efforts to discredit McKee and the *Globe-Democrat.* The *Republican* even tried to implicate McCullagh in the whiskey ring, and charged that McKee had bought McCullagh's silence by printing some of the latter's "Robber Roost" paragraphs, written when McCullagh was still working for Fishback. On January 25, the *Republican* headed its editorial column with this caustic sentence: "Mc——ee to Mc——ug, 'Et tu, Brute.' "

McCullagh did not remain silent on the editorial page but his comments were restrained and there was no attempt to vindicate the principal owner of the *Globe-Democrat.* When the *Republican* printed a story suggesting that McKee's health was breaking down under the strain, McCullagh wrote that McKee was not a man of the "breaking down" kind and asserted that his health had never been better.[10] In one of his few attacks on the *Republican* during the trial, McCullagh reprinted an editorial from the *Republican* and answered it. The *Republican* had charged that the *Globe-Democrat* and the *Times* were conveying the idea that McKee was an "injured being" and urged the jurors not to be influenced by the newspapers. It was the accepted practice then to permit jurors to read the newspapers and this was an overt attempt to sway them. McCullagh replied that the purpose of the *Republican* editorial was transparent and added: "It is hard to think that men so brave of heart and nature would print an article of this kind while the individual at whom it is aimed is on trial, according to law, with what is dearer to him than life or liberty. It is hard to believe that men could be so base and blackhearted as the Knapps, proprietors of the *Republican*. Their manifestation of hatred is a toothless rage of imbecility. How brave, how honorable, how Knapp-like that article is."

The jury deliberated ten hours in reaching a verdict. It was reported that on the first ballot seven jurors voted to acquit McKee, but when the verdict was read in court all were found guilty. On April 14 McDonald received a three year penitentiary sentence and a $5,000 fine and Avery two years and a $1,000 fine. McKee's sentence was two years in jail and a $10,000 fine. The following day, April 26, McCullagh's editorial read:

> We have at no time attempted to make the *Globe-Democrat* the special champion of Mr. McKee . . . We were unwilling to have it said that he was making use of a newspaper in which he happened to be a large owner, to obtain a vindication before the people, after his vindication or condemnation had been submitted to judicial determination. Now, however, that final action has been taken and final judgment rendered in the courts, we think we but echo the popular sentiment in pronouncing the sentence extremely, if not unwarrantably harsh and severe, but out of all proportion to the degree of criminality legally established and proven. After pointing out certain well defined circumstances of mitigation, the judge proceeds to assess the maximum penalty both as to fine and imprisonment; after stating the distinction which the law draws between official and non-official offenders, he gives a non-official offender four times the punishment he recently gave to an official offender. This seems to us a little remarkable . . . we do not think it will stand the test of reason or fairness.

McKee was later pardoned, but lived a little more than three years after his trial. He died on December 20, 1879 at the age of sixty-four. After his death, Houser became president of the corporation, and McCullagh was named vice president. McCullagh's handling of the story, a touchy one for any editor, demonstrated his insistence on objective reporting. He believed in aggressive news coverage. In *King News* in 1941, M. Koenigsberg wrote: "No journalist of McCullagh's time exceeded his contributions to the development and evaluation of newspaper standards."

Several years before he became dean of the world's first

School of Journalism, Walter Williams[11] had this to say of McCullagh's policy: "He understood how this kind of journalism impressed the public, and hence at all times he enjoyed some prodigious feat, as telegraphing or cabling pages of some great event at enormous expense, scooping all his rivals and editorially vaunting the magnitude of the achievement and making the world believe there was no other such paper as the *Globe-Democrat*. He would do these feats at such intervals as to keep the public in a constant state of admiration and amazement and thus the *Globe-Democrat* grew like Jack's beanstalk. He possessed the rare journalistic instinct of knowing what the public wanted, and he spared no expense to give it to them. Whenever any important event occurred the public could rely upon it being fully and well told."

The same policy of vigorous competition and liberal spending applied to local news as well. Late each night McCullagh had the foreman of the composing room bring to his desk the proofs on all local items.[12] Frequently he would select the stories that seemed to be wordy and in a florid style, and go through them, striking out words, and even entire sentences. Then he would take the proofs to the city editor and call attention to his editing as an example for his guidance. McCullagh was a stickler for verifying all statistical matter. An editor whose arithmetic was in error could expect the Chief's wrath to descend on him every time a column of figures was not correctly added.

McCullagh made it clear that every member of the staff was expected to read the *Globe-Democrat* every day before he reported for work. He reminded his staff that the habit of reading the paper must be as regular as eating breakfast.

An example of the thoroughness with which local news was covered, was the train wreck on December 8, 1881 at St. Charles, Missouri, some thirty miles from downtown St. Louis.[13]

The railroad bridge spanning the Missouri River gave way under the weight of a trainload of livestock, and the *Globe-Democrat* got a head start on their rivals because McCullagh had a regular correspondent in St. Charles, George S. Johns, who was later to become the editor of the editorial page of the St. Louis *Post-Dispatch*. Johns wired the *Globe-Democrat* and the city editor, Walter Stephens, with four reporters hired a hack and rushed to the scene ahead of all the rival papers. They hired the only two rowboats available on the east bank of the river to ferry them across and even purchased one of the boats to prevent its owner from returning to pick up reporters from the other papers. Then they proceeded to tie up the telegraph wire by persuading the operator to plead illness and permit a *Globe-Democrat* operator to take over. For his timely tip, Johns received a $5.00 bonus from McCullagh.

An example of thorough local coverage was the *Globe-Democrat*'s detailed report on the disastrous fire which swept through the old Southern Hotel on April 11, 1877, in which eleven persons were killed. Cliff Sanders, a *Globe-Democrat* reporter helped save several housemaids from the burning top floor and wrote a graphic first person account. Fires, natural disasters, lynchings, and violence of all kinds made gripping reading and the *Globe-Democrat* exploited them.

The success of this aggressive news policy was soon evident. In October 1876, a little more than a year after the merger, the sworn seven-day circulation of the paper was 21,900. The same issue that carried that announcement also carried this editorial paragraph, calling attention to the circulation for the previous Sunday: "The regular circulation of the *Globe-Democrat* was 28,804. This is all because of a conspiracy on the part of the newsboys to sell the paper which everybody calls for."

McCullagh used a number of ways to impress his readers with the *Globe-Democrat*'s steady circulation growth, and to challenge his competitors, which were understandably reluctant to reveal their circulations. In October 1878 at the top of the editorial page there appeared in bold type for several weeks the figures showing the amount paid in postage for each of the English-language dailies in St. Louis for the fiscal year ending June 30, 1878. In that period the *Globe-Democrat* had paid $10,378. The *Republican,* its closest rival, paid $6,537; the *Times* $2,855; the *Dispatch* $202; and the *Journal* $528. These figures included the weekly editions, and as McCullagh pointed out, the *Globe-Democrat* paid $260 more than the other four papers combined. Since all out of town circulation, except for copies sold by news vendors on trains, went by mail it was a convincing comparison. The following February McCullagh announced in an editorial paragraph that "The daily circulation of the *Globe-Democrat* was 26,792 and Sunday circulation reached 33,049." He added: "There are only four other daily newspapers in the United States which can make a better showing than this, and they are the Boston *Herald,* the Philadelphia *Ledger,* the New York *Herald* and the New York *Sun.*"

The aggressive news policy paid off financially as well. By the end of the third year after the merger, the *Globe-Democrat* had paid off all the debts incurred by the purchase of the *Democrat* and had a safe balance of $90,000.[14]

In an era when there was no formal education for journalism, McCullagh liked to describe the *Globe-Democrat* as "the best school of journalism in the country." Just as the New York *Sun* under Charles Dana was regarded as a "newspaperman's newspaper" in the East, so was the *Globe-Democrat.* Theodore Dreiser, who worked for the *Globe-Democrat* in the 1890's, wrote in his *Book About Myself* that when he informed John T. McEnnis, the city editor of the Chicago *Globe,* that he had accepted a job as a reporter for the *Globe-Democrat,* he was told that to work for "Mack" was one of the best opportunities he could have. McEnnis, who had previously worked for McCullagh, added that "It was one of the greatest papers and McCullagh was one of the greatest editors that ever lived."

There were many others who profited from McCullagh's tutelage and he was proud of his "students." He did not resent it when they moved on to other papers. When John A. Dillon took a front page advertisement in the *Globe-Democrat* on January 1, 1878 to announce the launching of the St. Louis *Evening Post,* McCullagh welcomed the venture in an editorial:

> Having filled various prominent pulpits and dignified professorships with graduates from its editorial staff, the *Globe-Democrat* now sends forth another graduate to establish a first-class daily evening paper, such as St. Louis has long needed. Mr. Dillon, who announces in our advertising columns his forthcoming paper, the St. Louis *Evening Post,* is a graduate of the best school of journalism in this country, having served faithfully for four and a half years on the *Globe,* and, after the consolidation on the *Globe-Democrat;* if he does not make a first-class editor it will not be for

want of training, and as the field before him is almost clear, all the circumstances conspire to insure his usefulness.

Mr. E. H. E. Jameson, a former editorial attaché of this journal, was ordained for the Baptist ministry last night under very favorable circumstances. The press is the best possible training school for the pulpit; a few years of editorial labor are better than half a lifetime in college to fit men for the gospel mission. We do not intend that Mr. Jameson shall be the *Globe-Democrat*'s only contribution to the army of Christian workers, or that no sect but the Baptists shall receive the benefit of our careful training and education. We have now in our office on the way to speedy graduation with high honors, several young men destined to be shining lights of the church before many years.

Dillon later joined Joseph Pulitzer when the *Post* was consolidated with the *Dispatch,* and when John Cockerill, who had worked for McCullagh on the Cincinnati *Enquirer,* moved to New York, Dillon replaced him on the *Post-Dispatch*. O. K. Bovard, the *Post-Dispatch*'s managing editor for many years, began his career on the *Globe-Democrat*.[15]

Among other alumni of the McCullagh school of journalism to achieve national fame was William Marion Reedy, the brilliant and eccentric editor of *Reedy's Mirror,* in which appeared the first writings of such well known literary figures as Sara Teasdale and Edgar Lee Masters.

Another newspaper which reflected the influence of McCullagh was the New York *Times*. George S. Ochs, brother of Adolph Ochs who purchased the *Times* in 1896, was the *Globe-Democrat*'s correspondent in Chattanooga. McCullagh frequently sent staff correspondents into the area on tips furnished by Ochs and his brother had the opportunity to study McCullagh's news policy before he went to New York. Another nationally known editor trained by McCullagh was Casper S. Yost, for many years editor of the editorial page of the *Globe-Democrat* who became a founder and the first president of the American Society of Newspaper Editors.

The *Globe-Democrat* was more than an excellent training school for the men fortunate enough to work under McCullagh's direct supervision. His new policy caused it to become a practical correspondence school for the hundreds of *Globe-Democrat* correspondents. The influence of that training was evident in the papers of the West and Southwest long after McCullagh's death.

He insisted on simplicity and clearness in writing and had little patience for wordiness. It was his practice to edit the galley proofs and eliminate useless words and details. Accuracy was a fetish for him. Homer A. Danford, who worked for the *Globe-Democrat* for thirty-nine years, said: "McCullagh delighted in catching writers and speakers in misquotations. Woe to the man who misquoted! McCullagh would go after him red-eyed and round-shouldered. Then he would give him this bit of advice: 'Always verify! Always verify!' The proofreader who read Mr. McCullagh's paragraph happened to have a book of quotations. Referring to it, he discovered Dr. Cave was right. When Mack's attention was called to it and he was shown the correct quotation, he crumpled the page of paragraphs in his hand and as he fired it into the wastebasket, he growled: 'All right. We'll give him the benefit of the doubt this time.' A day or so later an editorial paragraph appeared in the *Globe-Democrat* something like this: 'A proofreader is a gentleman employed in the composing room to prevent the editor from making an ass of himself.' "

In his daily relations with his staff, McCullagh was reserved and usually gruff. He seldom bothered to remove the perpetual cigar when he answered a question, and sometimes was difficult to understand. C. S. Webb, who worked for him for many years, recalled that he seldom praised good work. Usually he expressed his appreciation with a gift, or with a raise in salary.

CONTROVERSIES AND STUNTS

6

Nothing whets the readers' interest more than a public donneybrook in print, and McCullagh was a master at breathing life into the embers of controversy. In the last half of the nineteenth century there was little of the ecumenical spirit in America, and especially in the Midwest where Catholics and Protestants were deeply suspicious of each other. It was a period when the people took their religion seriously. McCullagh was aware of the fact and early he began to refer to the *Globe-Democrat* as "The Great Religious Daily." He gloried in the phrase and used it on every occasion.

What McCullagh promptly labeled "The Great Controversy" began in December, 1877. Bishop P. J. Ryan, who was later to become an Archbishop in Philadelphia, was regarded in St. Louis at that time as the most eloquent priest in the city. He delivered a public lecture at the Mercantile Library on "What Catholics Believe." Sensing the news potential in the lecture, McCullagh assigned one of his best reporters to cover it and the following morning a verbatim report filled five columns in the *Globe-Democrat*. For most editors that would have been the end of the story. McCullagh, however, invited the clergy of St. Louis to air their views. Perhaps with tongue in cheek, he extended the invitation in an editorial which read:[1]

Bishop Ryan's Sunday evening address was certainly very bold and very frank. It is not to be allowed to remain unanswered, however. Doctor Sonneschein has already been mustered into the service of the opposition, and will on Sunday evening, the 30th inst., point out what he considers the Bishop's mistakes. Doctor Sonneschein is a learned and logical man, and he will, of course, command a large hearing. But the Protestant divines of this city, against whose faith rather than against the faith of Israel the Bishop's argument was directed, can hardly remain silent. We trust they will be heard in the important controversy inaugurated by the Catholic bishop. As the organ of all creeds and denominations, the *Globe-Democrat* is anxious for the fullest and freest discussions, and will do its duty as a religious daily newspaper by publishing both sides.

The *Globe-Democrat* did not wait for contributions to the debate to come in. Its reporters interviewed thirty-two St. Louis clergymen and a week after the first invitation, published their views. The next week there were more interviews, twenty-one with Protestant ministers and fourteen with Catholic priests, including two bishops. On January 12 in the "Supplemental Sheet" of features for the Sunday edition, there was a full page feature under the heading "Modes of Faith," which was introduced with the statement that "a great controversy is now raging in the religious circles of St. Louis." Four days later McCullagh fanned the flames with this editorial paragraph: "If the ladies would like to take part in the Great Controversy, the columns of the *Globe-Democrat* are open to them. It is true that St. Paul commanded them to be silent in church, but he never forbade them to write for the *Globe-Democrat*." On January 21 the Great Controversy occupied three full columns on page 1 and all eight columns on page 3.

From then on it was not necessary to stir up the public. Church laymen joined in the fight and deluged the *Globe-Democrat* with letters. Clergymen preached sermons on the subject and the *Globe-Democrat* faithfully reported them. The only problem was to keep the debate within bounds. McCullagh reminded the readers of the limitations in an editorial paragraph: "We have received, as a contribution to The Great Controversy, a long communication intended to show that the Roman Catholic religion is inimical to American institutions. This is not the point at issue, and we shall not print anything on the subject.

The discussion is about religion in its relation to Christianity, and not its relation to politics. Within its proper limits we have allowed it to assume the attitude of a free fight, so to speak, but it must be kept within these limits."

The Great Controversy continued to rage for some three months, and of course whenever it was the subject of conversation the *Globe-Democrat* was mentioned. Circulation rose and in February 1878, McCullagh reported on the editorial page that the daily circulation was up to 32,915 and Sunday circulation to 33,049. Moreover, the paper gained a loyal following among the clergy, which it never lost in McCullagh's lifetime.

It is interesting to note that McCullagh valued the paper's reputation as the "great religious daily" so highly that on occasion he refrained from printing news which would have gained circulation, and at other times apologized for catering to the readers' desires while pointing out their error in demanding such news. The Great Controversy had scarcely died down before a church scandal, replete with juicy details broke in St. Louis and got into the courts. The *Globe-Democrat* could have reported the testimony of the court trial without fear of libel, but McCullagh ignored the testimony and explained his stand in an editorial:

> The *Globe-Democrat*, as the great religious daily and the organ of all the churches, would naturally be expected to publish reports of the Blank-Blank suit. But really the details have become so nasty of late that we are obliged to omit them. We presume, however, that they will be found in all their luxuriant grossness in the columns of the *Republican*. The *Globe-Democrat*'s patrons do not relish morbid sensationalism of this kind, even in the secular department. We hope, for the sake of morality and religion that the Blank suit will be brought to an end as soon as possible. It is doing more harm than an army of Ingersolls.

Earlier, it will be recalled, McCullagh did not suffer from such qualms. As managing editor of the *Globe* he had played the trial of the Rev. Henry Ward Beecher on a charge of adultery in full with all of its spicy testimony. Another illustration of his changed policy appeared on September 4, 1882 when an editorial announced: "The Temple of Truth regretfully announces that there will be a temporary profanation of its sacred edifice on Monday, Tuesday and Wednesday nights, in order to inform the public of the program and results of the feast of fists in New Orleans. Announcements will be made through a magic lantern as fast as dispatches are received from New Orleans. The *Globe-Democrat* is opposed to prize fighting and only adopts the scheme to keep people from going to worldly-minded newspaper offices for information it seems they are determined to have." On September 8 the *Globe-Democrat* carried a front-page report of the knockout of John L. Sullivan by James J. Corbett and a picture of the winner. McCullagh commented on the victory in two short paragraphs. One noted that "Sully is a very badly sullied man this morning." The other read: "The wife-beater was whipped by the wife-lover. Glory." Presumably the comments added a moral tone to the coverage of the story.

McCullagh's interest in religion is intriguing. Throughout his adult life he was not a member of any church and rarely attended church services. He was immune to the Catholic influence of his early boyhood in Ireland. His only church affiliation of which there is a record was his attendance at the Methodist Sunday School as a youth. But his writings show that he was familiar with the Scriptures and frequently quoted from them. How much of his interest was inspired by his conviction that it was good newspaper policy can only be speculated, but he never scoffed at religion or made light of any faith.

He gave the agnostics full coverage in the news columns, but reserved the right to point out the flaws in their statements. Robert G. Ingersoll's lectures in St. Louis received more space in the *Globe-Democrat* than in any other St. Louis paper. McCullagh answered his skepticism with comments like these on the editorial page:

Bob Ingersoll is still pillaging in the garden of Christianity for flowers with which to decorate his infidel ideas. In a dispatch to a gentleman who had charge of the funeral of the late Charles R. Thorne he said "The tragedy has ended. The curtain has fallen. Applause cannot lift it again, but memory and hope remain." We can understand how Memory can remain to Mr. Ingersoll and those of his peculiar views, but where does Hope, which is the twin sister of Christian Faith, come to their assistance? If, as Mr. Ingersoll asserts, death ends all, what part is there for Hope to play after death?

An ex-priest of the Catholic Church, after having been mobbed a week ago, was allowed, by the presence of several companies of militia, to lecture in Toledo yesterday on why he left the Catholic Church. In St. Louis Bob Ingersoll was allowed to tell why he left the Presbyterian Church, and not only was he not disturbed, but he got $1,600 for telling it. We like the St. Louis plan best, although in a country where salvation is free it seems a little high to charge a dollar for reserved seats for damnation.

Bob Ingersoll's infidel convention in Cincinnati does not seem to have accomplished anything of note. There was a good deal of railing and cheap scoffing about religion and the Bible, but most of it was very old and stale to those familiar with the ribaldry of Tom Paine and writers of his class. It is evident that the people of this country are not prepared to flock in large numbers to a political party which calls itself "Liberal" and which shows no liberality except that of abusing institutions and ceremonies which are held sacred by civilized people. When Mr. Ingersoll, with his pockets filled with the revenues of blasphemy, asks what this government owes to Christianity, we reply by asking him, what in the name of decency this or any other country owes to infidelity—except that France owes to it its long and terrible reign of vice and bloodshed. Thus far in his career as a peddler of paganism, Mr. Ingersoll has injured no one but himself."

McCullagh was not always so restrained. Stephen C. Tammany,[2] now retired, who was a printer for the *Globe-Democrat* during McCullagh's last years, recalls that during a mud-slinging match with Father Phelan and his paper, McCullagh commented: "If Hell was given an emetic, the last dregs would vomit Father Phelan."

A little more than a year after The Great Religious Controversy died down, McCullagh managed to stir up another dispute. He realized that if he was to win additional circulation and outstrip all his rivals in St. Louis, he must extend the *Globe-Democrat*'s circulation area. He also knew that one of the most effective ways to increase circulation was to make the *Globe-*

Democrat a frequent topic of conversation. Texas, he decided, offered tempting possibilities. The state was just emerging from the unsettled years that had followed the Civil War. Its people were uninhibited and seemed to enjoy violence. Indicative of that era in Texas was the advice given on the floor of Congress suggesting that Texas "ought to raise more hominy and less Hell." General Phil Sheridan, who had lived in the state for a time after the war was quoted as saying after his departure that since he owned Hell and Texas, he would rent out Texas and reside in Hell.

McCullagh proceeded to hire correspondents in every city in Texas of any size and his instructions were to wire all news of interest. Soon, as could be expected, special dispatches began to appear in the *Globe-Democrat* which were hardly the news preferred by chambers of commerce. Understandably Texas newspapers began to register protests and to charge that the *Globe-Democrat*'s dispatches were "Malicious and unwarranted."

Thus in the summer of 1879 began what came to be known as "The Texas Boycott," so called because of the widespread attempts to persuade Texans to refuse to buy copies of the *Globe-Democrat*.

McCullagh was able to keep the controversy at the boiling point for many months, aided by what in retrospect seems extraordinarily poor judgment on the part of the St. Louis *Republican*. The *Republican* saw in the controversy an opportunity to attack the *Globe-Democrat,* thereby playing directly into McCullagh's hands, or more accurately, the venom of his pen. His reply to the first editorial blast of the *Republican* appeared on the editorial page. He said:[3]

The *Republican* yesterday printed one of its periodical lectures on the proprieties ef journalism, taking the *Globe-Democrat* and its Texas news as a text. We are always glad to receive advice, and we know of no newspaper in the country less fitted to give it in this case than the *Republican,* which at the end of seventy years' existence exhibits all the infirmities of age and none of the wisdom of experience. As to Texas news, the difference between the *Globe-Democrat* and the *Republican* is just this. The *Globe-Democrat* keeps a corps of correspondents in Texas under instructions to report events as they occur. The dispatches are printed without comment or prejudice. The *Republican* prints all the Texas news it can get for nothing, or rather for its Associated Press membership. It has never omitted an "outrage" or any item of any kind that came to it in this alms-basket fashion. It draws the line, not on the quality of the news, but on the expense of it. Nothing is too bad for its columns, except when it costs extra labor and expense to obtain. It is constantly printing the vilest of nastiness because it comes gratis and constantly omitting the most important news of the day because it is unwilling or unable to pay for it. It is not an unusual thing for the *Globe-Democrat* to pay ten times as much for a day's special telegram as is paid by the *Republican*. Its last appeal is to the people of Texas to take it on the ground that it prints news from that state. This is a good scheme, and applied to all other parts of the country, will assuredly give the *Republican* the largest circulation in the world. Wherever the minimum of news will bring the maximum of circulation, the *Republican* is bound to boom.

The *Republican* continued to snipe at the *Globe-Democrat* and thereby provided McCullagh with more ammunition to keep the feud alive, and readers talking. In another blast at the *Republican,* McCullagh wrote:

It gives the *Republican* "the hydrostatics to such a degree" as Mrs. Malaprop says, to think that in the Democratic State of Texas, the *Globe-Democrat* exceeds it in circulation about six to one. This is no worse than in the Democratic State of Missouri. Our Democratic brethren in both states are troubled on the newspaper question. If they buy the *Globe-Democrat* they swear at what's in it, and if they buy the *Republican* they swear because there is nothing in it.

Our correspondents in Texas are instructed just like our correspondents in other states, to send news that is of general or special interest. If, for instance, one of them should see a man reading the St. Louis *Republican* down there, he would be in duty bound to telegraph that fact because of its novelty. We should print it just to show that there was one man in Texas who was easily imposed upon in the matter of newspapers. That man hasn't been found yet, however. A correspondent in a note printed elsewhere, says that in his recent travels in Texas he actually saw a man reading the *Republican*. We hope that he does not intend to question the intelligence of this individual in the remark that he read the paper upside down. The *Republican*'s readers do that in the vain hope of finding an item of news and it may be said of the *Republican* that it is quite as interesting when read upside down as when perused in the ordinary way.

Texas editors who were brave enough to enter the fray also were lectured by McCullagh, who promptly branded them jackasses.

The chawbacon editors of Texas, he wrote,[4] who are just now engaged in the work of "killing" the *Globe-Democrat* in that state, should remember that there is only one case on record in which a jackass whipped a lion. It was a sick lion, too, and even at that the jackass died soon after the fight. The Texas jackasses are kicking at a very lively lion and the first thing they know they'll all be lame. While the hoodlums and yahoos who edit a few of the Texas papers are denouncing the *Globe,* the better class of people in that state are more than ever in its favor, as the more they study it, the more nearly they find it up to the highest requirements of modern journalism in that wonderful combination of religious and secular to be found in our columns. Indeed, we understand there is a movement in Texas to invite some members of our staff to lecture before the Y.M.C.A.'s in the different cities of Texas. It is an excellent idea, too. We can promise if the contract is entered into, a series of most interesting discourses. No compensation will be asked except a trifle to cover life insurance.

The Galveston *News* interviewed one of the *Globe-Democrat*'s correspondents and reported that the correspondent insisted he was not instructed by McCullagh to specialize in news of crime. McCullagh tempered his comment, but was unwilling to permit the incident to pass unnoticed.

The delicate sensibilities of the Galveston *News* are aroused to frenzy by the thought that the *Globe-Democrat* circulates so largely in Texas, which the *News* has always regarded as its own particular province and backyard, he wrote. Indeed the *News* regards it as the highest sort of treason to the State of Texas for any citizen to read any other newspaper. It is a good local paper, in which can be found the latest news of the Galveston police court. It does not, however, fill the bill as a newspaper on a large scale, such as the *Globe-Democrat* may fairly claim to be, and hence we are not surprised that the circulation of the *Globe-Democrat* in the State of Texas, down to within a short distance of the city of Galveston, is about twice the circulation of the *News*. We can't help this but perhaps the *News* can.

The attacks on the *Globe-Democrat* did not abate, even after McCullagh pointed out that the *Globe-Democrat* was benefiting from the free publicity. McCullagh put it this way:

The *Republican* is worrying itself intensely about the *Globe-Democrat*'s Texas circulation. It publishes from a scrub journal of Texas a call upon the papers of the state to unite in denouncing the *Globe-Democrat*. All right. But remember that we do not pay for advertising unless we have previously made an agreement to do so. Let the choruses of jackasses begin, with the *Republican* in the lead. Let the shout be all along the line, "Don't take the *Globe-Democrat*." The only fear we have is that some day the *Republican* will be converted into a newspaper, and then we may be compelled to look to our Texas circulation. But at present there are no alarming symptoms in that direction.

Long before book publishers learned the secret that to be banned in Boston was a sure-fire way to promote a best seller, McCullagh was practicing this principle. The pious guardians of public morals might have taken a lesson from the attempts to discourage the reading of the *Globe-Democrat*. One Texas community went so far as to propose a municipal ordinance prohibiting the sale of the *Globe-Democrat* within its corporate limits, but it was never enacted. Marshall Texas, however, discovered an old blue law prohibiting the sale of newspapers on Sunday and arrested a news butcher of a Texas and Pacific train. The newsboy, David Jones, was brought to trial. The *Globe-Demo-*

crat reported the trial and McCullagh added this editorial comment:[5]

At Marshall, Texas yesterday a newsboy was tried by a jury of his peers for selling the *Globe-Democrat* on Sunday, and was fined $25 and costs. The boy sold a big bundle of *Globe-Democrats* and a single copy of the *Republican*. The specific offense being the sale of newspapers, there was no harm in selling the *Republican,* except to the misguided Texan who paid his nickel for a copy.

The trial at Marshall seemed to turn the tide of the Texas boycott of the *Globe-Democrat*. Some of the Texas papers began to speak up. Typical of their comments was the piece in the *Christian Advocate* of Galveston, a publication of the Methodist Church. It said: "Some of the Texas papers, loudly seconded by the *Missouri Republican,* are saying harsh things about the *Globe-Democrat*'s misrepresentations of Texas. We do not greatly admire the *Globe-Democrat* but it certainly is a better newspaper than the St. Louis *Republican,* and fully as honest. The *Globe-Democrat* misrepresents Texas politically; the *Republican,* adopting the infidel hobbies of would-be scientists, misleads its readers religiously. We believe, of the two, we would be conscientious in giving preference to the *Globe-Democrat*. It is the least of two immense evils."

This indorsement was faint praise, but McCullagh did not let the opportunity pass. He reprinted the *Christian Advocate*'s comment and added:[6]

The *Advocate* is the organ of the M.E. Church South, which will sufficiently explain its hostility to the political course of the *Globe-Democrat*. We have often received complaints of the infidel tendencies of the *Republican,* and have endeavored to correct them. Especially in its Sunday issue that journal indulges in lengthy displays of Huxley and—dishwater, which are calculated to do great harm to the cause of religion, mainly through the inability of the writers to distinguish between the true and false in science. A chapter from Huxley could do no harm, but Huxley, after passing through the alembic of the *Republican* editor's brain, is infidel nonsense—just the thing against which St. Paul warned

Timothy when he wrote, "O Timothy keep that which is committed to thy trust, avoiding profane and vain babblings, and oppositions of science, falsely so-called."

As the attempted boycott lost its steam, the *Globe-Democrat* continued to build its circulation. McCullagh kept it going as long as he could with such pithy shots as:

" 'Although they all cuss the *Globe-Democrat* down here,' writes a correspondent, 'they all take it.' The boy on the Texas and Pacific, between Texarkana and Sherman, takes sixty *Globe-Democrats* and ten *Republicans* every day. This is no doubt a truthful statement, but we would like to know what that boy does with ten *Republicans*."

In addition to the special dispatches and the controversies, McCullagh sought to intrigue the readers with bizarre and sensational stories from the exchanges, both in this country and abroad. Such items culled from other papers appeared regularly on the second page of the paper.

Years later McCullagh told Walter Williams[7] that "Spending money is the only way to make a newspaper. I never hesitate to lay down one dollar when I can see I can thereby pick up two." It was sound advice in the nineteenth century and it is equally sound today.

More than half a century before the old *Literary Digest* first attempted to poll the voters, a venture which reached disastrous proportions in the election of 1936; and before Dr. George Gallup developed his method of sampling the public pulse, McCullagh was polling the public on subjects ranging from a knowledge of the Bible to national politics. What was described at the time as "the catechism," was another of the new ideas in journalism from the editor's fertile brain. It provided another opportunity to get the public talking about the *Globe-Democrat,* and it was highly successful.

The first time it was used was on June 21, 1879. A large group of Ohio editors on a junket to the Middle West arrived in East St. Louis that morning and were met at the Relay Depot on the east side of the Mississippi River by thirty reporters under the direction of the city editor and the railroad editor. Each reporter had pinned to the lapel of his coat a white satin badge which read:

> A soft answer turneth away wrath.
> **Globe-Democrat** Interview Corps.
> With Malice toward none,
> But with Questions for all.

Each reporter was well stocked with cards containing the questions to be asked and blank spaces for the answers. They also had a supply of yellow cards which read: "Pumped. Keep this check in your hat to avoid further disturbance." The interviews filled eight columns in the *Globe-Democrat* the next day. More important for McCullagh, virtually every editor on the junket went home and wrote about it.

McCullagh instructed his interviewing corps on the technique to be used.[8] They should not allow time for reflection. Questions should be restricted to the outline provided in advance. On one occasion he sent his interviewing team to the floor of the Merchants' Exchange in St. Louis to query the local bigwigs on their knowledge of the Ten Commandments, with results that delighted the readers of the paper. He organized an interviewing corps to visit the New York Stock Exchange and to test the members' knowledge of history. Another variation of the "catechism" persists today in the "Inquiring Reporter" features used by many newspapers.

The "catechism" which attracted the widest national attention was the sampling of the political knowledge of the members of the House of Representatives in Washington in 1891 on the opening day of the session. That year the voters had given the Democrats a majority in the House and there was a bitter contest being waged between Charles F. Crisp and Roger Q. Mills for selection as Speaker of the House. Interest in the news from Washington was high. McCullagh laid his plan carefully. In a letter to Walter Stevens,[9] his Washington correspondent, he wrote:

Could you organize a corps of reporters—say twenty—to run a catechism class on the floor of the House the first day of Congress? I will prepare the questions—all to relate to political history. The

CONTROVERSIES AND STUNTS 121

thing to be conducted like the New York Exchange matter. I think you know the modus operandi. Answer by telegraph and I will write further instructions.

As the plan developed, McCullagh decided to extend it to the Senate and to members of the Cabinet. In a letter to Stevens, he explained:

I am extremely anxious to make a success of the catechism and think the material is there. Some of the questions are quite "catchy" and will fool the boys. For instance, "How many ex-Presidents died on the Fourth of July?" Well, they will remember John Adams and Thomas Jefferson, but most of them will forget James Monroe. Our success, of course, will be proportioned to the number who can't answer. You might send four or five men among the Departments to tackle the Secretaries. If you can find a man with nerve to tackle the White House it would be well. I am having nice badges made, each reporter to wear one. I will send the cards to you by express. Be careful and do not let them get out. If they should work out a "key" in advance the joke would be on us.

In a subsequent letter he wrote:

Enclosed is a proof of the badge for the interview. It will be printed on fine silk. The motto is a thing which Mr. Sumner would have said had he lived long enough, I think. Will send by express, probably Saturday night, 600 copies of catechism and 75 badges. Do not open the bundle until the morning of the raid. I am terribly afraid of the list of questions getting out and spoiling our fun. Take the bundle to your room and lock it up. I will have the answers set up and printed on proofslips and forwarded to you to be given to the reporters. I think you had better not distribute them until after the raid, as it is just as well that reporters should not know the answers when presenting the questions.

The letters reveal McCullagh's attention to detail. His instructions were carried out to the letter. On the morning of December 7 the reporters pinned on their white silk badges. The badges bore a picture of the nation's capitol and the motto which McCullagh attributed to Senator Sumner. Approximately 25,000 words were sent by telegraph that day and the entire story was in the office of the *Globe-Democrat* by midnight. The story and interviews filled fifteen columns in the issue of December 8. McCullagh wired his commendation to Stevens: "Catechism a great success. Hope it worked up the people in Washington." Three days later, after he had time to appraise the public's response and had read the comments of other newspapers, he wrote to Stevens: "I need hardly say how well everybody at this end is pleased with the catechism work. It was splendidly done and amply repaid all effort, not to speak of my own nervous excitement concerning its fate in advance."

The story with six decks in its head indicates the kind of writing McCullagh strove to achieve on the *Globe-Democrat*. This is the way the readers saw it on December 8, 1891. The complete story which preceded the interviews appears in Appendix II.

CONGRESS CATECHISED

The **Globe-Democrat's** Class in Political History Descends on the Capital

- - - - - -

An Attempt to Ascertain What Our Statesmen Know About American History

- - - - - -

Fourteen Simple Questions Prove Too Much for the Great Politicians

- - - - - -

Not a Dozen Public Officers Knew How Old Washington Was When He Died

- - - - - -

The President Smiled and Smiled—Four Southern Congressmen Who Remembered Their Lessons—Some Very Bad Breaks by Very Good Statesmen—None of the Senators Could Answer Them

- - - - - -

Special to the **Globe-Democrat**

WASHINGTON, D.C., December 7.—Men were fuming and steaming and sweating blood almost. It was a great party crisis. To the 232 men who were in it the whole world seemed to be holding its breath, when suddenly there confronted them with this:

Who was the first Speaker of the House of Representatives?

The tension relaxed with a snap; lines of anxiety melted into broad grins; the storm center changed in a twinkling. The issue of the hour was not the speakership of the Fifty-second Congress; it was the St. Louis *Globe-Democrat*'s class in political history.

Washington will never meet the fate of the worm. It rises leisurely. Today, however, it was astir earlier than usual. The speakership contest, after seventeen fruitless ballots on Saturday, was to be resumed at 10 o'clock this morning. By 9 o'clock the Congressmen were up and beginning to move toward the big Capitol on the hill, a mile away. At the same hour down Newspaper Row marched a column forty strong. White silk badges fluttered on their breasts. They bore this strange device:

St. Louis Globe-Democrat
INTERVIEWING CORPS
Mission for the Promulgation of Political History in the Halls of Congress

"No American Education is complete which does not include an accurate knowledge of the political history of this country."—*Charles Sumner*

McCullagh continued to make use of the catechism as long as he lived. An example of the variety of uses to which it was put was the twenty-fourth reunion of the Army of the Tennessee in St. Louis in November 1892. The issue of November 17 gave a full page of coverage to the convention program and on an inside page was a five column feature, with the heading: "The Gallant Officers Surrender to the *Globe-Democrat* Interviewers Corps." The lead paragraph described how the corps descended upon the convention, demanding: "Give us your best war stories." The second paragraph was one sentence: "These are the spoils."

Another variation of the catechism, which also was obviously inspired by his development of the technique of the interview, was the column which appeared each day in the *Globe-Democrat* under the standing head: "Heard in the Corridors." McCullagh insisted that the St. Louis hotels be covered by the local staff every day. Reporters were instructed not only to check the hotel registers for tips of newsworthy visitors to the city, but also to interview every guest if possible. If the interview did not produce a story important enough for separate treatment, it was used in the column. The interviews were usually short, one, or at the most, two paragraphs, but they were bright and sometimes humorous. The subjects varied from the report on the crops in outstate Missouri, to politics or human interest experiences. It was a rare day they did not fill a column in the paper. It was human nature for the person interviewed, to buy one or more copies of the issue and to talk about it when he returned home, which again made people talk about the *Globe-Democrat*.

Searching for other ways to exploit the interviewing technique and to add to the *Globe-Democrat*'s impressive list of correspondents, McCullagh announced a new feature in an editorial on January 22, 1893. Headed "Our New List of Correspondents," the editorial explained that the paper had obtained the mailing list of the Commercial Travelers Association and was extending an invitation to all traveling salesmen to become correspondents of the *Globe-Democrat*. The editorial gave explicit instructions. Except in rare instances they should report by letter and the letters should be not more than 300 words in length. No letter should contain anything that is scandalous or libelous. An account would be kept for each contributor, he explained, and the amount due him would be forwarded at regular column rates once a month. He noted that "more than 100 acceptances have already been received." The editorial pointed out that:

"The *Globe-Democrat* has made a great many new departures in journalism during the last fifteen years and added many new features to lift the newspaper above the dull monotony of crime and politics. We think a very interesting departure of a daily newspaper can be made up from letters written by commercial travelers, giving what is odd, curious and unique, what they see and hear that is worth preserving in print."

Two days later he wrote: "Letters are coming in by every mail. When in operation this will prove to be the best and biggest of all journalistic schemes." The feature was launched in the issue of February 4 with a three-column illustrated head and it appeared thereafter every Saturday. Typical headings in the first letters included: "Why He Quit Smoking"; "Philosophical Headwaiter"; "Efficacy of a Drummer's Prayer"; and "An Accommodating Conductor."

Another variation of McCullagh's use of the interview technique he dubbed the "unspoken speech." He tried it out on a convention in 1890 and wrote to Stevens: "I have struck a new way of reporting conventions. You will see it in an article in Sunday's paper on 'Among the Blind.' I sent McAnally to the convention with instructions to listen and talk with others and make this kind of a report." McCullagh felt that most of those who attended conventions never had a voice in the proceedings and should have ideas and recollections worth printing. A tactful reporter should, he explained, be able to elicit ideas and items of interest to the public.

McCullagh wrote to Stevens instructing him to do some "unspoken interviewing" at the American Medical Congress in Washington.[10] He wrote to Stevens after it was over: "The Medical Congress was admirably done. The *Globe-Democrat* ought to take out a patent on that particular form of reporting." The success in Washington encouraged McCullagh to adopt the idea as a regular feature. The general format included the name, home address, and from 100 to 400 words of what was said in the talks with delegates. McCullagh amplified his idea in a letter to Stevens in 1893: "It may be that I will ask you to go to Cincinnati to the Hotel Keepers Convention. I have wired to find out if it will be a big thing. If you go, do it up on the 'unspoken speech' plan. For instance, ask some of the big fellows how they like to take care of opera singers; whether they don't give a great deal of trouble. Also how they like certain men, etc. Many ideas will suggest themselves to you."

The Chief frequently sent explicit instructions to Stevens.[11] Some of the original letters in his handwriting are preserved in the Missouri Historical Society in St. Louis. On March 12, 1886, he wrote: "Your work has been so efficient that I do not like to complain of special matters, but please state facts and avoid elaboration." November 20, 1887 he suggested: "For a series of Washington letters you might write up unpublished features of the Smithsonian Institution and oddities in the Patent Office." January 5, 1888 he admonished: "Don't forget Congressional summary every Tuesday night. The Sunday *Post-Dispatch* is a great failure." In 1890 he wrote that Steven's salary would be $70 a week and added: "Select your own time for a vacation. If you go to Kansas, write up Wichita boom." In 1893, after the "Great Catechism," he notified Stevens his salary would be increased to $75 a week.

While others are usually given the credit for the development of the human interest story and feature stories generally, McCullagh was making effective use of all kinds of features regularly long before his rivals began attracting attention. Rule 46 in his instructions to correspondents, drafted shortly after he took over at the *Globe-Democrat* emphasized his interest. It read: "The *Globe-Democrat* makes a specialty of stories about old people, ghost stories, faith cures, spiritual manifestations, stories about animals and rare and curious incidents generally. Much of this matter can be conveniently sent by mail."

Imitation is usually sincere flattery, but McCullagh never proposed to permit rivals to get ahead of him. He cautioned his readers in an editorial shortly after the stories of snakes began to appear in the *Globe-Democrat*:

Some weeks ago the *Globe-Democrat* started a new department devoted to natural history—chiefly snakes. A number of journals have since adopted the idea, but we observe that many of them go entirely beyond the bounds of truth and probability in what they write. Our snake department is edited by an expert and is therefore reliable. We caution the public against the romancing of some of our contemporaries; ours are the only genuine snake stories published. The *Republican* is evidently jealous of the *Globe-Democrat*'s snake department. If the *Republican* should start a snake department, it would take ten years to bring the subject down as late as Aaron's serpent. The Cincinnati *Commercial* has been cooperating with the *Globe-Democrat* in the collection and publication of the phenomena of natural history vulgarly called snake stories. We have hitherto given the *Commercial*'s stories full credence and belief, but now comes one relating how a snake drew sustenance from a cow after the manner of a full-grown calf. This might be received in evidence before the Louisiana Senatorial investigation, but the *Globe-Democrat* cannot accept it. We must draw the line somewhere, and we draw it on the cow's teat.

The average life span in the last half of the nineteenth century was much shorter than it is today and McCullagh early realized there was interest in longevity and those who had achieved it. Regularly the *Globe-Democrat* printed a feature on oldsters, which ran from two to four columns. Limited to approximately three-hundred words, the individual stories gave the name, address, and age of the octogenarian, a brief biography and frequently the reason attributed for the impressive age. In fact, the *Globe-Democrat* published so many of these stories that some unkind critics suggested that they were fiction.

Ghost stories, which probably bordered on fiction, and faith cures appeared frequently. Rather than using one story, which would not attract much attention, McCullagh saved them until he could fill two or more columns at a time. He played them in what was for that period dramatic typographical fashion and they attracted wide readership.

McCullagh supplemented the spiritualist stories sent in by correspondents with staff coverage of spiritualist camps. Walter Stevens was sent to New York from Washington in 1893 to report the forty-fifth anniversary observance in Carnegie Hall of the start of modern spiritualism and his report appeared in the *Globe-Democrat* on April 2. It is an interesting, but not conclusive sidelight, that the St. Louis *Republican* in its obituary of McCullagh, reported the rumor that he was a spiritualist. Casper S. Yost, his assistant managing editor in McCullagh's later years, continued this interest in the occult long afterwards.

Early in the 1880's the *Globe-Democrat* was running a regular weekly hunting and fishing column, usually with illustrations. While American newspapers began to increase the use of illustrations in this period, following the development of zincographs, line cuts etched by acid on zinc, it was possible to speed up the old wood cuts and McCullagh was among the first to take advantage of the process. Cartoons appeared from time to time on the front page and illustrations in the news pages as well as in connection with feature stories.

By 1890 a typical Sunday edition of the *Globe-Democrat* was forty pages. November 18 of that year, the paper's Sunday features included a story on "Marriage Superstitions," "The German Reichstag," an article on artists' models, another on advice in creating "Cosy Corners and Artistic Nooks," a long feature on birds, a feature on Robert Ingersoll, a full page feature on New Mexico, another on Chile, a women's feature entitled "Ballroom Toilet," a feature story on St. Louis Postmaster, and a piece on "The Polar Seas." That issue included more than fifty illustrations, as well as the words and music of a popular song, which was a regular Sunday feature. There were two columns of "Questions and Answers" and another regular feature, "Multum In Parvo." This feature occupied two full columns of one sentence paragraphs, presenting a long discussion of a subject. One issue was the history of printing. Another presented a collection of famous quotations.

In variety and scope the Sunday *Globe-Democrat* compared favorably with any of its contemporaries in New York and other large cities. In St. Louis it stood head and shoulders above its rivals and its success was attested by the steady growth of its circulation.

CRUSADES AND COMPETITION

7

With the purchase of the St. Louis *Democrat* and its merger with the *Globe* in 1875, the St. Louis *Republican* remained the only serious rival for circulation and prestige. It was obvious from the scant editorial attention McCullagh gave the evening newspapers in St. Louis that he did not regard them as important. The *Republican,* however, was a formidable competitor. It was the oldest newspaper west of the Mississippi River, having been established by Joseph Charless in 1808, a month after St. Louis had become a town by act of the territorial legislature.[1] The first issue appeared July 12 of that year as a weekly newspaper. It was sold in 1818, but was repurchased by Charless' son Edward in 1822 and was renamed the *Missouri Republican,* reflecting the Jeffersonian politics of the owner.

Thus it began in the era referred to by historians of journalism as the period of the "Party Press." In the first three decades of the nineteenth century, and in fact, up to the Civil War, the partisan press was concerned predominantly with politics. Its editors were either politically ambitious, or worked for politicians who aspired to office and power. It was an era of vituperation and insult. By the 1880's this personal journalism was beginning to abate, though it was not until the end of the decade that it began to die out.

The *Republican* had been acquired by George and Charles Knapp in 1836. It was generally regarded as the voice of the Democratic Party in Missouri, and in the 1870's as the spokesman for the conservative and wealthy families in St. Louis. The circulation was a closely-guarded secret, but was estimated at somewhere between fifteen and twenty thousand.[2] However, its weekly and semi-weekly editions had a substantial circulation over the state. More important, it claimed to have the largest circulation in the business and society circles of the city, which added to its prestige as an advertising medium.

If the owners and the staff of the *Republican* were inclined to be superior, even smug, in the 1870's, there was justification for their attitude. The *Republican* had the largest news staff in the city and local newsmen assumed that it paid the highest salaries. Its managing editor at that time was William Hyde,[3] a college graduate, with thirty years of service to the paper. Daniel M. Grissom, who wrote the "leaders" was recognized as one of the foremost editorial writers in the West. He, too, was a university graduate. Thomas E. Garrett was acknowledged to be the most highly respected drama critic west of the Mississippi River. William H. Swift had given the paper leadership in business and financial news. Frank R. O'Neil was agreed to be the star reporter of the city. One of the bright young lads on the staff was William Marion Reedy.

McCullagh and Hyde had known each other as rival reporters in St. Louis before the Civil War, but seldom met as rival editors. After McCullagh's death Hyde explained: "We were good friends but when I was editor of the *Republican,* Mr. Knapp on my side and Mr. McKee on his, did not think it the wisest thing for us to be too intimate and so we drifted apart to some extent for business reasons." It was the *Republican*'s policy that its staff should not associate with rival staffers. *Republican* reporters did not join the Press Club. They were instructed not to cooperate with their rivals in covering news stories.

In its earlier years the *Republican* had attracted wide attention with its news beats. In the era of the stage coaches it had consistently beaten its rivals with the first publication in the West of Presidential addresses to Congress. Hyde while still a reporter had made a trip by balloon, which won him national attention. The paper featured weekly letters from the best known correspondents in the East and in Europe.

The *Republican* was published in one of the most imposing

CRUSADES AND COMPETITION 131

newspaper plants in the nation. The five-story building at Third and Chestnut Streets had been equipped at a cost of $100,000, including a press purchased from the *Times* of London which was capable of printing thirty-thousand copies an hour.

But despite all its advantages the signs of complacency and age were beginning to show. If power corrupts, so does success. More important, the owners of the *Republican* failed to recognize that the readers' interests were changing. The *Republican* was dull, and McCullagh was persistent in pointing it out. Day after day his editorial paragraphs poked fun at his rival:

> The *Missouri-Republican* prints a facsimile of its progenitor, the *Missouri Gazette*, first issued in 1808. So far as we can discover, it has not materially degenerated. It is nearly as good a newspaper as it was then.
>
> A correspondent inquires what we will pay for "original stories, such, for instance, as are published in the Sunday *Republican*." Three cents a pound.
>
> The *Republican* took the city advertising not so much for the money there is in it, as for the purpose of giving a little spice and liveliness to its columns. An ordinance for the paving of an alley reads like a soul-stirring sensation in contrast to the average *Republican* editorial.
>
> The *Republican* is becoming a journalistic doubleender, so to speak. The man who controls the eighth page made fun of White and Bliss (the revivalists) on Monday, and the man who controls the fourth page felt bound to make amends on Wednesday. Too many cooks do not more inevitably spoil the broth than do too many "responsible" editors spoil a newspaper. We have a whole army of professional wits on the *Globe-Democrat* but we do not allow any of them to exercise their marvellous faculties at the expense of Christian ministers of any sect or denomination whatever.
>
> We will pay a round sum to any man who will give us the secret, which the *Republican* seems to possess, of publishing the dullest newspaper in America. Put every man in our office under the influence of opium for a month, and the *Globe-Democrat* would still be a marvel of animation compared with the *Republican*.

However, as we have seen, the *Globe-Democrat* was rapidly overtaking the *Republican*, both in circulation and in advertising. The weekly and semi-weekly editions of the *Globe-Democrat* were also challenging the *Republican*. The newspaper which was in time to offer the keenest competition to the *Globe-Democrat*, did not appear on the scene until nearly the end of 1878. On December 10, 1878 a news story on page 4 of the *Globe-Democrat* reported the sale of the bankrupt St. Louis *Dispatch* at an auction on the courthouse steps the previous day. Joseph Pulitzer was present but did not participate in the bidding. He was represented by an agent, Simon J. Arnold, and the newspaper was finally sold for $2,500. The *Globe-Democrat*'s story noted that "The tall graceful figure and mephistophelian face of Mr. Pulitzer, with its expression of keen irony" was present at the sale.

On the editorial page that day, McCullagh wrote: "There are so many rumors afloat about evening journalism in St. Louis that we should not be surprised, as the result of all of them, to hear the newsboys crying out 'the *Dispatch-Journal-Post-Star*.'" In a second paragraph, noting that Pulitzer was in fact the new owner, he commented: "What he failed to accomplish with an eloquent tongue, he may yet achieve with a brilliant pen. If the world was made no better by Mr. Pulitzer as an orator, it will, we trust, be made wiser by Mr. Pulitzer as an editor."

The following day after the first issue of the *Dispatch* appeared under the new owner, McCullagh wrote: "The editorial salutation is always more or less prolific of promise but we know of no editor who has in one article of this kind, mapped out for himself a wider field of usefulness and activity than that assigned to himself by Mr. Pulitzer. Mr. Pulitzer has taken a very large bite but, although his teeth are excellent and his mouth is good for a seven-inch smile, we doubt his capacity to chew it all."

Less than a week later, when Pulitzer persuaded John Dillon to join his *Post* with the *Dispatch,* McCullagh saluted the new *Post and Dispatch* editorially:[4]

Great events always follow in the wake of Mr. Pulitzer. When he arrived in St. Louis a few days ago we hardly knew what to expect, but a column of double-leaded Democratic thunder in the

Dispatch partially solved the problem, although we were prepared for a new reform movement or something much more serious. We felt relieved when we saw that Joseph has found a journalistic 'scape valve for his superfluous ardor. Without this we feared an explosion. And now another great thing has happened in the consolidation of the *Evening Post* and the *Dispatch* under the management of Mr. John A. Dillon. Mr. Dillon has made a conspicuous success of the *Post* and the consolidation can only be looked upon as a personal triumph for him, which can be explained by two facts: (1) that he is a man of ability in the newspaper line, and (2) that he graduated in the greatest journalistic university in the country, the *Globe-Democrat* office. He is now confronted with the greatest task he has yet assumed—that of taming down the crude products of Pulitzer's fiery and untamed brain to the shapely dimensions of average newspaper dissertation. When he shall have shown his ability to do this, he may well quit the field of journalism for the more remunerative occupation of harnessing the zebra in its native wilds.

There was editorial bickering between the *Globe-Democrat* and the *Post and Dispatch,* particularly after Pulitzer brought in John A. Cockerill as managing editor in December 1879. Cockerill, who had worked for McCullagh briefly on the Cincinnati *Enquirer,* came to St. Louis from Baltimore, where he had been editor of the Baltimore *Gazette*. Both men were masters of the editorial paragraph, and it was natural that frequently their editorial lances would be leveled at each other. But the venom in which McCullagh dipped his pen when attacking the *Republican* was seldom evident in his editorial comment and advice to the *Post and Dispatch*.

Relations between the two publishers were friendly. Pulitzer had consulted Daniel Houser about the purchase of the *Dispatch* and Houser had encouraged him to buy it. Some accounts insist that the *Post and Dispatch* was printed for a time on the *Globe-Democrat* presses and that the *Post and Dispatch* had office space in the *Globe-Democrat* building.[5] No mention of it appears however in the files of either newspaper. It is an interesting sidenote that the *Globe-Democrat* is now printed by the *Post-Dispatch* under contract in the modern newspaper plant built by the *Globe-Democrat* in the early 1930's.

On March 10, 1880 the *Post and Dispatch* moved into its own building and the name was shortened to the hyphenated form, the St. Louis *Post-Dispatch*. When their press broke down four years later the paper was printed temporarily on the *Globe-Democrat* presses. McCullagh noted the emergency in an editorial paragraph on February 2, 1884:

> An accident to the machinery of the *Post-Dispatch* yesterday gave the *Globe-Democrat* an opportunity to tender the courtesy of its assistance to our evening contemporary. Hence, yesterday's issue of the *Post-Dispatch* partook of the physical perfection of the *Globe-Democrat*. The moral beauty of the *Globe-Democrat* was not there, however. This is a thing which machinery cannot impart.

Occasionally the editorial exchanges were complimentary. McCullagh reprinted one of the *Post-Dispatch*'s favorable comments, but he could not resist adding: "Thanks for the above kind notice. But please don't use that abominable word 'gotten' in any paragraph in which you mention the *Globe-Democrat*."[6] The *Post-Dispatch* promptly retorted: " 'Gotten' is not an abominable word; it is good English, and we cannot consent to discredit it at the request of an editor who uses the expression 'native-born Senators.' "

McCullagh then proceeded to give his rival a lesson in grammar. He replied:

> "Gotten" is, as Polonius says of "beautified," a vile phrase. It is a dudish effort to be hypergrammatical. As well say "has hadden" as "has gotten" for "has got." The expression "native-born" is strictly correct, rendered necessary for the sake of contradistinction to "foreign-born Senators." The Constitution of the United States declares that "no person except a natural-born citizen" shall be President. "Natural-born" is here synonymous with "Native-born," having the same root in "natus."

Careless writing seemed to wave a red flag at McCullagh. He could never resist the temptation to point it out to the offender. A *Post-Dispatch* news story announced Pulitzer's annual Christ-

CRUSADES AND COMPETITION

mas gift of turkeys to the employes. The lead of the story read: "All the employes of the *Post-Dispatch* were presented with a Christmas turkey today." McCullagh's editorial reproof follows:[7]

At first glance the above is somewhat discouraging. It leads to the impression that a solitary turkey sufficed as the "typical expression" of Mr. Pulitzer's generosity to 250 employes. Further on, however, we learn that there was a turkey for each instead of a turkey for all—twelve barrels of birds in fact—and that to each bird was attached a tag bearing the compliments of the giver. "Careful discrimination," we are informed, "was used in the distribution of the turkeys." This announcement is supplemented by an explanation that the number of people in a family was carefully considered, and that the size of the turkey was, in each case, proportioned to the size of the family. We cannot indorse this kind of discrimination as of the best. The line should have been drawn on appetites rather than on numbers. Some families of three will consume more turkey than other families of six. In cases of this kind, however, it is cruel to be critical. The fact remains that the annual distribution of turkeys to the *Post-Dispatch* employes has again thrown a ripple of sunshine upon a dark and cheerless world, and that Mr. Pulitzer's newspaper has once more paid a glowing tribute to Mr. Pulitzer's generosity.

McCullagh's attitude toward the *Post-Dispatch* and toward Cockerill was clearly demonstrated in his handling of the biggest local story of 1882: the fatal shooting of Alonzo Slayback, a St. Louis attorney and politician, by Cockerill in Cockerill's office on the second floor of the *Post-Dispatch* building. Slayback was a close friend and political supporter of James O. Broadhead, an attorney who was seeking a seat in Congress. The *Post-Dispatch* had been waging an editorial campaign against Broadhead, and Slayback publicly accused the *Post-Dispatch* of being a "blackmailing sheet." The dispute came to a head when Cockerill ran a "card" from John Glover, the recently defeated candidate, which accused Slayback of being a coward.[8]

Late on the afternoon of October 13, Slayback and another lawyer, William Clopton, went to the *Post-Dispatch* and confronted Cockerill. The precise details of what transpired remain in doubt to this day. But it was established that Cockerill took a revolver from his desk and fired. Slayback died in a few minutes before medical aid could be summoned.

The *Globe-Democrat* played the story the following morning for two columns on page 1 under the head "A Shot in the Sanctum." The remainder of the page was filled with advertisements, and the story continued for most of page 2. McCullagh on the editorial page urged that judgment be suspended until all the facts were known. In a double-leaded editorial he wrote:

> Our local columns this morning contain the details of one of the saddest tragedies that have darkened the pages of our local history in many a day. We have been at pains to get an impartial statement of all the facts in the case and to present them in their fullness in order to let the reader form his own judgment of their merit. As usual in such cases, there is conflicting evidence on the vital point of responsibility for the fatal termination of the sad recontre. There must be more or less mystery about the matter until the facts are carefully sifted before a competent tribunal. In the meantime, the feeling of all good citizens must be one of unfeigned sorrow for the loss of an estimable and a brave man thus suddenly cut off in a community in which he was widely known and respected.

In contrast to the *Globe-Democrat*'s handling of the story, the *Republican*'s account reflected that newspaper's vindictive antagonism for the *Post-Dispatch*. The headlines indicating the tone of the story, read: "Alonzo W. Slayback Shot and Killed by John A. Cockerill"; "Singled out by the *Post-Dispatch* as a Victim of Its Venom"; "He Visits the Sanctum of That Paper to Vindicate His Manhood; And Finds the Editor With a Revolver Ready at Hand"; "Great Excitement Throughout the City"; "Fruits of Aggressive and Sensational Journalism of the *Post-Dispatch* School."

The *Globe-Democrat* covered the Coroner's inquest in a full page report on October 15 and on the following day McCullagh sharply reproved the *Republican* editorially for demanding Cockerill's conviction even before Cockerill had been charged with a crime. Seven weeks later a grand jury heard the evidence in the case, including testimony that Slayback had been armed when he entered Cockerill's office, and voted a no-bill. McCullagh later wrote several editorials urging contributions for a fund for Slayback's widow.

In charging the *Post-Dispatch* with "sensational journalism" the pages of the *Republican* must have exuded a distinct odor of sour grapes. There was a new school of sensationalism in St. Louis, as elsewhere, but the *Republican* was aiming at the wrong target. The newspaper which was responsible for the new "sensational journalism" was the *Globe-Democrat,* and the man responsible for it was McCullagh. It was recognized by others, if not by the *Republican.* Writing on "Western Journalism" in *Harper's New Monthly Magazine* for October 1888, Z. L. White pointed out: "McCullagh is what the western people call a rustler. He was said to be sensational, but if he was, it was a sensationalism that was popular and everyone read what appeared, and liked to read it too . . . There was a snap in his editorial comments that St. Louis had not been accustomed to. There was an air of sensationalism about its news department that was new in the field . . . The *Globe-Democrat* became one of the leading papers of the country, and a very valuable property."

There is no evidence in McCullagh's editorials, nor elsewhere, to suggest that he regarded the *Globe-Democrat* as sensational. There is ample evidence that he firmly believed it was the duty of a newspaper to print the news, violent or unpleasant though it might be. He had a strong aversion to faking and inaccuracy, and he never hesitated to point out the shortcomings of other newspapers in this regard, usually to remind his readers that the *Globe-Democrat* had reported the facts, even though it did not make as good a story. For example, in an editorial on May 13, 1893, he took the *Post-Dispatch* to task: "Yesterday's *Post-Dispatch* contained the most flagrant piece of faking known to the history of journalism." The news story to which he referred was a dispatch relating in detail the execution of a convicted murderer, even to describing his final words and how he died. McCullagh continued: "The *Globe-Democrat* yesterday contained a special dispatch stating that the execution of Elias Loving for murder was postponed on account of a reprieve from the Governor." He added: "There is nothing in the way of faking it now seems that is too mendacious for a newspaper with a lottery annex and a 5-cent guessing attachment." The final comment obviously referred to some of the promotion and circulation projects of the *Post-Dispatch*.

On another occasion, McCullagh chided the *Post-Dispatch* for "cribbing." On June 10, 1889 he reprinted the following from the Cincinnati *Enquirer*:

> The St. Louis *Post-Dispatch* is what is known in the Newspaper World as a "cribber." In its issue of Sunday, June 9, it published as original matter under the caption "Written for the Sunday *Post-Dispatch*" the article on "Hypnotism" written expressly for the *Enquirer* of Sunday June 2 by Dr. M. C. Lockwood. The article was stolen bodily from the Enquirer by the *P-D*. The paper even had the cheek to quote the closing paragraph of the *Enquirer*'s article as "an interview with a physician by a *Post-Dispatch* reporter." (Cincinnati *Enquirer*)

Then McCullagh added:

> The stolen article appears also in the New York *World* of June 9 as original. The closing paragraph of the *World*'s story held an interview with a physician, etc. The simultaneous publication in New York and St. Louis would seem to indicate an interchange of fakes between the two establishments.

The *Globe-Democrat*'s policy was set out in a house advertisement which appeared in the issue of January 2, 1879:

> The *Globe-Democrat* owes its unprecedented success to the fullness and accuracy of its news reports, and the fairness and candor of its criticism on current events. Recognizing the truth to be the highest obligation a newspaper owes to its readers, we shall at all times publish the essential facts relating to public affairs and public officials, and shall reserve the privilege of commenting upon them as they appear to us to be related to right or wrong.

"Fullness and accuracy" were the key words to McCullagh's news policy and they explain in part why some referred to it as "sensationalism." To report the news fully meant then, as it should today, not to ignore its sordid aspects. In a literal sense the *Globe-Democrat* merely reflected the era and the area it served. In the last quarter of the nineteenth century Missouri and the territory to its west and southwest was still the frontier. Jesse James and other robber barons were in their heyday. Gunslingers and law men were performing the exploits that have become part of our folklore. Horse thieves were still being strung up to the nearest tree and gamblers plied their trade on the Mississippi River packetboats and in frontier saloons. In St. Louis, as in most cities across the land, local political bosses stuffed ballot boxes and grew rich on corruption. Prostitution and gambling flourished openly while the affluent oligarchy tried to pretend the evils did not exist and stealthily pocketed their share of the profits.

It was the very fact that the *Globe-Democrat,* and then the *Post Dispatch* exposed and emphasized the violence and the sordidness of the times, that disturbed the *Republican* and the entrenched leaders of business and society. The *Republican* in the first decade after the Civil War had been the most influential spokesman, not only of the Democratic Party, but of business interests of St. Louis. But it was first of all a party organ and its editor, William Hyde and its publishers George and Charles Knapp were more concerned with manipulating elections than with seeking out the news. By the time of Slayback's death, the *Globe-Democrat* had drawn ahead of the *Republican* in circulation and undoubtedly the *Republican* recognized a new exponent of aggressive journalism in the *Post-Dispatch,* which was even more flamboyant in its news coverage and headlines.

Typical of the bickering between the *Republican* and the *Globe-Democrat* over the charge of sensationalism was the skirmish in the fall of 1878.[9] The Republicans at their city convention in St. Louis nominated for sheriff Major Julius Hunicke, a well known and respected citizen. The *Republican,* in its attempt to discredit the opposition, recalled a highly sensational incident from the past. The day after the convention the *Republican* commented: "Who would have thought that the once brilliant Callahan banquet, where police commissioners from Cincinnati and St. Louis supped in splendor with the demimonde, should drift into sight through the aid of a Republican convention. It is the case of the sins of the youthful politician returning to plague him. Mr. Hunicke should have thought of this."

It is a good rule in politics, as in editorial writing, to first make sure of your facts, as McCullagh pointed out in his editorial the following day:

Ordinarily we hesitate before challenging any assertion of the *Republican* which involved the habits, modes of life, or other proceedings of the demi-monde. It is a wise law of nature which ordains a division of labor in this world. "Each to his business and desire shall point." The principle obtains in journalism as in other professions, and pursuits, and in obedience to it, the *Republican* has become the organ and oracle of female frailty. In all that happens within the many temples of Venus, within the city of St. Louis, the *Republican* is regarded as indisputable authority. We should as soon think of questioning *Bell's Life* or the *Clipper* respecting an event in the prize ring as of doubting the *Republican's* record of anything transpiring in a *maison de joie*. And yet we are constrained to correct that usually accurate journal when it says, as in its issue of yesterday, that Mr. Hunicke, the Republican candidate for sheriff, was present at a banquet given some years ago at the residence of one "Madame Callahan." We have no idea who Madame Callahan was or where she resided, but the *Republican* speaks of her in terms of familiarity which indicate a long acquaintance. Mr. Hunicke was not present on the occasion made memorable by the Madame's organ. His absence from the city —he being then a resident of Nashville, Tennessee—will partially at least account for his absence from the banquet. We do not want to be misunderstood as generally arraigning the *Republican* for want of accuracy in a single instance of this kind. The fact that its editor can recall the great event of the feast after ten years is creditable to his memory and to the watchful zeal with which he stores his great mind with the kind of information he most highly prizes. People may differ as to literary or editorial ability, but as historian of events like the "Callahan" banquet the individual referred to is without a fellow in the firmament of journalism.

The *Republican* was forced to retract, but in doing so charged the *Globe-Democrat* with "indecent journalism," thereby providing McCullagh with the opportunity to reply. He wrote:

> We dislike personal journalism but we cannot help dipping into it once in a while just to remind the old reprobates at Third and Chestnut streets that they cannot be allowed to abuse their betters with impunity. If they do not change their course, the treatment they will receive from the *Globe-Democrat* will make them think they have suddenly been struck in the softer parts by a quarter section of the day of judgment.

Later, after another exchange of insults, the *Republican* commented at some length on "the wicked, desperate and malignant character of J. B. McCullagh." McCullagh's answer was restrained:

> We assure the two old scoundrels at Third and Chestnut streets that they do not know Mr. J. B. McCullagh. He is not "wicked, desperate and malignant." On the contrary, he is noted for his sweet disposition, and his strong point is excessive modesty. If Poker George and Monte John will call at the *Globe-Democrat* office, we will take pleasure in introducing them to Mr. McCullagh and those associated with him in the conduct of the great religious daily.

By January 1880, the *Globe-Democrat* had such a safe lead in circulation that the price was increased 20 per cent to thirty cents a week for local subscribers and $12.00 a year by mail. McCullagh rubbed salt in the wound of the *Republican*'s pride with this editorial:

> The circulation of the Sunday *Globe-Democrat* is steadily and rapidly increasing, which is not at all remarkable, considering its merits as a newspaper, and comparing them with those of its contemporaries. The poor old *Republican* is getting duller and more dish-washery every week. The newsboys are stuck with it every Sunday and agonizingly offer three copies for five cents before 10 A.M.
>
> A correspondent—and he is one of a very large class to which he belongs—writes to us that he hates the *Globe-Democrat,* but he

buys it regularly "to find out what is going on." We are sorry to incur the hatred of any of our fellow-men; but a large experience in the newspaper business has taught us that no man's love will go as far as his nickel in paying printers and telegraphers.

The *Globe-Democrat* is a strictly Republican paper, and yet its report of the Democratic State Convention will be read by five Democrats in the State of Missouri where one will read any other paper, and not one who makes the comparison but will admit our report is more full, free and fair, better written and better worth reading than any given by the organs. This explains how it has come to pass that in a democratic state a republican paper has the largest circulation.

Another aspect of the new journalism which certainly disturbed the Republican and no doubt some of its staunch supporters, was the crusades of the two papers not only against corruption in local government but against social evils as well. It is not surprising that some of the more respectable elements of the community regarded such exposures as not only sensational, but in poor taste.

The battle strategy of McCullagh on the *Globe-Democrat* and that of Pulitzer and Cockerill on the *Post-Dispatch* present an interesting contrast and in fact persisted long after those antagonists had passed from the scene. Both papers attacked vigorously on their editorial pages. It is fair to note that in time the *Post-Dispatch* became more aggressive in its news columns, and indeed instigated more crusades. Pulitzer undoubtedly recognized his crusades as an effective way to attract attention and circulation, but in fairness it must be added that both papers believed that exposing evil and advocating reforms were legitimate obligations of a newspaper.

McCullagh never spelled out his own convictions on the role of a newspaper as a crusader, but more than thirty years after his death E. Lansing Ray, then publisher of the *Globe-Democrat,* explained his philosophy, which undoubtedly reflected McCullagh's views, this way:[10] "The *Globe-Democrat* will fight for what it believes should be exposed or improved", he said, "but it is not a common scold. Because it is not constantly campaigning for something, I believe it can be more effective when it does campaign for something."

In the decade from 1870 to 1880 there were enough evils to keep both papers fully occupied. Typical was the campaign against gambling, and more specifically lotteries in 1879. St. Louis, perhaps as a result of the influence of the riverboats, was known as a wide-open town. In the 1840's the state legislature had voted to charter a Missouri State Lottery to finance building a plank road from the village of Franklin to the Missouri River. By 1879 the road had been abandoned, but the lottery continued to operate under the guiding hand of a former river gambler, William C. France. Its annual profit was estimated by the newspapers at more than $180,000, much of which found its way into the pockets of local officials. The *Globe-Democrat* vigorously protested the lottery and as a result a group of St. Louisans filed a suit attacking the lottery's legality, only to have the Missouri Supreme Court uphold it.

Early in 1878 Alanson Bankson, alias Alanson Wakefield, also an ex-river-gambler, gained control of the lottery and was able to put pressure on local politicians to persuade the Governor to name Dr. James C. Nidelet and David Ladd to the St. Louis Board of Police Commissioners. Both were rumored to be linked with Wakefield. As the result of the publicity of the newspapers, the legislature refused to ratify the appointment of the two commissioners and a grand jury investigation followed Wakefield's operations. Interestingly the foreman of the grand jury was the editor of the *Globe-Democrat*. Wakefield was indicted on a charge of perjury and was tried and sentenced to two years in prison. Dr. Nidelet was censured by the grand jury for unbecoming conduct, but was not indicted.

The 1870's were decisive years, both for McCullagh and the *Globe-Democrat,* and for Pulitzer and the *Post-Dispatch.* Both men in that period were influential in popularizing the "new journalism." It was a decade of highly personal journalism and two of its practitioners, McCullagh and Cockerill, were masters at it. Undoubtedly the readers enjoyed the verbal jousts. McCullagh, as has been noted, occasionally chided his rivals for indulging in personalities, but the gusto with which he attacked suggests that he must have loved to match sarcasm and venom with his contemporaries. For example, he lashed out at both the *Times* and the *Republican* in one editorial:[11]

The *Times* is indulging in another series of unjustified attacks upon the *Republican,* its founders and its founderers. This is very improper, and quite beneath the dignity of metropolitan journalism.

The journalistic Jumbo of the *Republican* calls attention to the fact that a few days ago he "designated" the editor of the *Globe-Democrat* as a Bohemian. Well, what if he did? We have heard the same journalistic Jumbo "designated" as a drunken loafer and a gambler's pimp. These "designations" you see, are not always reliable.

The *Globe-Democrat,* perhaps, will be expected to take some notice of the allegation several times repeated in yesterday's *Republican,* that certain matter published in our columns as having been received from San Francisco did not come by telegraph at all, but was written in our office. We notice the assertion only to say that its author is a brainless ass and an unmitigated liar.

The *Republican* reminds the *Globe-Democrat* that judicial records are stubborn facts. True, O King. And nobody knows it better than the two old beats of the *Republican,* who, according to judicial records, are self-acknowledged blackmailers and convicted blacklegs.

There is a good deal of talk in the newspapers about the Big Horne route. Colonel George Knapp knows all about it. The trail is first struck at the *Republican* office, thence to Jacoby's, thence to the Southern Hotel, then up Fourth Street to the Planter's House and Lupe's, thence up Olive Street to a half a dozen points.

The Big Booby of the *Republican,* having spent a great many years in ineffectual attempts to learn the use of a pen, is wise enough to fall back on the scissors when he would enliven the dreary waste of his editorial columns. We congratulate the Bog Booby on the judgment with which he selects from the files of the deceased *Democrat.* The *Republican* calls our Mississippi River Expedition a "k-news fleet." The wit is supposed to be deeply embedded in the k and the hyphen. As Colonel John once remarked, "Bill doesn't often do his best but there's a hell's sloo o' humor in him when he gets started."

CRUSADES AND COMPETITION 145

In the decade from 1870 to 1880, McCullagh's eye was undoubtedly centered on building the *Globe-Democrat*'s circulation, and he was quick to recognize that he had a worthy rival in Pulitzer's *Post-Dispatch*. It is an interesting sidelight that for the most part he refrained from attacking Pulitzer's news columns. But he did not hold back his comments on *Post-Dispatch* editorials or Pulitzer's promotion methods. He was scornful of the *Post-Dispatch* contests and what he called lotteries. For example, as late as 1893 on Thanksgiving morning this paragraph appeared:

The *Globe-Democrat* finds many reasons for thanks at this particular season, but it esteems as the highest inspiration of its gratitude that abounding grace which has enabled it to rise above the temptation of lotteries, coupons and all kinds of fakes into which most of its contemporaries here and elsewhere have fallen.

Earlier that year he commented on the circulation statement of the *Post-Dispatch* in these words:[12]

When the Old Testament revisers had proceeded with their work as far as Ecclesiastes, Chapter Two, verse 11: "All is vanity and vexation of the spirit," someone handed them a copy of the sworn statement of the circulation of the *Post-Dispatch* and they immediately changed the familiar text to "All is vanity and striving after wind."

Even in the early years, however, McCullagh made it clear that he was aiming at more than merely circulation and advertising. He was aware of the importance of the kind of readers who subscribed to the *Globe-Democrat,* and he recognized that circulation was not the only factor in attracting advertising. He told a visiting editor[13] on one occasion:

You will find that you cannot judge a man's politics by the fact that he is reading the *Globe-Democrat*. If he is reading the *Republican* you can be sure he is a Democrat. Before I came to St. Louis, I edited the *Republican* in Chicago for a time. The Chicago *Times* was at that time by far the biggest newspaper in the West. But it used to come out day after day with a very small amount of advertising—much less than the *Tribune,* although it had four times the *Tribune*'s circulation. Storey did not care very much because he had other ways of getting money. But I was surprised that the *Times* had so small a share of advertising, and meeting the advertising manager of Field, Leiter & Co. one day, I asked him about it. He told me his firm advertised in the *Tribune* simply because the *Tribune* reached the people whose custom they wanted.

While McCullagh knew that sensational news stories and editorial stunts were effective in getting readers to talk about the *Globe-Democrat,* he was building for permanence and gradually the paper became more dignified, though certainly not dull. But he was reaching out for wider and significant news coverage. Less emphasis was given to local reforms. New features and wider news horizons were sought. He insisted many times that the ideal newspaper should accurately and comprehensively record current history. On one occasion he summed his concept up this way in a Sunday editorial:[14]

Today's *Globe-Democrat* consists of 24 pages. It is the equal in size of three numbers of any paper printed in New York. Its contents will speak for themselves, whether in news or advertising. In the former the history of the world is given; in the latter nearly every merchant of this great city speaks of and for himself. The issue as a whole is one of which we have reason to be proud. It is objected by some that these double and triple numbers of the *Globe-Democrat* are "too big." Did anybody ever object to a hotel's bill of fare because it is too big or contained too many dishes? No guest is supposed to eat all there is on a bill of fare at a hotel, and no reader is obliged to take in every line there is in a newspaper. But a great newspaper, like a great hotel, must be conducted on the theory that tastes differ—and the best newspaper, like the best hotel, is that which prepares the largest variety of entertainment for the largest number of guests. It's a very queer taste that cannot find five cents worth to suit in today's *Globe-Democrat*.

One of the new areas of news in which McCullagh pioneered was education. While his interest in this field came in the next decade, it is appropriate to note it here as indicative of his widening interests. In an editorial on June 17, 1893, he called attention to it:

CRUSADES AND COMPETITION

The *Globe-Democrat* has for several years made a special feature at this season of the year of the news of college commencements, lists of graduates, etc. Since the first of the month we have printed as much as four columns a day, giving reports of as many as 26 commencements in one day. No other half dozen newspapers, east or west, have printed half as much as has appeared in the *Globe-Democrat*. Editors who think such matters of too little importance to be chronicled, greatly mistake the true nature of a newspaper's vocation, which is to get as close as possible to the people through the family, and what family is not interested in the school career of its members?

Features like this make the *Globe-Democrat* the most popular newspaper in the West, and make its columns of peculiar value to advertisers. Nor do we, to make room for the schools, neglect any other branch of legitimate newspaper work. We record all events of the active, thinking and working world from a baseball game to a heresy trial, to a double murder. We do not believe that all the space of a newspaper should be divided between those who practice politics and those who commit crimes, or that the morning supplication of a newspaper reader is "Give us this day our daily rape case."

As the decade of the 1880's drew to an end, the personal journalism, in which McCullagh excelled and the readers undoubtedly enjoyed, was beginning to disappear. The pot shots from his Ivory Tower became less frequent and less personal. By the end of its third year the *Globe-Democrat* had liquidated all the debts that had accumulated in the competition between the *Globe* and the *Democrat* and the expense of the purchase of the *Democrat*. Circulation was showing a steady and at times spectacular growth and advertising was increasing. McCullagh had his eyes set on national prestige for the paper.

He could never resist, however, a personal comment on occasion. When Pulitzer retired from the active direction of the New York *World* in 1890, McCullagh commented on October 24:

Mr. Pulitzer's retirement from active journalism calls forth many congrats on his New York success. He certainly has transformed the best-written and least-read newspaper in New York into the worst-written and most read newspaper in New York.

On December 1, 1893, he rebuked his friend Charles Dana, of the New York *Sun* for a literary lapse: "For shame, Mr. Dana. You ought to be able to quote Shakespeare more correctly than that. Shakespeare does not say 'Imperial Caesar,' but 'Imperious Caesar.'"

"POINTED AS A TACK"

8

Eugene Field, who cut his journalistic teeth in St. Louis, was an admirer of McCullagh, although he never worked for him. Field moved on, first to St. Joseph, Missouri, and then to become managing editor of the Kansas City *Times*. Later he took over as managing editor of the Denver *Tribune* where he started a column he called "Nonpareil Column." In 1883 Melville E. Stone persuaded Field to join the Chicago *Daily News* and there Field began his famous "Sharps and Flats" column, which he continued until his death in 1895. It was urbane and witty and was widely imitated. Hence Field could appreciate McCullagh's talents as an editorial paragrapher and he paid poetic tribute to them when he wrote:

> But the paper he is running makes the rusty fossils swear—
> The smartest, likeliest paper that is printed anywhere!
> And best of all, the paragraphs are pointed as a tack,
>   And that's because they emanate
>   From Little Mack.

McCullagh's national recognition as an editor rests primarily on the new ideas he brought to journalism in gathering and writing the news. Walter Williams, who edited the *Missouri Editor,* a monthly publication for Missouri weekly newspapers in the 1890's, commented on McCullagh's contribution to the new journalism in an editorial that appeared shortly after McCullagh's death. Williams wrote: "The best resolution a newspaperman can make at the beginning of the year is that he will spring a series of surprises upon his readers, that he will think up something that no one else has thought of or that he will steal some idea of someone so far from his readers that they will think it is his own, and thus give zest, interest and originality to his paper. McCullagh's success as a journalist lay in that he thought of things that occurred to no one else."

Certainly McCullagh recognized the importance of the news departments of the newspaper, but much of his own time and attention was given to the editorial page, and the conclusion seems inescapable that it was his greatest personal satisfaction. Significantly, most of the editorial tributes from papers across the country at the time of his death mentioned his editorials, and particularly his editorial paragraphs. Melville Stone[1] said: "His particular forte was paragraphs. His work was clean-cut, sharp, and incisive. He was a dangerous man to attack. His only rival, I think, was John Cockerill and it is a singular coincidence that the two men would have come from the same paper."

The Chicago *Times-Herald,* in its editorial tribute after McCullagh's death declared that McCullagh was a "master of fencing, knew the tierce and carte of public discussion thoroughly, but he preferred the flail."

McCullagh expressed his own ideas on editorial vigor when he told a member of his staff: "When you have to go after a man, don't pour a barrel of vinegar over him. Apply a drop or two of vitriol." [2]

In St. Louis both Cockerill and McCullagh had their ardent admirers. There were sharp differences of opinion as to which was the more caustic. Orrick Johns, the poet and son of George S. Johns, later editor of the editorial page of the *Post-Dispatch,* called it a draw. In *The Time of Our Lives,* he said of Cockerill: "He was an adroit phrase-maker, and a master of the short and deadly paragraph, the equal of J. B. McCullagh of the *Globe-Democrat.*"

However, the rivalry lasted only a few years, for Cockerill joined Pulitzer on the New York *World* in 1883. In any event, McCullagh was unquestionably the superior in the new ideas he brought to the editorial page, in the scope of his interests and in the editorial page's influence upon its readers.

McCullagh used a number of devices to lure the readers to

his editorials. He used the top of the editorial columns each day to print the weather forecast in italics, reasoning that the forecast was one service the reader wanted each day and that the reader's eye would inevitably be attracted to the paragraphs which followed. For a number of years the top of the column also contained a succinct summary of the previous day in Congress as well.

In an era when terseness was not the virtue it is acknowledged now, McCullagh was a firm believer in short editorials and he was convinced that the most effective editorials of all were those that were condensed into one short paragraph. He did not write all of them, of course, but they all passed under his careful scrutiny. D. R. McAnally, the son of the man who had given McCullagh his first job in St. Louis, was hired by McCullagh as an editorial writer. McAnally had taught English at the University of Missouri. After McCullagh's death,[3] McAnally recalled that on one occasion he had asked McCullagh: "How is it when I give you a long editorial you pass it on almost without reading it, while if it is something short, or a paragraph, you revise it carefully?" McCullagh replied: "Because people read the short editorials and they don't care a d———n for the long ones."

McCullagh believed that brevity in the soul of both sense and nonsense. He summed up the election of Grover Cleveland in 1884 in eleven words. His comment which led off the editorials for the day was: " 'Tell the truth' vs. 'Burn this letter,' verdict for the plaintiff."

Editorial paragraphing is becoming a lost art in the United States. Today the effective paragraphers in this country can almost be counted on the fingers of one hand, and not one can match the impressive volume of daily output that McCullagh achieved. Each day the entire first column of the editorial page was devoted exclusively to editorial paragraphs. The daily average was twenty or more, and frequently much of the second column was also devoted to paragraphs. Politics was a perennial subject, but the paragraphs covered a wide range of interests, from observations on the weather, to sports.

In reading the *Globe-Democrat*'s editorial pages of that period, there is the distinct impression that McCullagh achieved the concept and feeling of the *New Yorker* magazine's "Talk of the Town" nearly half a century before it became the trademark of Harold Ross. The *Globe-Democrat*'s paragraphs were a daily running commentary on the unusual, the foibles, and the bizarre as is the "Talk of the Town," today. McCullagh's comments were briefer, and the style of writing was perhaps not as sophisticated, but the similarity is striking.

In an era when newspapers did not have promotion departments to extoll their virtues and emphasize their value as an advertising medium, McCullagh, if not an innovator, was certainly a pioneer. Pulitzer, when he took over the *Post-Dispatch*, quickly followed McCullagh's lead. While the *Globe-Democrat* did from time to time run house advertisements, McCullagh's favorite spot for promotion was on the editorial page. It seems a logical assumption that he reasoned the promotion would receive more attention there. It might also be assumed that perhaps it seemed less ostentatious to brag about the newspaper on a page devoted to the expression of opinion.

McCullagh was aware of the importance of classified advertising, both as a source of revenue and as a circulation builder. Typical of his editorial promotion of want ads is this editorial paragraph on April 2, 1894: "Yesterday's *Globe-Democrat* contained 2752 small ads—and all the other morning papers combined did not contain nearly as many. Circulation goes with the small ads and small ads go with the circulation."

By that time the *Globe-Democrat* was publishing from six to eight pages of classified ads. Pulitzer took a leaf from McCullagh and the *Post-Dispatch* consistently plugged its classified section, as did the *World* in New York.

As we have seen, McCullagh frequently used the editorial columns to call attention to news beats and to new features. He reminded his readers, "The *Globe-Democrat* Gossip Department is booming today. St. Louis, Chicago, Washington, New York, Boston and San Francisco are represented and the whole array makes a symposium of surpassing interest and instruction." On August 31, 1893 the *Globe-Democrat* devoted its entire front page, with a runover on page 2 to the text of the address in the Senate of Senator John Sherman of Ohio on the silver issue. Five days later, McCullagh called attention to this news beat this way: "If the thing were to do over again several of the great

"POINTED AS A TACK" 153

newspapers of the country would print Senator Sherman's speech in full, instead of leaving the task exclusively to the *Globe-Democrat*. In matters of this kind, foresight goes for a great deal and hindsight for nothing."

When the *Globe-Democrat* was preparing to move to its new building, a six-story structure, in 1892, McCullagh reminded readers of the move at frequent intervals. He named it "The Temple of Truth." On New Year's Day in 1892 he wrote: "The *Globe-Democrat*'s next New Year's greeting will be issued from the Temple of Truth, now almost completed at the southwest corner of Sixth and Pine Streets."

When the actual move to the new building was at hand McCullagh announced the dedication of "The Temple of Truth" in a longer editorial:[4]

A portion of today's edition of the *Globe-Democrat* or rather a portion of the first section of it—pages 1 to 12—will be worked on the magnificent new press just put up in the basement of the Temple of Truth. As we write this paragraph there are wagons waiting at Fourth and Pine to carry the twelve stereotyped pages, especially cast for the purpose, to the T of T where everything is in readiness for the trial trip of the new machine, which we have christened Lady Veracity.

Yes, we shall probably allow a few lawyers to occupy apartments in the Temple of Truth. They must be very select members of the profession, though. We know of a lawyer in this town who says he "wouldn't give a damn to acquit an innocent man; that his only joy is in getting a verdict in favor of a man whom he knows to be guilty." No such lawyer can find an abiding place in the Temple of Truth; rather shall the bats and the owls fill its stately corridors and hold carnival under its lofty ceilings. To be eligible to this honored tenancy a man must use the law not less as a sword to punish the guilty than as a shield to protect the innocent. Otherwise he must find apartments with the *Chronicle,* the *Star-Sayings* or some other newspaper whose moral tone is less excellent than that of the great religious daily.

The Temple of Truth is still in the hands of its interior decorators, but the tenants are impatient and insist on taking possession, several having already moved in. It will be a great building, that T. of T. at Sixth and Pine. What columns would have been written about it ere this, were it intended as the home of any of our contemporaries. But then, as the poet says: "The shallows murmur, but the deeps are dumb."

On May 16 the editorial comment was shorter:

This is moving day for the Great Religious Daily. Today, with the *Globe-Democrat,* the old order changeth, giving way to new.

It is interesting to note that there was no mention of the move in the news columns. The front page on that day was devoted to floods in East St. Louis. The following day McCullagh ended his editorial discussion of the move in three words: "We have moved."

McCullagh delighted in reprinting favorable comment from other papers and made sure it was brought to the attention of the readers of the *Globe-Democrat.* In 1875, the Springfield, Massachusetts *Republican,*[5] which had won a reputation as one of the better newspapers in the East, said in an editorial: "Whatever may be thought of the *Globe-Democrat*'s peculiar tactics, politically or otherwise, there is no gainsaying the fact that it is a first-class newspaper and popular with the masses."

McCullagh reprinted the comment and added:

A "first-class newspaper and popular with the masses" is the highest praise that can be given any journal; and as long as our contemporaries render this verdict in our favor, they are welcome to their own estimate of all the rest. On these hang all the law and the profits.

He also reprinted a comment of the New York *Herald*:[6]

St. Louis is every day interested in the column of paragraphs in the *Globe-Democrat,* which in every department is one of the spiciest papers west of the Alleghanies. McCullagh's comment was: It is not often that the New York *Herald* condescends to a favorable notice of a contemporary, especially in the West.

In its issue of April 16, 1896, *Reedy's Mirror* commented it "was the general opinion that McCullagh was St. Louis' best all-around editorial writer." Reading his editorials nearly a century later, the first impression is their honesty and sincerity. There was never any doubt as to where he stood. He scorned the subterfuges of the Ivory Tower. There were obviously in his mind no shades in between black and white. He could be tolerant on occasion, but he was a relentless adversary, as those who incurred his wrath discovered to their sorrow. As have nearly all editorial writers, he had his favorite "hates" and those who were thus unfortunate received no mercy.

Among his favorite targets were Gen. William T. Sherman, Carl Schurz, St. Louis politician and one time mayor, Chauncey I. Filley, and college graduates, particularly those from Harvard. His dislike of Sherman stemmed from his experiences with the fiery general during the war. Ironically, both McCullagh and Sherman are buried in Bellefontaine Cemetery in St. Louis. Perhaps their ghosts still enliven the silent nights with their bickering.

Schurz came to St. Louis shortly after the Civil War and took over the coeditorship of the *Westliche Post,* then regarded as the most influential German-language paper in the West. It was Schurz who gave Joseph Pulitzer his first job as a reporter. The *Westliche Post* was Republican. Schurz belonged to the left-wing of the party and was successful in politics. He was elected to one term in the United States Senate. President Hayes named him as Secretary of the Interior in 1877. But he was not a party regular, which was one of the reasons for McCullagh's animosity. Hence Schurz was frequently the target of paragraphs in the *Globe-Democrat*.

Carl Schurz sprained his ankle a few days ago, trying to catch a train at Lawrence, Mass. He sprained his conscience several years ago, trying to catch up with a Democratic procession.

Carl Schurz is on our side this time, but we think we can win this fight, nevertheless.

In 1880 Schurz was among those who sought to block the nomination of General Grant for President, and among other things cast aspersion on Grant's war record. The attack inspired a number of sharp paragraphs from McCullagh. An example was this one:

Major General Schurz, U.S.A., continues his fearless criticism of Grant's military record. At the close of yesterday's article in the

Westliche Post there was not enough left of the little man from Galena to make a second lieutenant. The truth is that there was no real military genius displayed in the late war, on the part of the Federals, except at the battle of Chancellorsville, where Gens. Schurz, Schimmelfenning, and Siegel were in command. Schurz killed a great many rebels there. But he killed them after the manner related by a noted Mexican scout named Bill Chowder. Bill was six-feet-three and was one of many sitting around a campfire and telling how each had killed his man. "You killed your man, didn't you, Bill?" "Oh, you bet I did." "Did you shoot him?" "No." "Run him down?" "Well not exactly that either, but he died tryin' to run me down."

McCullagh found a letter written by President Lincoln in 1864 and quoted from it:[7] "I also received yours about Gen. Carl Schurz. I appreciate him certainly as highly as you do, but you can never know until you have the trial how difficult it is to find a place for an officer of so high rank when there is no place seeking him." McCullagh added his own comment: "Mr. Lincoln's sarcasm was very gentle. An officer of high rank for whom there was no place in the most critical period of the war. But Carl drew his pay like a little man, all the same."

The feud with Filley continued for nearly twenty years and provided McCullagh with a perennial target. Filley had served St. Louis as mayor during the Civil War. He was the city's postmaster when McCullagh became editor of the *Globe-Democrat*. For years he was the head of the St. Louis Board of Trade and he was generally regarded as a leader in the Republican party in Missouri, particularly of the wing of the party known at first as the Radical Wing and later as the Stalwart Wing. McCullagh was convinced Filley's kind of machine politics was not good for St. Louis, nor for the party.

Such overt infighting was unusual for that era. Newspapers were frankly partisan and rarely publicized interparty disputes. The *Globe-Democrat* was the leading Republican paper of Missouri and for McCullagh to attack one of its leading spokesmen, was rank heresy. The feud emphasizes McCullagh's belligerent independence and if future events cast their shadows before them, perhaps it was an indication of the independent editorial policies of newspapers today. The surprising thing was that Filley was able to remain in control of the party under such heavy attack, and that the *Globe-Democrat* continued to increase its circulation. The persistence, as well as the vigor with which McCullagh pressed the attack is indicative of his mettle as an editorial fighter.

To his credit, Filley was a worthy antagonist. He never asked, nor gave, quarter. It is interesting that he used the Democratic newspaper in St. Louis to strike back. He wrote letters to the editors at great length. Usually he was on the defensive, replying to a McCullagh paragraph. Certainly the *Globe-Democrat* provided ample ammunition with paragraphs such as these:[8]

Mr. Cheeky I. Filley says he is going to sue somebody for his character. He will do nothing of the kind. He has no character to lose, except a very bad one. He is a political deadbeat and an infamous and villainous liar."

The new year starts out badly. A terrible railroad accident and a letter from Filley on the same day. Poor little 1884.

"The Republican party has great need of Filley," says one of his admiring newspaper friends. Yes, about as much as the passenger on the rear platform of a street car has for a fan with the thermometer twenty degrees below zero.

Mr. Filley has his faults, but he has at least one trait of character that challenges admiration. He is probably the most malicious liar in St. Louis; he is undoubtedly one of the greatest poltroons in America; if he is not a common swindler his own blood relations do him gross injustice; he will for the sake of a paltry office, dive deeper into the dirt of personal humiliation than any other living man; he has not the semblance of a sense of personal honor; the qualities which are the objects of hatred, and the qualities which are the proper objects of contempt, are evenly and exquisitely balanced in him; if hell were dosed with tartar emetic, the last dregs of its last vomit would be a few men of his kind.

On one occasion Filley gave an interview to the *Missouri Republican*,[9] in which he accused McCullagh of being a cheap plagiarist. He was referring to one of McCullagh's paragraphs blasting him and he accused McCullagh of quoting from a noted British historian without giving credit to the source. McCullagh's reply was prompt, and to the point. He wrote:

> The *Republican* makes a charge of plagiarism against the *Globe-Democrat* because in an article of column length on Mr. Cheeky I. Filley we use twenty words from Macaulay without credit. Well, when Macaulay used the phrase he was gunning for bears; when we borrowed it we were gunning for skunks, and we were ashamed to put the label on the ammunition.

The *Republican* let itself be used by Filley in the feud, and of course did not escape McCullagh's attention. He fired a broadside at both in this paragraph:

> We are somewhat astonished, but not at all grieved by the statement in yesterday's *Republican* that Mr. Filley "knows more about Missouri politics in an hour than the St. Louis organ (to wit: the *Globe-Democrat*) has learned in a lifetime." How much political knowledge Mr. Filley can compress into the short period of sixty minutes we have no means of ascertaining, but on one occasion he imparted a good deal of information to the Postmaster General in a very few lines thus: "I dare not tell you on paper, but will when I see you, how I captured the *Republican* and made it come begging. Chauncey I. Filley."

The long feud ended in 1892 at the Republican national convention in Minneapolis. Filley, who had been Missouri's representative on the Republican National Committee through many campaigns was defeated for reelection by the Missouri delegates. The vote was 19 to 13. It is an interesting sidelight on the characters of both men that they later became friends and formed the habit of meeting at the St. Louis Club. When McCullagh's health forced him to be confined to his room, Filley, whom the public still assumed was an implacable enemy, was among his visitors. After McCullagh's death, Filley told a reporter:[10]

> We often met in the last two years in friendly personal conferences and were personal friends. Our meetings were at the St. Louis Club and consequently were unknown publicly. He will be missed throughout the country. Journalism loses one of its brightest lights. Socially, he was genial and kind; politically erratic.

From Filley that was high praise and it reflected the respect he accorded McCullagh as a worthy foe.

McCullagh's editorials sometimes were scholarly. His remarkable memory made it easy for him to quote from the Scriptures or literature. Occasionally his editorials were light and humorous. For example, he commented on the postal service in an editorial entitled "Kisses By Mail," as follows:

> "Now I have paid you the money, and I suppose you want the kisses."
>
> "Yes," she said, "if he sent me any kisses I want them too."
>
> It is hardly necessary to say that the balance of the order was promptly paid, and in a scientific manner at that, and eminently satisfactory to the country maiden, for she went out of the office smacking her lips as if there was a taste upon them she had never encountered before. After she arrived home she remarked to her mother: "Mother, this Post Office system of ours is a great thing, developing more each year and each new feature seems to be the best. Jimmy sent me a dozen kisses along with the money order and the Postmaster gave me twenty. It beats the Special Delivery system all hollow."

Sometimes his whimsy evoked comment in other publications. In 1882 McCullagh vented his disgust at the evils of corsets for women, which inspired the following comment from the St. Louis *Hornet*,[11] a weekly literary magazine:

> "With deep regard for the human welfare, he undertook to discuss the absorbing subject of corsets, in all its various branches, viewing it commercially, statistically, morally, and hygienically in such a familiar manner that considerable wonder was excited among the readers of The Great Religious Daily as to how its bachelor editor, who had resisted the wiles of the fair sex for 40 years, became possessed of his overwhelming knowledge of the subject."

As a paragrapher, McCullagh was familiar with all the tricks of that demanding trade. He was a master of the simile, metaphor, exaggeration, and the unexpected punch line. His avid reading of the exchanges provided much of the grist for his pointed paragraphs. Here are a few samples, selected at random:

> "A whole whale was captured on the Maryland coast a few

days ago and a five-gallon demijohn of whiskey was found in his stomach. He must have been on his way to a Democratic caucus."

"A child without a mouth has been found in Mississippi. If Senator Farrell could swap faces with it, his chances of re-election would be materially increased."

"They have in the Washington Navy Yard a new machine for rifling guns, but we have in the St. Louis City Hall an old machine for rifling taxpayers which beats it all to pieces."

"The regular semi-annual death of the last survivor of the Battle of Waterloo has just been announced."

"The Emperor of China is studying the English language. His example is worthy of the consideration of the average American congressman."

"Lent may be defined in a practical sense as a matter of getting used to Democratic rule."

"The city of Oklahoma is two days old and has not yet organized a baseball team."

"Do donkeys talk is the title of a leading article in a recent magazine. The *Congressional Record* would seem to have strong affirmative evidence on the subject."

"The Rev. Sam Jones is so sick he cannot preach. This is one of the Almighty's methods of helping the cause of true religion."

"A correspondent piteously inquires 'How long are the people of Missouri to be robbed?' We cannot answer as the Legislature has not fixed the date for adjournment."

"A line to Mr. Tennyson on reading his verses entitled 'The Fleet,' published recently in the London *Times*. 'Alf, old boy, don't write any more poetry.' "

"Two New Orleans editors met on the field of 'honah' yesterday—and one of them was a majah—but we regret to say that neither was hurt very much."

On one occasion when McCullagh admitted the *Globe-Democrat* had erred, he apologized this way:

We were ready for the chastening rod of affliction, but we did not expect a cat-o-nine-tails." Another time under similar circumstances he wrote:

Here's about the only consolation we can get from Shakespeare

"POINTED AS A TACK"   161

concerning a recent event which shall be nameless because painful. It is from the mouth of Hamlet: "Our indiscretions sometimes serve us well, when our dear plots do pall!"

He could also dispose of critics with biting terseness. "We are informed," he wrote in one of his paragraphs, "that Mr. C. D. Boisseau offered a resolution in the Republican caucus at Jefferson City condemning the *Globe-Democrat*. Who's Boisseau?"

McCullagh used many semantic devices in his editorials. We have seen his emphasis on "The Temple of Truth" and "The Great Religious Daily." Another of his favorites was "The *Globe*'s Towline."

On January 1, 1893 he led off the column with some twenty "Happy New Years," beginning with: "The Temple of Truth, January 1, Happy New Year to all."

Long before Walter Winchell, McCullagh used one of Winchell's tricks with paragraphs like this:

"What reputable clergyman of the city is willing to make a tour of the Holy Land on a ticket won in a lottery?" Or he would take a sarcastic growl at an attempt of the advertising department: "When the advertising agent undertakes to steer the paper, he should be called the Damaging Editor."

He was expressing his own editorial philosophy when he wrote:

The Great Religious Daily belongs to the church militant, and when a Yankee tramp smites it on one cheek, it generally makes things hot for the tramp's left cheek and one or both of his eyes.

With tongue in cheek, he would write:

Now let there be a tax on editors. The *Globe-Democrat* is the only newspaper in St. Louis that could be affected by it, but the Great Religious Daily is willing to pay its share of the public burden.

It was not surprising that his blunt charges and insulting adjectives brought occasional libel suits. In December 1892 John H. Pohlman, a Democratic politician objected violently to McCullagh's assertion that Pohlman had been false to his party vows when he assisted in the illegal election of E. A. Noonan as mayor four years earlier. Pohlman filed suit for libel. Mc-Cullagh's reply was typical:

And now comes Mr. John H. Pohlman to swear that the editor of the *Globe-Democrat* has libeled him, and then comes the editor of the *Globe-Democrat* who thanks Mr. Pohlman for this tribute to his mastery of the English language, he, the aforesaid editor, having previously supposed that the action attributed to him by the aforesaid Pohlman was beyond the limits of the vernacular.

The following day, McCullagh added fire to the feud:

The *Globe-Democrat* wishes it to be distinctly understood that it is not putting the slightest impediment in the way of Mr. Pohlman and his attorney in their daily pilgrimage to the shrine of justice in pursuit of a warrant for the arrest of the editor on a charge of criminal libel."

As might have been expected, nothing came of the suit except a little more heat lightning, a phrase McCullagh liked to use in a different connotation. Of those editorial writers who were prone to intersperse their conversation, and sometimes editorials with d——s and dashes, he said they indulged in "heat lightning profanity." [12]

Earlier he had expressed his opinion of Noonan this way:

There is not a man on the City Council who is not better fitted to be mayor than E. A. Noonan. This is official and is nailed down.

When the *Globe-Democrat* supported a candidate for mayor, McCullagh left no one in doubt of its support. In 1893, the paper saw in Cyrus P. Walbridge, a civic and business leader, the chance to oust the local Democratic machine. In March there were frequent reminders to voters to register. On March 14, after each paragraph, in italics, was the reminder: "Last day of registration." On April 2, McCullagh noted: "Only 2,880 minutes until the election of C. P. Walbridge as mayor of St. Louis." On April 3, the day before the election, this warning appeared: "The First, Second, Seventeenth and Nineteenth Wards will bear watching tomorrow." On April 5, the editorial page presented a cartoon of a rooster crowing and the lead story on the front page carried the headlines: "A Clean

Sweep; Walbridge Elected." At the top of the column of paragraphs, McCullagh's comment was succinct: "The Temple of Truth, Wednesday morning. Got 'em." Another paragraph read: "The tow line seems to have got its work in this time."

Despite the victory, there apparently were irregularities in some precincts as McCullagh had warned. In a longer editorial the *Globe-Democrat* charged some six-thousand fraudulent votes had been cast. In one short paragraph McCullagh wrote: "Open the ballot boxes, count the votes, locate the crimes, and send the criminals to the penitentiary."

McCullagh wrote many leaders and longer editorials but it is obvious that his preference was the short pointed paragraphs. His leaders usually were comparatively short, both by comparison to most of his contemporaries and by modern standards. Occasionally he revealed his personal convictions. On New Year's Day in 1885 he expressed his views on objective news:

> Washington Irving relates in his *Knickerbocker* that the progenitors of the sturdy men whose history he there relates were once visited by a man who called himself a philosopher, who introduced strange notions in the name of progress, and that the people rose en masse and disapproved all his assertions by banishing him from town. Most of the New York papers seem to us to be edited in the old Knickerbocker spirit; they disapprove what a great man says by not printing it. Some of them omitted Mr. Beecher's remarkable sermon of last Sunday, for the purpose, doubtless, of punishing Mr. Beecher for his recreancy in the last campaign. It never occurred to them that the omission was a greater punishment to their readers than to Mr. Beecher.
>
> The *Tribune* and the *Sun* suppressed Mr. Cleveland's letter on civil service reform, because, perhaps, the editors of those journals did not wish Mr. Cleveland to be known as a civil service reformer. And so on, from day to day, the important news of the country is published or suppressed in the "great dailies" of the metropolis as it may happen to please or displease the persons who are clothed with editorial functions. Out here in the Wild West this style of journalism would hardly succeed. The *Globe-Democrat* has never tried it, at any rate, and never will. We take it for granted that the people who buy a newspaper expect to find in it all the im-

portant news of the day, without regard to the views of the editor as to its effect upon parties, politics, or individuals.

As Gibbon says of his father's interference with one of his love affairs, "I sighed as a lover, but obeyed as a son." So the editor of a great newspaper, though he may often be tempted by the news of the day to suppress it as a politician, should always yield to the higher demand to print it as a journalist.

McCullagh's last editorial to appear in the *Globe-Democrat* was printed on January 6, 1897, six days after his death, with the explanation that it had been found in his desk and had probably been written several years before.

Next to Christmas day, the most pleasant annual epoch in existence is the advent of the New Year. There is a lachrymose sort of people who usher in the New Year with watching and fasting, as if they were bound to attend as chief mourners at the obsequies of the old one. Now we can't but think it a great deal more complimentary, both to the Old and the New Year that is just beginning to dawn upon us, to see the old fellow out and the new one in with gayety and glee.

In the 1880's McCullagh strengthened his editorial page staff. He hired Capt. Henry King in 1883, a Civil War veteran. Walter B. Stevens, the paper's Washington correspondent and roving reporter, described King as "one of the most polished, forceful writers of his generation." King had edited several newspapers in Kansas and was an occasional contributor to magazines. He became McCullagh's right hand man and was the logical choice[13] to take over as editor after McCullagh's death.

Another addition to the editorial page staff was Charles M. Harvey who was lured from New York. Harvey was recognized as something of an authority on American history and contributed historical features to the editorial page.

One of the features McCullagh began in this period was a solid page of essays on Sunday, utilizing the talents of the new members of his staff. All of the essays were signed, as was the practice in that year. Capt. King regularly contributed two columns, usually in a light, philosophic vein. Harvey wrote on historical subjects, and supplied two more columns. The remaining three columns were filled by other writers not on the staff. McCullagh insisted that the essays be written to fit the space. He believed the typographical appearance of the page was more attractive if every essay ended at the bottom of a column.

McCullagh invited a local pastor to become a contributor and warned him that he should not exceed the limit of one column. When his first contribution ran over the limit, McCullagh cut it to fit. The following day when the minister went to the editor's office to complain, he found Martin R. H. Witter, foreman of the composing room in conference with the "Chief." McCullagh did not wait for the minister's protest.[14] "There's the man. I told you he would do it if you ran over the column. Talk to him."

The affronted pastor, in relating the incident, said: "His appearance (McCullagh's) proves that a man can smile and smile and still be a villain."

One of McCullagh's devices to attract attention to the editorial page was to select a subject and run a full column of one and two-line items related to it. A typical one appeared on February 18, 1894 and was entitled "Feminine Fashions." In it the reader was informed that corsets were found on mummies in Egypt, that the wire hairpin was invented in England and that the longest dress train in history was forty-eight yards and was carried by ten pairs of pages. A frequent Sunday feature was a column of poetry, reprinted from current poets and entitled "Gems in Verse."

An omnivorous reader, McCullagh culled from the exchanges not only intriguing articles for reprinting in the paper, but spice and variety for the editorial page. He considered the material from other papers one of the best features of the paper. In the first decade of the *Globe-Democrat,* reprinted pieces filled from six to ten columns a day. One of his favorite quotations was "mighty interestin' reading," which he attributed to James Gordon Bennett. It applied, he felt, to the exchanges.

As McCullagh's health began to fail during the last two years of his life, he apparently left more and more of the editorials to Capt. King and others. The paragraphs, and the editorials became longer. The sparkle that was his distinctive trademark was missing. Since his death, McCullagh's ability as an editorial writer has been overshadowed by his other contributions to "the new journalism." Certainly he was one of the great masters of abusive prose of his time. He could sting and torment a victim with the light touch of a rapier, but more often he chose an Irish shillelagh. In the period of highly personal journalism, he could hold his own with the masters of invective. But when personal journalism died out, he was among the first to discard it. If he was intolerant of malfeasance and misfeasance in public office, he was also a constructive force in building his city. He could be witty or erudite as the occasion demanded, but he was the product of his Irish inheritance and he gloried in a free-swinging editorial fight.

An unintentional acknowledgment of McCullagh's reputation as an editorial writer and his inimitable style appeared in the *Post-Dispatch* in the summer of 1895. *Reedy's Mirror* took notice of it:[15] "An editorial in the *Post-Dispatch* states that the editor of the *Globe-Democrat* has taken to writing for that 'bright, if somewhat pert, sheet, the St. Louis *Mirror*.' If in these reflections, we have at times attained a combined clarity of purpose calculated to create the impression that the powerful pen of Mr. Joseph B. McCullagh is engaged in our service, and support, we are of course, immensely gratified. We should very much like to have Mr. McCullagh on the list of our valued contributors.

"No, Mr. McCullagh is not writing for the *Mirror*. He is writing within the narrow limitations of his field well and inspiringly to the great horde of the common vulgar."

Readers of the *Globe-Democrat* would agree with the opinion expressed by the Rev. William G. Eliot,[16] one of the outstanding reformers in St. Louis in his day, when he told his son: "Whenever the pinch comes, McCullagh is always found on the right side."

It was an epitaph any editorial writer could take pride in having earned.

BOOMING ST. LOUIS

9

One of the greatest satisfactions any man can earn surely must be the recognition that the community in which he makes his home is the better for his contribution. Certainly this must be true of a newspaper editor, whose profession implies the responsibility of leadership. McCullagh loved his adopted city and he served it with militant zeal. He was aware of its shortcomings and on occasion he would refer to "Poor old St. Louis." The phrase was one of his devices to jolt civic complacency, but he was never a pessimistic obstructionist. The *Globe-Democrat* "Towline" was always ready to pull the city out of the doldrums.

While his sarcasm could be biting when he railed at civic lethargy, McCullagh was a "boomer" at heart. He is credited with originating the word "boom"[1] in the connotation with which it has become familiar, and it became one of his favorites in describing St. Louis. He used it the first time on July 19, 1879 when he wrote: "The Grant movement is booming," and a little later when he observed: "The Grant movement booms more boomingly than ever." A number of years later the editors of the *Century Dictionary* wrote to McCullagh that a number of newspapers claimed to have originated the word.

I replied, he explained, that the easiest way to determine the matter was from the files of the claimant newspapers. A careful investigation showed the *Globe-Democrat*'s use of it to be at least six months earlier than any other newspaper. Then the editor of the dictionary asked me to explain how I came to use it. I replied that the word came to me from a Mississippi river pilot, whom I once heard to exclaim as he looked upon the river overflowing its banks and sweeping everything before it, "By Jove, but she's a-booming." It was in this sense that I applied it to the Grant movement, of which the *Globe-Democrat* was then a strong supporter. The English papers ridiculed the word in its new application at first, but now they use it freely, and it is frequently found in their best magazines.

By the time McCullagh took over the editorial direction of the *Globe-Democrat,* St. Louis was in dire need of a civic prodder. To put it bluntly, the "Gateway to the West," symbolized today by the magnificent Gateway Arch that towers some six hundred feet above the West bank of the Mississippi River, was sunk deep in the comforting warmth of complacency. The city had survived the great fire of 1849, the cholera epidemics and the divided loyalties of the Civil War. Its business and civic leaders were ultraconservative and seemed unaware of the threat of competition from the upstart cities in what they regarded as their rightful trade territory.

From the time Pierre Laclede established a fur trading post in 1764, St. Louis had been a transportation center linked with the Mississippi River and its tributaries. It was low cost river transportation that enabled St. Louis to become a distributing and manufacturing center. The city had grown strong and wealthy on the river. It had survived the panic of 1873 much better than its rival cities. The census of 1870 showed St. Louis was the largest city in the West with a population of more than three hundred thousand.

But St. Louis business and civic leaders were mired deep in lethargy. The fur trade, which had been centered in the city since its founding was dying out. St. Louis had been the focal point for the Santa Fe trade to the Southwest and it was now being diverted to the railroads from Chicago, Kansas City, Wichita, and other cities that were rapidly gaining population. A revolution was taking place in transportation and it was bypassing St. Louis. Rail service had reached the east bank of the

Mississippi River before the Civil War and until Eads Bridge was built there was no service into St. Louis itself from the east. By 1880 Chicago had become the rail center of the West and was threatening to pass St. Louis in population.

During his first five years as editor of the *Globe-Democrat*, McCullagh had concentrated his efforts on making the paper talked about and a leader in circulation. He was ready to turn his attention to the critical problems of the city. As Walter Stevens recalled [2] in August 1882, he went to the city room and said to the city editor: "We will have a railroad department. Make all you can of it." Thereafter "The Railroads" became one of the dominant features of the *Globe-Democrat*. It was one of the first departments of its kind in American journalism and it became an impressive example of the power of the press in community leadership.

Railroad news, and even a railroad department, was not new. In St. Louis, the newspapers for many years published a "steamboat" column, devoted to personal news about the packet boats and their crews. The *Globe-Democrat* had a column headed "Railroad News" which had appeared fairly regularly for several years. It never ran much more than a half column and was made up largely of personals and reports of railroad accidents. The last of these columns appeared on August 31, 1882. On September 1, the new feature "The Railroads" appeared and it ran for a full three columns, with the lead story devoted to a report on the "glut" of freight cars impeding rail traffic in the St. Louis area. The following day there was a long report citing instances of rail rates which discriminated against St. Louis.

Each day thereafter "The Railroads" appeared, occupying three, four, and frequently five columns of space, usually on Page 5. McCullagh insisted that if news had to be cut down or eliminated, it must be taken from other news and departments. The "Railroads" were to be played up regardless of the pressure of other news. McCullagh was convinced that the continuing emphasis on the railroads could do several things. He wanted to impress upon St. Louis that its future lay in securing more rail transportation and preventing Chicago from achieving a rail monopoly. If St. Louis was to hold and expand its trade territory, it must have rail service to compete with its rivals. Moreover, he used it in his constant campaign to bring more railroads and better rail service to the city.

It was not wholly an altruistic effort. He was aware that better mail service was essential in expanding the *Globe-Democrat*'s circulation. Day after day the *Globe-Democrat* pounded away at the theme of more rail service. Sometimes "The Railroads" called attention to new services to other cities; other times it chided the railroads for not paying more attention to St. Louis. When he felt the railroads were in the right, he defended them.

McCullagh's editorial independence was never better illustrated than during the railroad strike of the southwestern railroads in 1886, including Jay Gould's Missouri Pacific Railroad. This was the period when the Knights of Labor were at maximum strength. Martin Irons, their leader, called a general strike that paralyzed rail transportation and filled the sidings with abandoned trains. McCullagh promptly denounced the strike and declared in an editorial "The trains must run." He followed up with other blasts at the striking trainmen. In one editorial he declared, "The way to end a strike is to shoot a hole in it."

The Knights of Labor struck back by urging its members and the public to cancel their subscriptions to the *Globe-Democrat*.[3] The effectiveness of their campaign began to be felt by the circulation department and Daniel Houser, president of the paper became alarmed. He instructed the foreman of the composing room to bring the proofs of the editorial page on one occasion to his home before the paper went to press and while the foreman waited, he blue-pencilled several of the more vitriolic paragraphs from McCullagh's editorial. The following day the foreman, Martin Witter went to McCullagh's office at the usual time.

McCullagh glanced up from the paper he was reading and remarked without anger: "You left out some of my paragraphs. I have no fault to find with you. Mr. Houser is the president of this company. He has the right to say what shall be left out. But he should give me the order. He cannot go over my head. I shall resign." McCullagh did submit his resignation, but it was not accepted and no more proofs were taken to Houser's home.

However, the *Globe-Democrat*'s fight[4] to end the strike paid off. Shortly afterwards Gould met McCullagh in the lobby of the Southern Hotel and thanked him for the paper's support. McCullagh replied that the *Globe-Democrat* had treated the labor dispute from the standpoint of law and order and had tried to do justice to all. When Gould suggested he would like to show his appreciation in a more substantial way, McCullagh's answer was prompt and to the point. The *Globe-Democrat,* he said, had found the Post Office Department willing to cooperate in a fast mail train to leave St. Louis for Kansas City at 2 A.M. Within a few weeks the train was put into operation.

In 1890 McCullagh's campaign paid off again with the inauguration of fast mail service to New Orleans. On May 1, the page one headline proclaimed:

FAST MAIL TO THE SOUTH

It will be run by the **Globe-Democrat**—The first train leaves This Morning.

A Great Gain of Time in the Delivery of the **Globe-Democrat** at Points in the Southeast—to New Orleans at 7 a.m. Instead of 10 p.m. and to Other Points in proportion.

The story featured a large map showing the route of the new service[5] and McCullagh called attention to it in editorial paragraphs for several days:

Special fast mail trains come high, but the *Globe-Democrat* must have them.

The *Globe-Democrat* special fast mail to the South and Southeast is a daisy. No Chromos.

When the *Globe-Democrat* undertakes to do anything in the way of enterprise it generally rises above the cheap trick of the guessing bee or the chromo. This time it has gone into the special train business. Any or all of our contemporaries can get it on the same terms—that is to say, by paying for the train. But fast trains can't be run on wind.

On August 17, 1890 McCullagh chided the *Republic*[6] for abandoning use of fast mail service in this editorial paragraph:

The *Republic* has discontinued its fast train service to the South via DuQuoin and the Illinois Central Railroad. We mention the fact simply to enable us to say that the *Globe-Democrat,* which inaugurated this particular branch of the fast mail service, will continue it. We are sorry to lose the company of our esteemed contemporary on this route, but we find such handsome additions to our circulation as the result of this enterprise that we shall not abandon it, but shall, on the contrary, endeavor to increase and extend it. Special trains come high, but the *Globe-Democrat* must have them.

Three days later he expanded on the same theme:

The *Globe-Democrat*'s special fast mail to DuQuoin and the South, is on our part an act of self-defense against unjust discrimination by the Post Office Department in favor of Chicago and against St. Louis. The Post Office Department recently gave Chicago a special fast train to the South, leaving that city at 1 A.M. and going direct to New Orleans at unusual speed. It is run for the benefit of Chicago newspapers and without a dollar of cost to them. Our special train, every dollar of the cost of which is paid by the *Globe-Democrat,* gets to DuQuoin early enough to connect with the Illinois Central train that leaves Chicago at 8 P.M.—five hours ahead of the fast mail train. In this way the *Globe-Democrat* on its way South and Southeast keeps ahead in point of time as it certainly is ahead in point of merit—of the Chicago papers which are carried at public expense. It is a piece of private enterprise which we are glad to know is appreciated by the public in the section of the country benefited by it.

McCullagh frequently reminded his readers that they got later news in the *Globe-Democrat* because of the fast mail trains. On December 7, 1889 he wrote:

These are the days of rapid communication. Jefferson Davis died in New Orleans on Friday at 12:45 A.M. At 1:05 A.M. the announcement of his death was in type and on the presses of the *Globe-Democrat* in time for the first edition, which catches the fast mail for the West and Southwest.

Again in 1893 when he learned the Burlington Railroad was considering inaugurating its fast mail service to the West, Mc-

Cullagh gave it the paper's full support. The *Globe-Democrat* paid nearly two-thirds of the operating cost of the service until it became self-supporting.

McCullagh used "The Railroads" and the editorial page to campaign for favorable freight rates for St. Louis. On May 22, 1882 he wrote: "Wholesale merchants of St. Louis will be interested in a letter from Springfield, Mo., in this issue of the *Globe-Democrat*." (He was using the term "letter" in its customary connotation of that period, a special dispatch to the paper.) "The main point so far as they are concerned, is that the freight rates between here and Springfield are so high that dealers in the latter city find it to their advantage to purchase goods in Chicago. The trade of Southwest Missouri naturally belongs to St. Louis and the railroads ought not to be allowed to drive it elsewhere."

In November of that year he noted progress in another editorial:

The movement now in progress to secure fair railroad freight rates to and from St. Louis should receive the hearty support of every merchant in this city, and with their support and cooperation it cannot fail to succeed. The railroads will do in the matter precisely as much as they are compelled to do, and no better. Their managers know very well that there are unjust and unfair discriminations against St. Louis now existing, but they will not of their own unsolicited motion offer any relief. Hence the reason for an aggressive movement all along the line by merchants and others interested in fair rates of transportation.

Not all the blame could be placed on the railroads. On December 20, 1882, he pointed out that St. Louis businessmen were also at fault. He put it this way:

We published yesterday some facts of the efforts of Chicago to get the trade of the territory belonging to St. Louis. We do not wish to be understood as making a case against the Chicago and Alton Railroad, or the Chicago merchants. On the contrary, the case is made against the merchants of St. Louis for allowing their trade to be stolen from them, for doing nothing either in the way of prevention or retaliation. The *Globe-Democrat* finds no difficulty in competing with the Chicago newspapers on every line of railroad in Central and Southern Illinois, and if the merchants of St. Louis will imitate our example, they will be able to compete successfully with the Chicago merchants.

Not all of the credit for the growth of St. Louis as one of the great rail centers of the nation could be claimed by the *Globe-Democrat,* but certainly the militant efforts of the paper and its zealous editor were a decisive factor. When the Union Station was completed in 1894, and the event impressively recorded in the *Globe-Democrat,* it was acclaimed as the biggest rail passenger terminal in the world. By that time St. Louis was served by twenty-four railroads and five of them maintained their headquarters in the city.

At times his editorials sounded like releases from the Chamber of Commerce. July 18, 1878 he wrote:

St. Louis is the greatest primary wheat market in the world, the daily receipts being three times the combined receipts of Chicago and Milwaukee. Let the dwellers of the lake front put this in their pipes and smoke it.

Indicative of how he constantly reminded St. Louisans of their lethargy and the need for progress, on April 2, 1882 the *Globe-Democrat* featured a two and a half page article headed: "ST. LOUIS, THE GREAT CITY OF THE WEST." The article reviewed the early history of the city, its progress and problems and singled out those who had contributed to its growth. On the same day he commented editorially:

Large cities do not spring up in a day. Time, brains, capital, and well-directed labor and enterprise make them. All these have been brought to bear to make St. Louis what she is now, but it is in reason to assert that she has just reached the threshold of that greatness which the near future has in store for her.

Disadvantages have been here from the time of her becoming a trading post, down through the town, village, and city experience to date. She had her booms of prosperity prior to the commencement of the war in 1861, but there followed for years a terrible dullness, and it took years to recover advantages lost. They were regained, however, and reasonable prosperity has since waited upon all classes of her citizens.

Another drawback to the city was the two sieges of cholera which she passed through—one in 1849 and the other shortly after the war. The idea obtained to a degree that St. Louis was a sickly city and capital was turned away from local investment and some desirable residence people were influenced in other directions. Unquestioned statistics now show that she is the healthiest in the United States among the larger cities.

With the increase of realty values, better prosperity was ahead. A general reconstruction of her streets, (which the *Globe-Democrat* campaigned for so much) is about to begin. The prospects are great for a real estate boom.

He even extolled St. Louis weather, though St. Louisans will readily concede that the city is hardly a summer resort. He observed in one of his editorial paragraphs in July 1891 that "the man who leaves St. Louis for the resorts just now may be suspected of not having enough money to buy the warm clothing needed for staying at home."

The previous July he wrote: "Chicago utters a sigh of joyful relief at finding the thermometer below 90 degrees for the first time since the early days of June. In St. Louis we have had delightful weather all along, with here and there a night when blankets were unnecessary." He recognized Chicago as St. Louis' most serious rival and he delighted in sly jibes like this: "A Chicago woman writes to one of the local papers asking how she can cure the habit of excessive blushing. Her best plan, we should say, would be to leave the town." Or: "How to make Chicago a paradise for strangers, is the title of an article in the Chicago *Tribune*. One plan would be for all the present inhabitants to move out."

His editorial skirmishing became more serious when he began to fight for a world's fair in St. Louis. Chicago was talking about a world's fair when McCullagh wrote in July 1889:

The *Globe-Democrat* has insisted all along that Chicago's $5,000,000 subscription to the World's Fair would not materialize, and now we are informed that not more than $2,000,000 of the money can or will be collected. If this be true the legal conditions upon which the fair was given to Chicago are violated and the matter stands as if no law had been passed to hold the fair anywhere.

In November he kept up a running barrage of editorial paragraphs:

Chicago and New York should "pool their issues" and unite in favor of St. Louis as the place for holding the World's Fair.

The only well-defined and steadily growing boom in this country today is that which St. Louis has organized for World's Fair purposes.

The question of the location of the World's Fair will have to be determined before Congress can get down to its regular work; and fortunately this matter does not require any great amount of thinking. St. Louis is so clearly the proper place that it ought to be chosen on the first day of the session.

In December he wrote:

Chicago is promising Southern Congressmen that if she gets the World's Fair, Illinois will go Democratic in 1892. The argument would be more forcible if it did not involve the ridiculous notion that Providence is willing to work a miracle for the benefit of the wickedest town in the country that Columbus discovered.

Again:

The subscription to the World's Fair guarantee fund in New York last Saturday was $96,006. On the same day in St. Louis the subscriptions were $483,000. These are official figures in each case.

In July 1890 he observed:

The $2,000,000 that Chicago can raise for the World's Fair was nearly all contributed by the railroads. The railroads did very little for St. Louis in World's Fair subscriptions, and yet $10,000,000 would have been raised here had this city been selected.

When Chicago opened its fair in 1893 the *Globe-Democrat* devoted all of the front page, except for the advertisements, and the entire second page, to covering the exposition. Staff reporters were sent to Chicago and the daily activities were reported in full. There can be no doubt that McCullagh's efforts were an important factor in securing the next World's Fair for St. Louis in 1904. That exposition is still regarded as one of the most successful in the nation's history and was a financial, as well as an artistic success. The present City Art Museum in St. Louis was one of the permanent buildings erected for the Fair.

McCullagh was aware of keen competition in the population race among the cities of the West. In 1870 the official census figures showed St. Louis had a population of 310,864.[7] Ten years later the census gave St. Louis 350,518 and Chicago 503,185. That year Cincinnati had 255,000, Kansas City 55,000, Denver 35,000 and Omaha 30,000. In June 1881 McCullagh noted in an editorial that St. Louis was the geographic center of population of the nation. The next decade saw all of St. Louis' competitors gaining at a much faster rate. Chicago by 1890 had far outstripped St. Louis and had a population of 1,099,850. Kansas City grew to 132,000, Denver to 106,713 and Omaha to 140,000.

The 1890 census gave St. Louis 451,770 but McCullagh thought it should be even higher. On July 22, he wrote: "There is a delightful possibility that the revised count of population in St. Louis may bring the revealed increase of the city in the decade up to nearly 33 per cent. Every citizen of St. Louis, whether in or out of town, should give all the aid required to the gentlemen who are making the revised count of the population of the city."

In August he wrote:

The *Globe-Democrat* has gathered more data on the census than any other paper in the West, if not in the country. So far as regards the figures of Missouri at least, no other paper has made any attempt to do anything in this direction.

The boundaries of St. Louis were fixed by the Missouri Legislature in 1875 and could not be extended without legislative approval.[8] This restriction, McCullagh believed, severely handicapped the city in the population race. Putting the best face on the situation he could, he noted on July 19, 1889:

St. Louis' increase in population has been 28 per cent, which is greater than that of any other large city whose territory has not been expanded. Its increase in bank clearances in the decade, however, have been 50 per cent, or almost twice as great as the gain in population. St. Louis has been a fairly active place since 1880.

McCullagh liked to describe the *Globe-Democrat*'s influence as "The Towline," and he referred to it frequently in civic problems, as well as in politics. He believed the paper should take the lead in exploring new ways to stimulate progress in the city. When he read of how the building associations had helped make Philadelphia a city of homeowners, he sent a member of his staff to that city with instructions to make a thorough study of the operations of the associations. The result was a series of articles on how St. Louis might make use of such associations. He became convinced of untapped mineral resources in the Ozark region of Missouri and several times he dispatched reporters to explore the mineral potential.

He used comparisons with other cities to nudge St. Louis on needed improvements and reforms. For example, on July 25, 1881 he pointed out in an editorial that St. Louis, a city twice the size of Cincinnati, had only about half the water reservoir capacity. A few days later he complained that while the water supply was critical, "the City Treasury does not have a dollar to spare for other than ordinary expenses." The *Globe-Democrat* began in 1881 to campaign for rapid transit for St. Louis and to urge an elevated rail system.

In May 1884, in one of his longer editorials he pointed out that the residential sections of the city were extending "to where the distance between homes and places of business becomes a serious matter." He continued:

> Happily the spirit of improvement is abroad in the community. The changes which have been wrought since 1882 are notable. Then there was not a single street running east and west paved to any considerable distance. Now there are three and arrangements are on foot for enlarging the number. Two years ago the Exposition Building was talked of as something in the dim future; now it is fairly on its way to completion, and the old houses are beginning to disappear in its vicinity to give place to new and better ones. Rapidly the aspect of affairs about the Federal Building is changing. On Washington Avenue and elsewhere the prevailing business blocks of the coming era are practically prophesied. West of Grand Avenue the growth is a revelation to the individual who has not visited that locality in the last twelve months.

There is a rate of progress implied in all this which calls for something better than the slow horse-car with the straining beasts, and its uncomfortably jammed load of humanity, not the least of whose grief is the time lost on the road. The men and the money are at hand to supply the remedy. The city legislators have but to use a fair amount of prudence to insure its speedy application. It devolves upon them to rise above personal conflicting interests and give St. Louis what it wants. West of the city is a magnificent park, but so far as the body of our population is concerned, it might be an oasis in the desert of Sahara. Capital waits eager for the chance to connect the people with their own. Is it possible that our legislative wisdom cannot devise some way to let it proceed to work? It is time that an irresistible popular pressure is exerted in this direction.

McCullagh sought cultural as well as business progress for his city, and he did not hesitate to lambast those who failed to appreciate cultural attainments. When the city failed to grasp the opportunity to obtain a valuable library in 1877, he spoke out vigorously:

One of the singular facts in the history of St. Louis is that, with the exception of the little group of benefactors who have stood by Washington University, there has not been in ten years a single gift to the cause of learning or literature or art in this city. While we are loud in our boasting, we stand behind every other great city in the Union in our contributions to such purposes. Our two struggling libraries represent the generosity of a generation which has passed away and left no successors. We have nothing whatever to show in the way of art, and have spent less money in all its forms than has been devoted to furnishing a permanent home for six bears and twenty-four monkeys at the Fair Grounds. This is the aspect which St. Louis wears in the light of its failure to secure the Toner Library and, though the picture is not a pleasant one, it is more wholesome to study it, than to continue the wild brag and bombast of culture and liberality which contrast so strongly with the real facts of narrow prejudice and stinginess.

When a movement was suggested to give St. Louis a new opera house, McCullagh was skeptical and again he chided the lack of civic spirit this way:

As nearly as we can understand the situation on the subject of the new opera house, it is this: Every one of our "best citizens" who owns property on Washington Avenue wants a new opera house, and is determined to have it, if some other "best citizen" will put up the money. The "best" citizen never allows himself to be beaten in vicarious enterprise. Indeed, we know of several "best citizens" who would rather see their neighbors in bankruptcy than let St. Louis fall behind in the march of progress.

However, he would counteract the jab of his sarcasm by praise when he felt it was deserved. When the Exposition Building was formally opened on September 3, 1884, in an editorial headed "Historical Monument to St. Louis," he wrote:

This is destined to be an historic day in the future of St. Louis. The greatest enterprise ever carried to completion by the voluntary aid of a city's own people will be inaugurated tonight. Where but a short while ago there was a park which many believed was more fruitful of evil than of good, which had ceased to be a breathing place and become a loitering place because the city had grown beyond it, there now stands the largest, most beautiful and in every respect the best edifice belonging to the class known as exposition buildings in the United States. Of its uses and its destiny we need not speak, since all are familiar with them.

But the special point of pride to the people of St. Louis is that this beautiful structure is a monument to their own liberality—to their desire not only to equal but to excel the rival cities of the East and West, and to do this in such a manner that every needed dollar came as an unenforced and almost unsolicited contribution. Probably no undertaking of such magnitude has ever before been so promptly completed in any other city in the United States. He must be critical indeed, who can point out flaw or mistake in any part of the movement, beginning with a suggestion, then leading to a consultation, soon crystallizing into a resolution and now bearing the splendid fruition which all can witness today.

McCullagh was an efficient watchdog in matters affecting the city's interest. The *Globe-Democrat* helped expose gambling and other forms of vice. It kept a constant eye on the City Hall. In exposing the evil-doers, the paper had the vigorous efforts of the *Post-Dispatch* to help, and credit for the reforms must be divided between the two papers, but the *Globe-Democrat* and the prestige it enjoyed under McCullagh certainly was a dominant factor. The "Gas Bill" of 1889 is an example.

On December 20 the City Council approved by a narrow vote of 7 to 6 a bill to authorize private interests to build a gas plant and lease it to the city for thirty years at $225,000 annually, and to sell it to the city at the end of the thirty-year period for $4,500,000. The *Globe-Democrat* reported the action fully the next morning and on the editorial page McCullagh warned: "The people of St. Louis will wake up this morning and find themselves robbed of $4,500,000." Hopefully, he suggested in another paragraph that: "Mayor Noonan can make himself famous by vetoing the gas bill." The following day a series of paragraphs appeared:

The City Council "combine" must go.

A public meeting to denounce the gas bill and the men who voted for it ought to be very largely attended.

A petition asking for the resignation of the seven men who voted for the gas bill would receive a large number of signatures.

The gas bill, according to City Counselor Bell, "Is not worth the paper it is printed on." We hope not; but it is intended to be worth a great deal to some of the legislators who voted for it.

In the next few days there were additional pointed paragraphs in which McCullagh centered his fire on the mayor:

Mayor Noonan is preparing to commit the great mistake of his life. He will sign the gas bill. The Noonan element of the Democratic Party is in favor not only of this particular bill, but of all other bills with money in them.

Mayor Noonan will stick to his friends, and his friends are all up to their eyes in the gas bill. This is official.

The constant needling proved successful and McCullagh praised the mayor for his veto of the bill. On January 2, McCullagh wrote:

In vetoing the gas bill Mayor Noonan met the wishes, if not the expectations of the taxpayers of St. Louis and placed himself on a high plane of independence in the discharge of his executive duties. The *Globe-Democrat* has never doubted the integrity of Mayor Noonan, and has never believed him capable of an act of personal dishonesty. It has recognized the fact that he is a man who is largely controlled by personal friendships and because the advocates of the gas bill seemed to be largely composed of personal friends, it feared that he would strain the balance of judgment in their favor. That he has not done so is greatly to his credit as an officer elected by the people to care for the interests of the people.

McCullagh recognized that financial and business news was important in building St. Louis, as well as in increasing circulation. In that period, when crop reporting was not supplied by any agency, the *Globe-Democrat* through its correspondents in the midwest gathered information on crop prospects and production which were published regularly on the paper's financial page. When Congress failed to appropriate money for weather reports to be sent out over the country, the *Globe-Democrat* arranged to have the weather forecast and summary telegraphed each night from Washington.

By 1880 the paper was running each day a column of financial news and for many years it was recognized that the daily results of the New York stock market, telegraphed each night, were the best in the city. The stock market report was usually headed by a cartoon, indicating whether the bulls or the bears had been in the ascendancy that day.

McCullagh's personal interest in the market was casual. One of his regular visits on Monday mornings was to the brokerage office of James Campbell,[9] which he referred to as "going to market." With Campbell, and later with other brokers, he discussed stocks and crops and occasionally gave an order to buy or sell. His real interest was to check on financial matters to make sure the *Globe-Democrat* was reporting them accurately. His brokers recalled after his death that "going to market" never proved very profitable to McCullagh.

It must have been a source of satisfaction to him that his efforts to build St. Louis in a critical period did not go unnoticed. There was a group of business and civic leaders who recognized that through the *Globe-Democrat* he had helped improve the city and they decided to express their appreciation in a material way. As a bachelor McCullagh had never owned a home in St. Louis. For a number of years he lived in a rented room at 610 Walnut Street and had moved in 1885 to 3837 West Pine Street, where he had two rooms. He always dined at downtown hotels. A movement was started quietly to raise a fund of $25,000 to be used to purchase a residence in keeping with the prestige of the editor and the project found enthusiastic support.

The committee must have sensed the delicacy of how to present the gift to McCullagh, and after considerable study it was decided to delegate the task to Campbell because of his personal friendship with the editor. McCullagh's response was courteous, but positive. He could not accept the gift. As he explained to Campbell: "Some of them might come around afterwards and want to run the paper." [10]

However, if the men who had subscribed to the fund wanted to express their appreciation, he said, they could give the money to the poor. The suggestion was accepted and the money was given to charitable institutions in the city.

William Vincent Byars, a St. Louis journalist, summed up McCullagh's efforts in building St. Louis in an article which appeared in the *Missouri Historical Review* in October 1920. He wrote: "It would be rash to undertake to guess how many millions in population, or hundreds of millions in 'increased values' Missouri and the West owe to the expert work of 'booming,' of which McCullagh and Morris Mumford were exponents."

Mumford, editor of the Kansas City *Times,* took a leaf from McCullagh's book and helped thump the drums for Missouri in the western half of the state.

SHREWD POLITICAL OBSERVER

10

From the time the followers of Alexander Hamilton and Thomas Jefferson first contested for victory in the voting booth, politics have been an absorbing and perennial interest of the American people—and of American editors. Certainly it was true of the last three decades of the nineteenth century. There were no crucial issues, such as slavery and states rights to divide the voters, but the thorny issues of tariffs, labor, sound money, and political patronage provided the fuel to keep political pots boiling and to furnish grist for the editorial writers.

It was not until after the turn of the century that newspapers slowly began to veer to the independent, nonpartisan policy they avow today. Editors in the 1870's, 1880's and 1890's would scorn such a stand as pussyfooting hypocrisy. McCullagh would have agreed. A reading of his daily barrage of scorn for the opposition and fulsome praise for his own party, gives the impression that he had an intense personal, if vicarious, interest in the outcome of every election. He suffered in print at defeat, but never for long. When Grover Cleveland defeated Benjamin Harrison in 1892, McCullagh conceded the loss this way: "Let's own up. We went for them—and where are we?" In another editorial paragraph the same day, he wrote: "For President in 1896—some man who was in no way connected with yesterday's razzle-dazzle." He was still suffering the following day when he wrote: "We came, we saw, but we let the other fellows do the conquering." There was some consolation in the fact that the Republican Party carried St. Louis and Missouri in that election. It also marked the first time the *Globe-Democrat* flashed election returns on a screen for spectators gathered outside the newspaper building.

In St. Louis the *Globe-Democrat* was recognized as the voice of the Republicans, and the *Republican* and later the *Post-Dispatch* were the most influential spokesmen for the Democrats. Politically, McCullagh was a striking contrast to both Pulitzer and Hearst. He never aspired to political office, nor did he see himself as a "King-maker." On March 19, 1883 he expressed his opinion on newspapermen in politics this way: "The editor who conducts his paper in such a way as to deserve an office is a man who cannot afford to accept it."

The only time he came close to the role of a "king maker" was in 1880 when he sought to "boom" General Grant for a third term. McCullagh had become disenchanted with President Rutherford B. Hayes. During one of his visits to Washington he wrote a series of editorial "letters" to the *Globe-Democrat*[1] emphasizing the growing dissatisfaction with the administration and suggesting Grant as the nominee in 1880. In the series he linked the names of a number of prominent Republicans with Grant, asking how each would do for vice president. In view of the graft scandal of Grant's second term, involving his Secretary of War, William W. Belknap, and the gold scandal of his first administration, which culminated in "Black Friday," it is difficult to understand McCullagh's enthusiasm for Grant.

Perhaps he felt Grant had been victimized by his friends. There was a personal friendship between the two men, which dated back to the siege of Vicksburg. Grant in his memoirs of the Civil War credited McCullagh with countermanding an order of his "which might have been disastrous." The suspicion also persists that McCullagh saw in the Grant "boom" the opportunity to "boom" the *Globe-Democrat* as well. This was during the early period when one of McCullagh's objectives was to get people talking about the paper. In any event, it succeeded. Other papers took it up and quoted the *Globe-Democrat*. The *Globe-Democrat* covered thoroughly Grant's trip around the world. When Grant landed in San Francisco at the end of his tour, the *Globe-Democrat* covered the homecoming in prolific detail.

An interesting sidelight of the *Globe-Democrat*'s campaign was the opposition evoked in St. Louis, which once had been Grant's home. The *Westliche Post* opposed Grant. Carl Schurz wrote a series of articles against Grant, which provided grist for McCullagh's paragraphs. A national convention was called to fan the opposition and McCullagh promptly dubbed it "The Tea Party." The *Globe-Democrat* gave five columns to the proceedings and pointed out no more than fifty of the delegates were from outside the city.

As the movement gathered momentum, the *Globe-Democrat* claimed the nomination for Grant, predicting he would have 425 delegates, more than enough to win. It was an overly optimistic prophecy, but a successful demonstration on how to get a newspaper talked about, not only at home but across the nation.

If he saw himself in any political role, it was as a keeper of the faith of the Republican Party. He explained his role perhaps in this editorial paragraph on April 20, 1889 shortly after the inauguration of Benjamin Harrison: "The *Globe-Democrat* is the official organ of the administration, and the President well knows that through its universally read columns he can reach the masses better than through any channel whatever. We may state confidentially that this fact explains the failure of the President to appoint the editor of the *Globe-Democrat* to a first-class foreign mission—he needs him for the promulgation of great principles at home."

The comment may be taken with a grain of salt. Perhaps it was written with tongue in cheek and as usual McCullagh could never resist getting in a plug for his paper. Perhaps there was an element of sour grapes, but if so, it certainly was not consistent with his insistence on aversion to any public office.

There can be no doubt, however, that he took pride in his recognized talent as an astute observer of the political scene. His reputation as a political prophet was national. The New York *Times* was only one of a number of newspapers which mentioned his stature in political reporting in editorial tributes after his death. The *Times* described him as "A man of ripe judgment, who could not only think quickly and soundly, but could grasp political situations so as to foretell their outcome."

Never was this uncanny ability to foresee the outcome more impressively illustrated than in the *Globe-Democrat*'s coverage of national political conventions. In this news field as in so many others, McCullagh blazed new trails in the new journalism. By 1880 he was ready to translate into action his ideas as to how these quadrennial events should be reported. More than a decade later he explained his ideas:[2]

It was the policy of the newspapers no further back than that (1880) to depend very largely on the reports sent out by the Associated Press. Prominent journals had been in the habit of sending correspondents to conventions to supplement or introduce, as the case might be, the reports of the Associated Press. The reports of these correspondents consisted mainly of opinions or expressions as to what the convention ought to do, but not as to what it would or might do. These expressions of opinion could have just as well been written without visiting the scene of the convention to take a survey of the field. The Associated Press makes no effort to solve the future but waits for the hereafter to reveal its own secrets before they are put upon the wires and given to the world.

It remained for the *Globe-Democrat* to introduce a new order of things. The idea of sending a corps of bright, energetic, wide-awake reporters to the convention city a week before the convention meets, with instructions to see every prominent delegate as soon as he arrives, to become thoroughly acquainted with every delegation and to learn beforehand just what it will do in the convention, so far as it is possible to obtain such knowledge, had never impressed itself on any newspaper before. Other Western papers followed the example of the *Globe-Democrat,* but those in the East, always slow to profit by Western enterprise, never undertook to anticipate the action of a convention until 1892. It may seem a little remarkable but true it is that only one paper in New York had ever made any effort to anticipate the convention news.

The reports of the *Globe-Democrat,* or rather its forecasts of national convention proceedings, have been the theme of extended comment by journalists and close newspaper readers for more than a decade. It has been the custom of the paper to publish everything before the opening day of the convention, so that when the routine began there was nothing to do but to report in perfunctory style just what the *Globe-Democrat* had been telling for a week. In 1888, the *Globe-Democrat* put a corps of reporters in Chicago with instructions to clean up the convention before it met, and they did it so satisfactorily that it revolutionized journalism in Chicago completely.[3]

Before the invention of photoengraving, pictorial convention coverage was skimpy. Rarely did any newspaper assign a staff artist to a convention. In 1892, McCullagh again showed the way. He organized a staff of twenty reporters and staff artists and sent them to Chicago a week before the Republican national convention opened. McCullagh explained the plan:[4]

They were not turned loose upon the city and told to bring in what they could, regardless of its value, but by visiting the hotels, watching the newspapers and using the wires, it was possible to learn just when each delegation would start, when it would arrive and where it would be quartered. This simplified matters greatly and enabled the reporters and artists to gather them in rapidly on their arrival. A book was kept showing just when delegations would arrive, where they would have headquarters and the names of each delegate who would be able to furnish desired information. On the arrival of a delegation a reporter and artist would be detailed to visit the hotel, and after the chairman or spokesman was pointed out to the reporter he would proceed to interview him, while the artist stood at a distance and made a sketch of the victim, which was usually completed before the interview was finished. Another member, and sometimes as many as half a dozen of the same delegation, would be treated in the same manner. After the work was completed the reporter and artist would return to the Leland Hotel, the *Globe-Democrat* headquarters, one to the artists' studio, the other to the reporters' room. There the artist prepared an engraving in chalk while the reporter wrote up his copy and got it ready for the wire.

Two shipments of the artists' plates were made every day. Five artists were engaged up to the opening day of the convention. Fifteen men were on the reportorial work. They were educated in the science of condensation and gave the views of delegates and their probable action in the convention in the fewest possible sentences. They left nothing unsaid, however, that would give full and fair expression to a man's views, and probably no attempt at interviewing and condensing has ever given such general satisfaction.

The immense sales of the *Globe-Democrat* in Chicago every day attested that fact. On the third day the demand for the paper was so great that the supply was exhausted in a few minutes after arrival, and the orders thereafter were doubled and in some instances quadrupled. Interviewing and illustrating a convention before it met was something never before undertaken by a newspaper and it was accomplished in Chicago before the other newspapers knew what was going on. If the twenty reporters and artists failed to come in contact with any delegate with ideas, to get an expression of opinion from him and to picture his features true to life, that delegate was not heard from.

McCullagh covered fifteen national conventions himself from the vantage point of the press section beginning with the nomination of Lincoln for reelection in 1864, when he reported the proceedings for the Cincinnati *Commercial*. He took pride in that record. There are men, he said,[5] "who have attended all the Democratic conventions in this time (1864–88) and there are men who have attended all the Republican conventions, but the number who have attended all of both sides is, I think, very small."

Supplementing the saturation coverage of the news staff were McCullagh's personal predictions on the editorial page, usually in an editorial paragraph as on June 3, 1892: "Temple of Truth, 2. A.M. It looks like Harrison."

McCullagh's eye for a picturesque phrase sometimes caught on nationally as in 1876 when Samuel J. Tilden won the Democratic nomination in St. Louis. A highlight of that convention was the speech of Henry Watterson, a close friend of McCullagh and editor of the Louisville *Courier-Journal,* lauding Tilden, McCullagh recalled it this way:[6]

Mr. Watterson was chosen as temporary chairman, and on taking his seat delivered a splendid oration, which elicited frequent applause and great admiration. It was in Tilden's campaign for the nomination that the now familiar phrase "bar'l o' money" to indicate the possession and use of funds with which to promote political success, was first used. Its original appearance was in the columns of the *Globe-Democrat* in a dispatch sent by me from Jefferson City in a report of the proceedings of a convention called to elect delegates to the St. Louis convention. I represented a delegate as saying that Tilden had a "bar'l o' money" and was bound to get the nomination. What he did say was a "bedtick full o' money" but I changed it to "bar'l" as a more expressive term, and "a more tenderer word" as Sam Weller says, and, above all, as a word of one syllable instead of two, and therefore more likely to catch on. It caught like fury. *Harper's Weekly,* in almost every issue during the campaign, had a cartoon on its first page with Mr. Tilden and a keg with a $ on it. The country press and the city press used the term and still use it, to express the idea for which it was originally intended. It has evidently taken up its permanent abode in the political literature of this country.

Of the conventions he attended, McCullagh insisted that the Republican convention of 1880 was the best, and the speech of Roscoe Conkling placing General Grant in nomination for a third term was the greatest convention address he ever heard. McCullagh was said to have stood on his desk in the press section and led the cheering after it was completed. The speech was described several years later by McCullagh:[7]

When the State of New York was called, Mr. Conkling stepped up to the reporters' platform, where he mounted a reporter's table, and having quoted the famous quatrain from Miles O'Reilly, "When asked what state he hails from," began a speech which for aggressiveness has never been equalled on a similar occasion. "Mr. President", said he, "Acting under instructions from the Republican Party of the great State of New York, instructions which I dare not (great emphasis on the I and much on the dare not) disregard." As he uttered these words he shook his fingers at the anti-Grant members of the New York delegation, who were seated very close to him, as if to say to them that they had disregarded their instructions in a shameful and traitorous way. He raised a perfect storm of hisses and applause when, a little further on, he said, "The candidate whom I shall present has no telegraph wire running from this hall to his home."

Everyone in the convention knew that this was a reference to the fact that there was a telegraph wire in operation between the convention hall and Mr. Blaine's residence in Washington. Another storm of hissing and applause followed. But the disturbance reached its limit when Mr. Conkling said that if his candidate was nominated no defensive campaign would be necessary. The Blaine men took this as an allusion to the Little Rock and Fort Smith matter, and raised such a hissing as was never before heard under any roof. It was not all hissing, though. The Grant men applauded quite as lustily as the anti-Grant men hissed, and divided the time about equally with their opponents. The storm would die down slowly and then rise slowly. In one of the intervals between bursts Mr. Conkling who seemed to be the only undisturbed man in the 20,000 which the hall contained, turned to the presiding officer and placidly observed: "This does not come out of my time, I hope," alluding to the time limit on nominating speeches, which, I believe, was fifteen minutes. Mr. Conkling kept General Grant's name out of his speech until he had reached the last sentence. When he mentioned it there was a pandemonium of forty-five minutes duration. His speech was something to be seen rather than something to be heard. As between a blind man who could hear and a deaf man who could see, the latter would have had the greater enjoyment. He was dressed nearly without a particle of gaudiness and his clothes fitted him as if they had grown on him. In the outside pocket of his coat he had a sheet of paper full of notes, to which he occasionally referred, but never to the detriment of his delivery.

McCullagh did not agree with some in the press section that James A. Garfield's nominating speech for Senator John Sherman had "more literary merit and finish," but he conceded that it did win for Garfield the nomination. McCullagh said:[8]

It was entirely devoid of the porcupine quills which were thrust into everything and everybody by Mr. Conkling. Mr. Garfield began by alluding to the tumult caused by Mr. Conkling's speech, and reminded his hearers that the depth of the ocean was measured from the ocean's calm and not from the topmost wave. Not here in this tempest would the contest be decided, but in the quiet of domestic life in the "chilly days of November." Someone afterward reminded him that the expression "chilly days of November" might be reduced to ridicule by the enemy during the campaign, and he changed it to a less vulnerable phrase in the speech given out for publication. It has often been said that Garfield's speech did more for Garfield than for Sherman, in whose behalf it was made. But Garfield was a favorite in the convention all the time, as was manifest from the applause which he received from the galleries every time he entered the hall. The friends of both Blaine and Grant might well have looked upon him as a dangerous man to both. Garfield's victory was not to be predicted until the thirty-fourth ballot. Then Wisconsin cast most of her votes for him, and the announcement was received with such applause that everybody could see that he was to win the prize, which he did on the thirty-sixth ballot.

It is interesting to compare his recollections of the convention with the issues of the *Globe-Democrat* just preceding and during the convention. On May 11 McCullagh wrote: "The Grant boomers beat the Blaine Boomers at their own game in Chicago," and another paragraph declared: "The towline is good for a strain of ten tons to the inch. The Cook County Kick is good for about five pounds to the inch. "On May 22 the *Globe-Democrat* published a list of the indicated vote by states, showing Grant in the lead, and McCullagh predicted that "Grant and Sherman will be the ticket sure as shooting." On May 23 he wrote: "A good towline handled by a great religious daily has a powerful moral influence on the nation." The entire editorial page on May 25 was devoted to editorials on the convention, and the news pages included eighteen special dispatches on the interviews with convention delegations.

The issue of June 2 contained this short editorial announcement: "The office of the *Globe-Democrat* was yesterday morning put in direct communication with Chicago by telegraph and a branch office of the Western Union set up in our sanctum. Our readers will not only have full particulars of Grant's victory, but they will have it served up fresh, with details carried down to the latest moment." There were thirteen decks on the convention story on page 1 and the story occupied all of the space on page 2.

Apparently McCullagh sensed that all was not well for Grant for on June 4 he wrote in one editorial paragraph: "The galleries are not running this convention." A little further down in the column was a word of advice: "One word to Grant men—stick." The head on the convention story on June 5 was "Hot as Hades." The *Globe-Democrat* also reported that morning that a large crowd had gathered in front of the paper's building at Fourth and Pine Streets to hear the convention bulletins. It was estimated at "no less than 3,000." On June 8 McCullagh wrote: "The dark horse is so dark at present that he is invisible."

Before that day was over the darkness had ended and Garfield emerged the winner with Chester A. Arthur as his running mate. The headline on June 9 was "Light at Last" and on the editorial page McCullagh conceded: "This is Garfield's boom." Other editorial paragraphs that day declared:

The canal boatman is greater than the Towline.

The Grant boom did not weaken, nor the Towline part.

It is Garfield against the bar'l; the canal boatman against the railroad wrecker.

We have immediate arrangements for the use of the Towline, which was formerly used on the Ohio Canal. It is guaranteed to pull him through.

McCullagh's recollections of the three national conventions of 1872 provided contrasting glimpses of two men: Carl Schurz who, as has been noted, was one of McCullagh's perennial "hates," and Horace Greeley, the noted editor of the New York *Tribune*. The Liberal Republican Party, with which Schurz was affiliated, convened in Cincinnati, the Regular Republican Party met in Philadelphia and the Democrats in Baltimore. McCullagh wrote:

The Republicans met to renominate Grant, which they did with great enthusiasm on the first ballot. The roll was called and every state responded with its full vote for the old Commander. The Liberal Republicans, which gave Greeley his first nomination, met on the first of May as was evidenced by the first sentence in the speech of Mr. Carl Schurz, who started the oratory. "This is moving day," said he. Mr. Schurz had changed in four years from the staunch admirer of and great champion of Grant, whom he eulogized extravagantly in the Convention of 1868, to the arch detractor of the great soldier, whom he denounced in all his speeches in 1872, making them ring out with the refrain, "Any man to beat Grant." Schurz was, however, much disappointed and chagrined with the result of the Cincinnati convention. He did not approve of Greeley's nomination, and, in the words I have quoted, he meant that while Greeley was not a very good candidate, he was good enough to beat Grant.

I once asked Grant if he knew why Schurz had undergone such a violent change of attitude toward him. He replied that he could not tell unless it was that he hadn't offices enough to give Schurz—that Schurz was the worst office beggar he ever saw—that he hung about the White House day after day, wanting to control every dollar's worth of patronage in the West, and much in the East too. "I was glad to have him turn against me, because then he could not bother me."

In 1872 McCullagh was the managing editor of the St. Louis *Democrat* and a strong supporter of Grant. His disenchantment with Grant did not come until much later and his disenchantment with Schurz had begun shortly after McCullagh returned to St. Louis.

His recollections were kinder to Greeley, for whom he had regard, at least as a great editorial writer. Of the Democratic convention he said:[9]

Greeley was afterwards nominated by the Democrats in Baltimore, in a convention which left little behind it that was worth remembering. He made a splendid personal campaign full of mental and physical energy, and made a series of speeches which have never been equalled for cogency and compactness. He was very confident of success at first, chiefly because he loved during his whole life to surround himself with flatterers, who purposely kept the truth from him. It is quite certain, indeed, that up to the last of September he believed he would be elected. The October elections, however, convinced him that his cause was hopeless. Ohio, Indiana, and Pennsylvania spoke to him in thunder tones and told him what to expect in November. Mr. Greeley died about three weeks after the November election, and before the electoral votes had been counted. His death reduced the number of electoral votes cast for him to three out of the sixty-six which had been carried for him in November, as against eighty carried by Seymour four years before. Grant profited by the Greeley movement to the extent of eighty electoral votes, receiving 294 in 1872, as against 214 in 1868.

McCullagh was aware of the public interest in political patronage, and in a few instances was not averse to using the *Globe-Democrat* Towline for someone he believed deserving of an appointment. Perhaps it was the times, or perhaps it was the myopic vision which afflicts so many in political situations, but there is little evidence that he was concerned, in print at least, with the evils of the "spoils system" until the election of 1884 which put Cleveland in the White House; the first Democrat in half a century. It was obvious there would be a wholesale turnover of political appointees and McCullagh was alert to the possibilities of the story. He launched his campaign to expose the extent of the spoils on New Year's Day, 1885 with a three column cartoon on page 1. It showed the closed doors of a building with the insignia over the door "Civil Service Institute" and the caption read: "Not Receiving Today." On January 3 there appeared a standing head which was to be used for many years thereafter. It read "What Are We Here For?" That day the story explained that the *Globe-Democrat* had sent instructions to all its correspondents, asking them to send short stories on the probable changes in federal positions in each correspondent's community and the names of those seeking federal appointments. Then followed two full pages of "special dispatches" from Missouri communities.

On the editorial page that day McCullagh wrote:

Our esteemed contemporaries in the East might do themselves credit by imitating the *Globe-Democrat* in securing lists of expectant office holders in their respective states. The *Globe-Democrat* will do the work in its own territory, which extends from the Alleghany Mountains to the Pacific Coast and from Lake Michigan to the Gulf of Mexico.

McCullagh was never modest in his claims for the sphere of

influence of the *Globe-Democrat,* a policy continued by the paper in this century, although on a more conservative note. For years the *Globe-Democrat* referred to itself as "The Newspaper of the Forty-Ninth State," and explained that the area included everything within a hundred-fifty mile radius of St. Louis. The slogan, devised by the late Douglas Martin,[10] continued to be used until Alaska became the official "Forty-Ninth State." McCullagh, however, made good on his promise. On February 14 he wrote: "We have already published the list of office seekers in Missouri, Illinois and Texas. Today we are covering Arkansas and Iowa, and several other states are being canvassed."

It was the response to this coverage that prompted McCullagh to establish the *Globe-Democrat*'s Washington Bureau. Few papers in the West had bureaus of their own in the national capital at that time. The *Globe-Democrat* had always published a great deal of Washington news and had been sharing a news service with several other large city dailies. It is interesting to note that the *Globe-Democrat* Bureau was set up without any fanfare in the paper. It was never in keeping with McCullagh's policy to be reticent about the services the paper supplied, but in this case there was no mention of the bureau. The only way it was indicated was by the pronounced increase in the number of stories from the capital.

Walter B. Stevens of the *Globe-Democrat* staff was selected to head the bureau and he continued in that post until 1901. Stevens had been city editor of the *Times-Journal* and had served the *Globe-Democrat* as city editor and as roving correspondent. Some of his "specials" such as "Missouri Minerals" and "Silver in a Silver Country" were later published in book form. After leaving the Washington Bureau, Stevens became secretary of the Louisiana Purchase Exposition in St. Louis, served two terms as president of the Missouri State Historical Society, and wrote several historical books including *St. Louis, the Fourth City,* as well as numerous articles. Among them was a series on McCullagh and the new journalism.

One of Stevens' first assignments was a satirical series under the general heading "The Drama of Politics." Frequently illustrated by cartoons, the series featured parodies of Shakespearean plays. The *Globe-Democrat* used the standing head, "What Are

We Here For?" long after the Cleveland administration to highlight news and gossip about office seekers and their prospects of success. In 1885 this feature was sometimes headed simply "The Spoils."

Few papers in the nation in McCullagh's day could compete with the *Globe-Democrat* in the comprehensive coverage of elections. McCullagh frequently reminded his readers of this service. For example, in October 1889 one of his editorial paragraphs said:

Municipal elections were held in the small cities of Illinois on Tuesday last. The *Globe-Democrat* received and published special telegraphic returns from sixty-six towns; the Chicago *Tribune* received and published returns from fifteen towns. The *Globe-Democrat* made no effort to get these particular items, and we mention the fact simply to show the efficiency of our news service in the field to the east of us.

When state legislatures were in session, the paper's coverage was both thorough and extensive. At least a column of news was published each day from each state. Included in the states covered regularly were not only Missouri and Illinois, but Kansas, Arkansas, Iowa, and frequently Texas.

In local politics and elections the *Globe-Democrat* was equally thorough, although not always as partisan. McCullagh was not always impressed with the virtues of some of the local Republicans, and vented his disgust in editorial comments such as these in the campaign of 1878. Of the local Republican organization, he wrote:

The Republicans of St. Louis might as well spare the labor and expense of nominations as to go into the campaign under the auspices of the bummers and barnacles who now constitute the central committee and try to dictate the policy and candidates of the party. A full stop must be put to the career of these men, and the present year is as good a time as any other for doing this.

He expressed his opinion of St. Louis' three Congressmen this way during the 1878 campaign:

We have three Republicans in the present Congress—they don't amount to much, but since God made them, we will call them such.

It was, of course, unthinkable and a confession of weakness for a paper to support any candidate of an opposing party, and despite his obvious misgivings, McCullagh waded into the local campaign vigorously. But as he did in other campaigns, when he felt the Republican nominees were weak, he concentrated his fire on the opposition, which was probably more effective in influencing the electorate. In 1878 he labeled the Democrats "The Donnybrookers." The significance is indicated in this paragraph:

The story was started by some wag that the Democracy of St. Louis mean to put an American on their ticket this fall; it is wholly without foundation in fact, and was doubtless invented to injure the party. Its absurdity will be more apparent when it is known that of the 100 knights of St. Patrick not more than two-thirds are now in office and that the outs are all as capable and eager as the ins. There will be no departure from the time-honored custom in this matter.

While McCullagh was an avowed partisan in both local and national politics, he could and did, fight vigorously against those he considered bad Republicans. As has been noted he waged a twenty-year feud with Chauncey I. Filley. He was a bitter and overt foe of James G. Blaine, and undoubtedly his dislike stemmed from the time a House of Representatives investigating committee charged him with using his influence as Speaker of the House to secure a land grant for a railroad in Arkansas and with selling the railroad's bonds at a handsome commission. Blaine had obtained possession of the "Mulligan" letters before they could be placed on the record and refused to surrender them.

When Blaine won the Republican nomination in 1884, the *Globe-Democrat* supported him, but it seems evident that McCullagh's heart was not in the fight that year. In 1892 at the Minneapolis convention when Blaine at a late hour announced his candidacy McCullagh was more disgusted than angry. In a blistering editorial at the close of the convention he wrote:

With the exception of Aaron Burr and his associates in iniquity the United States has not known a more desperate and unscrupulous band of political pirates then Clarkson, Quay and Platt. For no cause at all except such as is decidedly honorable to the President, these party bandits have, by treachery and falsehood been working day and night for months past in an endeavor to defeat him. They stooped to the lowest and most despicable devices to accomplish their designs. Professing a devotion to Blaine which they did not feel, they took advantage of the enfeebled physical and mental condition of that misguided man to induce him to repudiate his announcement of last February that he would not enter the race, and then abandoned him in the most cowardly and perfidious manner in the convention, as the vote revealed. Their intent was to beat Harrison by any means within their reach, even at the sacrifice of the man who in a moment of weakness was so unfortunate to give ear to their promises and plans. But retribution has come to them. These three men—Clarkson, Quay and Platt—are the most thoroughly beaten and humiliated of all persons who figured in the Minneapolis assemblage. Not one of them will ever have any influence in the Republican councils hereafter.

As to Blaine himself, McCullagh wrote this epitaph to "The Plumed Knight" the day after the convention ended:

> Poor Ichabod. His bitterest foe could not
> desire a more humiliating close to his career.
> So fallen! So lost! The light withdrawn
> Which he once wore!
> The glory from his gray hairs gone
> Forevermore.

It is a revealing facet of McCullagh's character that while he was an implacable foe in a political fight, he could be generous to an opponent once the battle was ended. His support of an arch rival, William Hyde, editor of the *Republican,* for postmaster of St. Louis was an example. After the inauguration of Cleveland in 1885 a half dozen candidates sought the appointment. By October the contest was reduced to two men, Hyde and John G. Priest. Stevens, who was keeping an eye on the aspirants in Washington, wrote later[11] in his recollections of that period that "The papers on the St. Louis postmastership outnumbered and outweighed, avoirdupois, those in any other case of patronage before the President that year. 'A hell's mint of 'em,' Congressman O'Neil called one collection of Hyde endorsements."

Priest, who had served on the Democratic National Committee, had the backing of the incumbent postmaster in St. Louis, prominent Democrats in the East, and among the indorsements was a letter from John J. Knapp of the *Republican*. Hyde's opponents raised the question of his personal habits and his presumed friendly relations with Robert C. Pate, a local Democratic leader and representative of gambling interests in the city. A scandal several years earlier involving the St. Louis gambling ring had been publicized nationally after a St. Louis grand jury had made a number of serious charges. McCullagh had served as foreman of that grand jury. McCullagh's sense of fair play prompted him to write a letter stating that Hyde had not been found to have any connections with the gambling ring, and this letter was sent to the President by Hyde's supporters. McCullagh backed up his statement on the editorial page:

Somebody has, it seems, sent to Washington a mass of documents intended to injure Mr. Hyde's chances for postmaster by connecting him with R. C. Pate and the gambling ring of some years ago. This is all rot. The editor of the *Globe-Democrat* was foreman of the grand jury which investigated the gambling business in 1879, and he is ready to give Mr. Hyde a certificate that after the most searching investigation, not a single fact to his discredit was brought forth. Other members of the "Big Twelve," as that somewhat famous body was called, will, no doubt, do the same thing.

Whether McCullagh's defense of Hyde tipped the scales in his favor is a matter of speculation, but in any event Hyde received the appointment shortly after the editorial appeared. Later Hyde repaid McCullagh's kindness by writing his reminiscences of his years as a reporter and editor of the *Republican* for the *Globe-Democrat*.

The postoffice fight stimulated McCullagh's continuing coverage of political spoils and he exploited the split in local Democratic ranks, labeling one faction "The Colonels" and the other the "Kids." From the Washington Bureau came frequent reports of the activities of the two factions in the capital. Papers in other cities reprinted some of the stories.

In appraising McCullagh as a political commentator, it must be remembered for most of his career virulent personal journalism was predominant. It frequently led to physical combat. McCullagh, for all his fiery Irish temperament, never came to blows over politics. Only once did he resort to fisticuffs and politics was not involved.[12] A former city official, Robert A. Watt, sought to use the newspapers in his campaign against the rates charged by the St. Louis Gaslight Company. McCullagh was suspicious of Watt's motives and refused to permit the *Globe-Democrat* to be used in the campaign. Watt went over his head and complained to McKee that McCullagh had been improperly influenced. If there was any charge that could provoke him, it was one against his and the *Globe-Democrat*'s integrity.

A few days later as McCullagh arrived at the *Globe-Democrat* he passed McKee's private office in back of the business department and saw Watt in conversation with McKee. Without saying a word he marched into McKee's office and struck Watt, knocking him to the floor. The two men were separated before any blood had been shed, but Watt swore out a complaint before a justice of the peace, charging assault and battery. McCullagh retained another fiery Irishman, James J. McBride, who turned the trial into a farce and McCullagh was speedily acquitted.

McCullagh contributed his share of the editorial infighting, but he did much more. He set a shining example in news coverage of conventions and campaigns. He was among the first to declare war on the powerful local political bosses and to focus attention on the evils of the spoils system. He was generally regarded by his peers as one of the shrewdest observers of his time, of the political scene.

THE TWILIGHT YEARS

11

McCullagh's newspaper career covered a span of thirty-seven years. For a quarter of a century he worked in St. Louis, and all but four years of that time he was the editor of the *Globe-Democrat*. The period in which his pioneering spirit and new ideas made their greatest impact on American journalism was the two decades from 1875 to 1894. In the last two years of his life, it seemed that the fire which had burned so fiercely began to die down. While his interest in the direction of the paper never lagged, more and more of the detailed management of the news and editorial departments were delegated to the hands of Captain King.

It is remarkable that his health stood up as long as it did under the rigorous regime to which he adhered. For years he spent approximately twelve hours a day in his office. He rarely took even a brief vacation. In the 1880's he visited Washington occasionally to check on the paper's capital Bureau and to get the feel of the political situation. Sometimes he would spend a few days at Saratoga, New York or some other resort city, but it was never a real vacation for he always sent back "letters" with the familiar signature "Mack" at the end of the dispatch.

The *Republic* in reviewing McCullagh's career in St. Louis on January 1, 1897, said: "In his early years at the *Globe-Democrat* he became set in his ways and he soon adopted a routine such as would have made an old man of any young man. For twenty years he came to the office at 12:30, went out for an hour at 3, had dinner at 7 and was back in his office at 9, where he remained until 12:30."

His dietary habits would have shocked the doctors of that time, and they were not as easily shocked in those days. Stephen Tammany, who as a young printer in the *Globe-Democrat* composing room in the 1890's, recalled that McCullagh "liked good whiskey," though he was never a heavy drinker. He smoked cigars constantly. Tammany said he could not remember any time when he saw "the Chief" without a stub of a cigar in his mouth. McCullagh, he said, never wore an overcoat, even in the bitterest weather. Before he acquired his own horses and carriage, he rode the cable cars, summer and winter, and the cable cars with no heat were a test of fortitude.[1]

Always inclined to be pudgy, he grew quite heavy as he got older. In later years virtually the only exercise he had was to walk from his office to his carriage. When the *Globe-Democrat* moved from Fourth and Pine Streets to Sixth and Pine Streets in 1892, one St. Louis paper carried a humorous story that insisted that McCullagh became lost in trying to find his way to his new office.[2] Tammany recalled that McCullagh always called for his carriage to take him to the Southern Hotel for meals.

Daniel Houser told a *Globe-Democrat* reporter after McCullagh's death that "Mack was one of the most peculiar men I ever saw.[3] I never knew a man so confirmed in his sedentary habits. In the early days, and even until just a few years ago, he was at the office the greater part of the time. He would never leave until the paper was out about 3:30 A.M. Then he would eat a hearty meal and go home, but by 11 o'clock he would be up and ready to go to work.

"In those days he wrote a great deal. He would sit in his office hour after hour reading and smoking. He kept a fine library right at his elbow and he was never idle. In the last three years he wrote very little, but he was always in harness. To have given up his work would have killed him then and there. I always wanted him to take a vacation, but he would never hear of it. He was engrossed in the newspaper as some men are engrossed in their families. He felt it was his creation and its glory was his glory."

For a number of years McCullagh suffered from asthma, and

in his last years from a kidney ailment. He became seriously ill in 1893 and never fully regained his health. At that time he moved from his bachelor quarters to live with his older brother John and his wife at 3637 West Pine Boulevard. When John McCullagh died, his widow married Peter Manion and moved to 3837 West Pine Boulevard. McCullagh moved with them and after Manion's death in 1895, he stayed on with his sister-in-law.

Theodore Dreiser, who worked for McCullagh in 1892 and part of 1893, described his first impression of "the Chief." [4] "McCullagh," he wrote, "was a short, thick, aggressive, rather pugnacious and defensive person of Irish extraction. He was Napoleonic, ursine rather than leonine. I was instantly drawn and thrown back by his stiff reserve. A Negro office boy ushered me into the great man's presence. I found him at a roll-top desk in a minute office, and he was almost buried in discarded newspapers. I learned afterwards that he would never allow them to be removed until he was all but crowded out. I was surveyed by keen gray Irish eyes from under bushy brows. 'Um, yuss' was all he deigned to say. 'See Mr. Mitchell in the city room.' He was chewing a cigar and mumbled his words.

"I often think of him in that small office, sitting waist-deep among his papers, his heavy head sunk on his pouter-like chest, his feet incased in white socks and low slipper-like shoes, his whole air one of complete mental and physical absorption in his work."

Dreiser's brief career as a reporter for the *Globe-Democrat* was colorful but erratic. He managed to score a beat on a train wreck at Alton, Illinois, and won commendation from McCullagh. Dreiser said that McCullagh sent for him when he returned to the office: " 'Mmm, yuss,' he mumbled in his thick, gummy, pursy way. His voice always sounded as though it was being obstructed by something leathery or wooly. 'I wanted to say that I liked that story you wrote, very much indeed. A fine piece of work. I like to recognize a good piece of work when I see it. I have raised your salary five dollars and I would like to give you this.' He reached in his pocket and handed over a yellow twenty dollar bill."

But more often Dreiser managed to get himself, and the paper into hot water. On one occasion he lost all restraint in reviewing a vocal concert by a young Negro woman. In his enthusiasm he wrote,[5] and it appeared in his review: "The purling of the waters, the radiance of the moonlight, the odor of sweet flowers, sunlight, storm, the voices and echoes of nature all are found here."

The *Post-Dispatch* could not resist the opportunity to get back at McCullagh. In an editorial the day the review appeared the *Post-Dispatch* commented:[6] "The erudite editor of the *Globe-Democrat* appears to have visited one of our principal concert halls last night. It is not often that ponderous intellect can be called down from the heights of international politics to contemplate so simple a thing as a singer of songs, a black one at that; but when true art beckons even he can be counted on to answer. Apparently the Black Patti beckoned to him last evening and he was not deaf to her call, as the following bit of word-painting fresh from his pen is here to show."

The editorial then quoted from the review, and continued: "None but the grandiloquent editor of the *Globe-Democrat* could have looked into the subtleties of nature, as represented by the person of Miss Sisseretta Jones, and there discovered the wonders of music and poetry, such as he openly confesses to have done. Indeed, we have here at last, a measure of the great man's insight and feeling, a love of art, music, poetry and the like, such as has not previously been indicated by him."

The editorial hit below the belt. It was well known that McCullagh never wrote musical or theatrical criticism. It revealed, probably unintentionally, the respect the *Post-Dispatch* had for McCullagh. But he did not reprimand Dreiser. His only action was to walk out to the city room with a copy of the edition carrying the review and tell Mr. Mitchell, the city editor: "I don't think a thing like that ought to appear in the paper. It is a bit too high-flown for our audience. Your reader should have caught it."

Dreiser's final assignment for the *Globe-Democrat* inspired one of the apocryphal stories still told to newcomers in the paper's city room. The yarn has taken on the patina of age and has been embellished with the fanciful details of reporters who have passed it on through the years. As it is told today, Dreiser was assigned to review a play to be presented by a traveling company scheduled to arrive in St. Louis that afternoon. It was a cold, blustery

Sunday in early April and Dreiser had other ideas for the evening, presumably romantic. The obvious solution was to write the review in advance, which Dreiser did, praising it extravagantly. Unfortunately, due to the weather, none of three touring companies scheduled for performances in St. Louis were able to reach the city and there was no performance. McCullagh, so the story goes, notified the city editor that Mr. Dreiser's services would no longer be required.

Dreiser's version bears little resemblance to that story except for agreeing that his review did appear in the paper and the traveling company did not appear in St. Louis. The review led off with the announcement, "A large and enthusiastic audience greeted Mr. Sol Smith Russell last night at the Grand Theater."

The fact that others on the staff erred as obviously as Dreiser lends credence to his version. It may well have been the amused chortles of the other papers, rather than McCullagh's wrath, which hastened Dreiser's departure from the staff. The *Post-Dispatch* took advantage of the opportunity to poke fun at the *Globe-Democrat*'s features on spiritualism in the following editorial:[7]

To see three shows at once, and those widely separated by miles of country and washed-out sections of railroad in three different states, Illinois, Iowa and Missouri, is indeed a triumph; but also to see them as having arrived, or as they would have been had they arrived, and displaying their individual delights to three separate audiences is truly amazing, one of the finest demonstrations of mediumship—or perhaps we had better say materialization—yet known to science. Indeed, now that we think of it, it is an achievement so astonishing that even the *Globe* may well be proud of it. It is one of the finest flights of which the human mind or the great editor's psychic strength is capable. We venture to say that no spiritualist or materializing medium has ever outrivaled it. We have always known that Mr. McCullagh is a great man. The illuminating charm of his editorial page is sufficient proof of that. But this latest essay of his into the realm of combined dramatic criticism, supernatural insight, and materialization, is one of the most perfect things of its kind and can only be attributed to genius in the purest form. It is psychic, supernatural and spooky.

The Evening *Chronicle* joined in the chorus of jeers and suggested the *Globe-Democrat* did not need a drama critic since the psychic mind of its chief was sufficient.

Dreiser's explanation was that he was also supposed to cover a police assignment and when he completed it, the theater was dark. But rather than explain, he wrote out his resignation and a few days later obtained a job on the rival *Republic*. He reported that he met McCullagh several weeks later in the lobby of the Southern Hotel and quoted him as saying: "I do not think you understand quite how I felt about that. I was sorry to see you go. I want you to know that it was an unfortunate mistake all around and I do not blame you too much." Time may have softened Dreiser's memory. It hardly sounded in keeping with McCullagh, who after other mistakes had fired the first reporter he met when he entered the office. Of course most of them were rehired within a few hours.

Dreiser in retrospect did not hold a grudge. He wrote that it was not until long after he left the paper, "when I was much better able to judge him and his achievements, that I understood what a really big man he was. He seemed to have the desire to make the paper not only good, but great, and from my own memory and impression it was both. It had catholicity and solidity in editorials and news. Its editorials were in the main wise and jovial, often beautifully written by McCullagh himself."

The other yarn which found its way into print and which remains in the folklore of the *Globe-Democrat* city room had its origin in the cyclone of May 27, 1896. McCullagh's illness was keeping him away from the office frequently by that time and when the big storm struck late that afternoon Casper S. Yost, who normally edited the Sunday edition, was in charge. Yost later became editor of the editorial page of the *Globe-Democrat* and served in that capacity until his death in 1941.

Silas Bent preserved the apocryphal version in print nearly thirty years later.[8] As Bent told the story, young Yost realized he had a big story on his hands and went to the composing room and discovered some 120 point wooden type which had been used for handbills and posters. Yost, Bent related, composed a "headline calculated to shock the most phlegmatic." Later versions insist it was the first seven column banner head in the history of the *Globe-Democrat*. When McCullagh went to his office the day after the storm, so the story goes, Yost laid a copy of the paper on his desk and asked the Chief what he thought about it. McCullagh is said to have shaken his head sadly and replied: "I guess it is alright, Mr. Yost, but I was sort of saving that type for the second coming of the Christ."

Bent accepted the story as "marking a milestone in American journalism." He pointed out that other newspapers had used type as big and bold, but "no newspaper so conservative as the *Globe-Democrat*." Unfortunately, neither Bent, nor those who have repeated the yarn since, heeded one of McCullagh's cardinal precepts—to be sure to check the facts. Had they taken the trouble to look in the files they would have discovered that the *Globe-Democrat* did use bigger heads than usual, not only on May 29 but every day for the next six days. On May 29 there were two single-line three-column heads on page 1. On the right hand side the head was "Wind's Deadly Work." On the left-hand side the head read: "East St. Louis in Ruins."

The *Globe-Democrat*'s coverage was as thorough as if McCullagh had directed it. The story occupied all of the first four pages and a part of page 9. There were a dozen artist's sketches of the damage. The storm killed one hundred-fifty persons, injured more than five hundred and caused extensive property damage on both sides of the Mississippi River. The eastern approach to Eads Bridge was demolished and a number of packet boats moored on the levee were destroyed. On May 30 there were two editorial paragraphs by McCullagh. He noted: "The cyclone was a McKinley boom, set to atmospheric music," and "The only comparison in the case of the cyclone is the destructiveness of Democratic rule."

It was another example of McCullagh's aggressive and thorough news coverage, but it was not until some time after his death that the first banner head appeared in the *Globe-Democrat*.

One of the indications that McCullagh's health was failing was his absence from the national political conventions. The last conventions of either party that he covered personally were in 1888. In 1896 the Republican convention that nominated William McKinley was held in St. Louis in June. McCullagh's only recognizable contribution was a full page article headed: "Recollections of Many Great Conventions." It is interesting to note that the biggest head used in reporting the convention was a two-column head on June 19 after McKinley was named as the party's candidate. McCullagh's capsule comment that day was: "The political cyclone has come and has done precisely what was predicted for it."

While he did not contribute as frequently to the editorial page in his last two years there was no evidence that he ever lost his touch. William Marion Reedy wrote in *Reedy's Mirror* on November 11, 1894 that: "Those who did not hear the ravings of the mad McCullagh before the election will probably have to wait another two years to hear him again." Reedy, in his own style, was as vitriolic as the man for whom he once worked.

In November 1895, when McCullagh returned to work after an absence because of illness, Reedy wrote under one of his many bylines, Uncle Fuller: "It looked like the good old times in the *Globe-Democrat*'s editorial columns Wednesday morning. Mr. McCullagh was very much in evidence. There were a half-dozen paragraphs that had all the old time flavor of the man, the badinage and persiflage with perfect dignity that used to make the *Globe-Democrat*'s editorial columns as necessary to a St. Louisan as a cocktail before breakfast. When I read the *Globe-Democrat*'s editorial columns last Wednesday morning at breakfast, the freshness and sparkle of them made me think for a moment it was Thursday and I was reading the *Mirror*. This is what I call high literary art and I lift me 'lid' to Little Mack."

While McCullagh obviously took pride and satisfaction in his editorials, he was first of all a newsman. One of his newspaper friends observed that "Mack never outlived the reporter habit." George E. Windegger,[9] who worked in the composing room in McCullagh's last years and who was for many years foreman of the composing room, recalled that "The Chief" usually skimmed lightly over the editorial proofs each night, but gave meticulous attention to the news proofs.

When an important story broke, the *Globe-Democrat* covered it in detail and the Pullman strike in 1894 demonstrated that he had not lost any of his vigor. For three weeks the entire front page was devoted to the strike, as well as most of page 2. In addition to staff reporters on the scene in Chicago, the paper carried special dispatches from correspondents in every city affected by the dispute. Each day the editorial page led off with a one line editorial: "Move the trains," followed by paragraphs like this: "Surrender first, then arbitrate" and "The thing to do with a riot is shoot a hole in it."

On July 9, the day martial law was declared in Chicago, the *Globe-Democrat* ran a reproduction of the American flag on page 1 with the caption: "In Hoc Signo Vinces." Attempts to bring pressure on the paper by the threat of a boycott in St. Louis failed. The paper reported on July 3 that a resolution had been introduced at a meeting of the striking unions to boycott the *Globe-Democrat,* but failed to pass. On July 12 two short editorial paragraphs told the story of the outcome: "The strike is beaten," and "The trains are moving." Three days later McCullagh summed it up in one sentence: "In Hoc Signo, we got there!"

There were other examples of McCullagh's thorough news coverage in his last years. On April 11, 1894 this editorial led off his column of paragraphs:

> The *Globe-Democrat* so rarely boasts of its own achievements that a brief reference to an exhibition of enterprise in yesterday's issue may not be out of place. We published as a special dispatch from Washington a verbatim report of the speech of Senator Hill on the tariff bill. It made nearly twelve columns, about 20,000 words. Other newspapers were content with the imperfect and incomplete synopsis of the Associated Press, but we threw that away and ordered the matter in its entirety.

Those who were critical of McCullagh in his last years felt that the *Globe-Democrat* had become dull. Reedy wrote the week after McCullagh's death that he "had a tendency to confuse dignity with dullness." There may have been some validity to the complaint. By the 1890's there were fewer and fewer headlines like "Bloodshed in a Brothel," "The Devil's Den," or "Lured by a Libertine." One reason was that the times had changed. St. Louis and the West were no longer the rough and rowdy frontier. The city had taken on a more urbane sophistication. To be sure the sensationalism which had won attention and circulation for the *Globe-Democrat* in the 1870's and 1880's was by the next decade blossoming into "yellow journalism," and perhaps it was an indication that McCullagh was becoming more conservative. On one occasion he paid for but refused to print a long and expensive story he had ordered cabled from England, on the ground the scandal it recounted was not fit for readers of "The Great Religious Daily."

Probably closer to the truth was that in his later years McCullagh's first concern was the paper's national prestige. Even before the 1890's the *Globe-Democrat* was recognized as one of the great newspapers of the country. Addison Archer, a newspaperman himself wrote in 1897[10] "From one end of America to the other, the *Globe-Democrat*, its publisher and its editor are known to the thinking classes, for the *Globe-Democrat* is one of America's greatest newspapers and is more widely copied than any except the New York *Sun*, the New York *Herald*, or the Chicago *Tribune*."

The paper's success was impressively reflected in its financial reports. The *Globe-Democrat* paid annual dividends ranging from 20 to 50 per cent on a capitalization of $500,000. Archer reported that the capitalization represented less than half of the actual value and a quarter of what it would require to purchase it. The paper paid more than $100,000 in bad years and the dividends went as high as $250,000. At the time of his death, McCullagh owned the thirty shares he had received when the *Globe* and the *Democrat* were merged. In his desk was found an uncashed check for $1,800 representing the dividend on his stock for one quarter. The stock netted him $7,200 in 1896.

It was generally accepted that the *Globe-Democrat* had the largest circulation of any newspaper in Missouri, both daily and Sunday. This claim was disputed by the *Post-Dispatch* which boasted daily on its editorial page that its city circulation was greater than that of any other two St. Louis papers combined. One clue to the validity of the claim is that the *Post-Dispatch* never published its circulation figures, as did the *Globe-Democrat*. In an era when circulation figures were consistently padded, McCullagh frequently challenged the opposing papers to make public their actual circulation figures. In the 1870's he adopted the practice of printing at regular intervals at the top of the editorial page the notarized statements of the foremen of the press room and the mailing department certifying the actual number of copies printed.

In 1896 Archer visited St. Louis and interviewed Houser of the *Globe-Democrat* and C. W. Jones of the *Post-Dispatch.* Houser told him: "The *American Newspaper Directory* did us an injustice this year in printing our circulation figures. We propose to furnish every advertiser a detailed statement that cannot be refuted or discounted. The statement will show that during the first seven months of 1896 the daily average number of papers subscribed for and sold was: January, 62,791; February, 66,275; March, 66,655; April, 66,197; May, 71,835; June 77,376; and July, 68,557."

For the Sunday edition Houser gave these figures: January, 74,688; February, 77,316; April, 75,197; May, 71,835; June, 79,797, and July, 75,285. The daily average for the seven-month period was 68,376 and the Sunday average was 77,641. The twice weekly *Globe-Democrat* had an average circulation of 115,872. Houser said about 50 per cent of the paper's circulation was in St. Louis, the mail subscriptions made up about 5,000 and the remainder went to news dealers and newsboys.

The *Post-Dispatch* circulation was listed in the *American Newspaper Directory* that year as 78,156 daily and 80,355 on Sunday. Archer reported that Jones showed him the paper's breakdown of circulation by months but insisted that the figures were not for publication. The *Republic,* the only other paper in the circulation race, claimed 68,204 daily and 71,042 on Sundays. Houser claimed that the *Republic*'s figures included sample copies and unreturned copies.

The *Globe-Democrat* was carrying more advertising than any of its rivals in St. Louis. Another reported that "St. Louisans read the *Globe-Democrat* as regularly as the day dawns, both readers and advertisers, and they advertise in it more liberally and at a higher rate, with better results than any paper in the field. I learned this from personal observation. I called on the five leading local advertisers of St. Louis, the firms that spend from $50,000 to $100,000 a year each, in St. Louis newspapers, and asked them to name the newspapers of the city in the order of their advertising value. Every one of them placed the *Globe-*

Democrat first, without a moment's hesitation, and what is most remarkable about it, not first for any one class, but first for all. These firms appeal to the entire purchasing population of St. Louis and there is no advertisement any of them ever published that does not go first and foremost into the *Globe-Democrat*. It seems to be a paper that is read by everyone, and while it is strong with the business men and strong with the masses, it is strongest of all in the homes of St. Louis."

Fred Goodwin, the advertising manager of Nugent's Department Store, told Archer: "We pay the *Globe-Democrat* the highest rates for it is worth the most to us. We use all the papers and know the exact value of each." J. F. Crawford, advertising manager of D. Crawford & Co., said: "The *Globe-Democrat* has undoubtedly the largest and best circulation in the city. I believe its sworn statement to be absolutely correct, but if it made no sworn statement at all I would place it first by all odds."

By 1890 the *Globe-Democrat* had ceased to run advertising on the front page, except on Sunday. Week after week the Sunday paper appeared with a full page advertisement on page one. The Sunday edition in that period averaged more than forty pages in four sections. The Saturday edition varied between sixteen and twenty-four pages. Most of the society news was still published on Saturday and there were a number of women's features as well.

In the development of Sunday magazine features the *Globe-Democrat* continued to show the way. Early in the 90's a regular Sunday feature, "Wheels and Wheelers" was added to cater to the current vogue in bicycling. The Sunday edition was printing serial fiction by such well known authors as Émile Zola. Another feature started in St. Louis by the *Globe-Democrat* was the words and music for a popular song. The Sunday feature stories were not as lurid as those which appeared in the *Post-Dispatch,* but they covered a wide range of subjects. The last Sunday in October 1896, for example, carried features on "Life in Iceland," "Roentgen Ray Photography," "The Tennessee Centennial," "Gossip of Fashion." All were liberally illustrated with chalk plates and there was a half page political map of the United States, showing the electoral votes of each state and the expected winner in each state. The previous Sunday there was a full page of pictures of the floats in the city's Veiled Prophet parade.

The sports coverage had expanded. By 1893 the *Globe-Democrat* was carrying special dispatches on football games in the East. The old St. Louis Browns, owned by Chris von der Ahe, won four consecutive pennants in the 1880's and their achievements were fully reported. During the racing season the paper carried the results each day. While McCullagh deplored boxing, the major boxing matches received full coverage.

Despite his ill health, McCullagh threw himself into the campaign in 1896 with his customary vigor. The *Globe-Democrat* began in October to run the American flag on page 1 each day with the slogan: "In Hoc Signo Vinces." On November 1 there were thirteen paragraphs all bearing the McCullagh trademark on the editorial page. The first page presented complete coverage of a parade for McKinley and Hobart with several illustrations, including a banner of the *Globe-Democrat* in the parade. The following morning there were sixteen McCullagh paragraphs and two long editorials urging votes for the Republican ticket. On November 3, election day, there was a full page sample ballot to show voters how to cast their ballots for "McKinley and Honest Money." On that day the last communique was issued from "The Temple of Truth." With the usual 2 A.M. dateline it read: "Mr. Hanna reluctantly concedes Texas and Arkansas to Mr. Bryan and Chairman Jones insists McKinley cannot carry South Carolina." The next paragraph read: "Honest men vote early. Let no vote be lost."

The day after the election there was a parade of seven roosters, the *Globe-Democrat*'s symbol of victory, strutting across the top of the first page and a three column picture of McKinley. The two column headline on the election story read: "The People Did It." At the bottom of the page was a seven column cartoon of a chorus of roosters. Two paragraphs on the editorial page proclaimed his personal satisfaction in the outcome. One read: "The campaign of education educated." The second was "Let us shake hands this morning with every other nation on earth and assure them that Uncle Sam pays 110 cents on the dollar every time." The *Globe-Democrat* "Towline" swept every

Republican candidate into office in St. Louis, but it failed to carry the state for the Republicans.

His efforts in the campaign were McCullagh's last contribution in the active direction of the paper. They brought on an acute attack of asthma, complicated by nervous depression. He never entered his office after November 10. Some of his friends were concerned about his health and without consulting him launched a campaign to raise funds to enable him to take a long voyage to recover his health. When McCullagh heard of the proposal, he asked that the project be dropped. He explained that he preferred to pay his own expenses.

THE RIGHT TIME TO DIE

12

Two days before death came to Joseph McCullagh, he told his personal physician, Dr. Charles Hamilton Hughes: "It is a good thing for a man to die at the right time." Dr. Hughes recalled that conversation after the editor's spectacular, and controversial, death made front page headlines across the nation on December 31, 1896. McCullagh, the doctor told St. Louis reporters,[1] apparently thought the end was near. "He maintained that in the light of history the assassination of Lincoln was a fortunate thing for his fame."

Dr. Hughes lived across the street at 3860 West Pine Boulevard. He had been a friend of the editor for thirty years and his physician since October 1894. In view of the personal relationship, it is difficult to understand the doctor's positive and somewhat contradictory statements after his patient's death. McCullagh, he said, would never admit he was ill, even when his efforts in the campaign that fall had resulted in nervous prostration. McCullagh had difficulty in breathing and Dr. Hughes ordered him to abstain from smoking and alcohol, a deprivation which undoubtedly contributed to the patient's depression.

There was in the doctor's opinion no pathological condition that would have resulted in immediate death and in his words, no "indication of softening of the brain."[2] He felt that McCullagh "might have been cured had he followed instructions," but he admitted that he had informed his patient there was no hope for recovery, apparently with the idea of inducing him to comply with his physician's orders. As the patient's condition steadily worsened, the doctor felt that his attacks of melancholy increased.

On December 29, McCullagh apparently felt that the end was near. He asked that one of his oldest and closest friends, Louis C. Bohle, be summoned. Bohle visited him that afternoon. Bohle owned the livery stable McCullagh patronized and had been his business advisor.

The following day McCullagh appeared to be stronger. The Rev. W. W. Boyd, pastor of the Second Baptist Church, and a personal friend, visited him that afternoon.[3] McCullagh talked at some length of his plan for a prolonged trip to California and expressed the fear he might not be able to go as soon as he would like. Dr. Hughes called that night. He found McCullagh tired from receiving his visitors and the editor told him he did not need any attention and wanted to go to sleep.

At 6:30 the next morning Henry Waters, Mrs. Manion's Negro stable boy, went out to sweep the rear steps as usual and discovered McCullagh's body lying just below the second story window of McCullagh's quarters. His body was clad only in a nightgown. The head had been crushed by the masonry protruding from the foundation. Waters awakened Mrs. Manion and then ran across the street to summon Dr. Hughes. When the physician arrived the body had been carried inside and the doctor pronounced him dead. Bohle, who was also an undertaker, was called.

The *Post-Dispatch* broke the news to St. Louis with an "Extra," which was being cried by news boys on the street by 8 A.M. The front page was given over entirely to the story, which described the death as a suicide. A diagram of the yard showed an X to mark the spot of the fall. There was a three column picture of McCullagh surrounded by a black border. The headline in bold-face type read:

KILLED HIMSELF
......
Suicide of Editor Joseph B. McCullagh of St. Louis
Globe-Democrat
......
Leaped From the Bedroom Window of His Home
In the Night

His Mangled Corpse Found In the Yard by Mrs.
Manion's Stable Boy

- - - - - -

Attempted to Take Life a Few Hours Before
By Turning on Gas

- - - - - -

Had Been Ill For Many Months And Is Supposed to
Have Become Deranged

- - - - - -

*Wore Out His Life at His Profession and Had Grown
Weary and Despondent*

- - - - - -

*Began His Career as a Printer's Apprentice and
Worked His Way Up to the Highest Rank of
Journalism*

The story, and Dr. Hughes's statements to reporters precipitated a dispute that persisted long after the editor was laid to rest. McCullagh's friends insisted he must have become dizzy and must have fallen when he went to the open window for fresh air for relief from a fit of asthmatic coughing. Dr. Hughes declared he ended his life deliberately, although he admitted that his patient had given no premonition of suicide when he saw him a few hours before his death.[4] At that time, the doctor added, he felt that "his brain was affected, but that his intellect was all right."

That conclusion seems contradictory, but Dr. Hughes flatly told a *Post-Dispatch* reporter: "There can be little doubt that McCullagh took his own life." He related that he had prescribed digitalis, a heart stimulant and had given him a four ounce bottle. Two days before his death, McCullagh told him he had taken more than an ounce at one time. Dr. Hughes explained that probably McCullagh's stomach was too weak to retain it.

Supporting the suicide theory was a statement made by Mrs. Manion and read at the Coroner's inquest. She said that shortly after midnight she had detected the odor of gas. When she entered her brother-in-law's room, she found one burner of a gas stove burning low and another burner turned on but not lit. McCullagh was asleep. She explained that she turned off both burners and opened the window to air out the room. Evidently her statement impressed the Coroner's jury which returned a verdict of accidental death caused when the editor "fell from an open window" while seeking fresh air from "escaping gas."

The *Post-Dispatch* quoted Houser as saying that he felt McCullagh had jumped from the window. However, the same day in an interview with a reporter for the *Republic,* Houser insisted he had been misquoted and said that McCullagh must have become dizzy and fallen during a siege of coughing. Bohle maintained that death must have been accidental and declared he was confident McCullagh would never have deliberately ended his life. Stevens agreed and said that in his mind there was no doubt death was accidental. The Rev. Mr. Boyd denounced the suicide charge when he spoke at a meeting of St. Louis newspaper men on January 3.[5] He told them that McCullagh was in "full possession of his faculties when he saw him at 4 P.M. on December 29." Others who spoke in the same vein included Casper S. Yost of the *Globe-Democrat* and George S. Johns of the *Post-Dispatch*.

A committee was named to draft an appropriate resolution. Members of the committee included Col. Charles H. Jones, publisher of the *Post-Dispatch,* Charles W. Knapp, publisher of the *Republic,* and Frank R. O'Neill and William Hyde, former editors of the *Republic*. The resolution unanimously approved at the meeting said in part: "Mr. McCullagh had won a conspicuous place in the foremost rank of the journalism of the country, and he won it not only by his native ability and adaptation for the work, but by that tireless energy, diligence and exalted conception of the duty to his readers and to the general public."

Newspapers in other cities took notice of the suicide charge. The Chicago *Tribune*'s story on January 1 pointed out that McCullagh had suffered from paralysis of the throat and that "every indication pointed to the conclusion that it was an accident." Had McCullagh jumped, the *Tribune* story said, the body would have been found much farther from the open window.

The *Globe-Democrat* discussed the controversy in an editorial on January 3, 1897 and declared: "The theory of suicide in the case of the late Mr. McCullagh, which in the early reports was given on the authority of one person, and which is still insisted upon by that person, was condemned by Dr. Boyd at the meeting of the members of the city press yesterday in vigorous and appropriate language. There was never any real reason for the suicide assumption. His own view, frequently expressed to his editorial associates and friends, was against suicide, the manner of his death, and all the circumstances connected with it, which on examination of the room and the ground on which he fell, are hostile to the theory of self-destruction."

McCullagh's impatience at the length of the final sentence can easily be imagined. It is certainly not consistent with the style he insisted on in *Globe-Democrat* editorials.

Even Reedy chided Dr. Hughes. He wrote in the *Mirror* on January 7, 1897: "There is no evidence to support the suicide theory other than on the evening Mr. McCullagh was killed he had been subjected to a three-hour visitation by Dr. Hughes." The doctor, he added, "in an attempt to gain notoriety makes an ass of himself." Moreover, he admonished, "a physician should no more say that his patient committed suicide than he should publish to the world that he died of a loathsome disease. Dr. Hughes has been false to his friend and traitor to his patient in insisting that Mr. McCullagh committed suicide."

An impartial review of the evidence from the perspective of more than half a century, tends to support the conviction of McCullagh's friends. He was Irish by birth and by temperament. He certainly was a fighter and his abhorrence of suicide was frequently expressed, as in this editorial on August 14, 1892 after the suicide of a friend, Judge Normille, in which he said: "The true and manly course is to go on trying for success, in spite of all the disappointments. That is what we are placed here for and we cannot do otherwise. The plea of despair, in short, is not a valid one." It can be argued, as some did, that he was mentally deranged temporarily, but this assumption is doubtful.

St. Louis paid its final tribute to the man who had done so much for the city, at a simple funeral service on January 3. Floral offerings had poured in from all parts of the nation. Personal condolences were received in profusion from Melville E. Stone, general manager of the Associated Press, Victor Rosewater of the Omaha *Bee,* John Russell Young of the Union League and W. C. Harrison, an old friend from Cincinnati.

H. V. Boynton, a contemporary of McCullagh in Washington

wired: "He was brilliant, but never sensational, critical but not abusive. If his caustic paragraphs fell like blows, it was because of the truth they contained."

The simple service was held in Mrs. Manion's home at 3738 West Pine Boulevard. Despite a cold, driving rain, a crowd began gathering outside the home long before the service began at 2 o'clock. In the parlor the body of the editor lay in state in a casket described by a *Post-Dispatch* reporter as "plain, but elegant." The casket bore a simple silver plate with the inscription "At Rest," and below it "Joseph B. McCullagh."

Although McCullagh took pride in referring to the *Globe-Democrat* as "The Great Religious Daily," and gave more space to religious news than any other St. Louis paper, there is no record of his affiliation with any church, and he rarely attended any religious services. This fact probably explains why the funeral was held at Mrs. Manion's home and why the service was conducted jointly by two Protestant ministers, the Rev. John Snyder, pastor of the Unitarian Church of the Messiah, and the Rev. Mr. Boyd.

The active pallbearers were all associates from the *Globe-Democrat*. They were Capt. Henry King, who was to succeed McCullagh as editor; Prof. C. M. Harvey and Capt. J. W. Miller, editorial writers; O. R. Lake, telegraph editor; W. J. Thornton, railroad editor; R. M. Witten, foreman of the composing room; and Joseph Kurtin, foreman of the pressroom.

There was a long and imposing list of honorary pallbearers, headed by Mayor Cyrus P. Walbridge. Henry Watterson, editor of the Louisville *Courier Journal* was on the list, as was McCullagh's long-time foe, C. I. Filley. Virtually every Republican officeholder and politician of any importance was included. Interment was in the McKee family lot in Bellefontaine Cemetery. Despite the rain which fell steadily during the graveside service, the *Globe-Democrat* reported [6] perhaps with understandable exaggeration, that the funeral was "one of the biggest" in the history of Bellefontaine Cemetery.

The only close relative present was a sister, Mrs. Rachel Souter of Brooklyn, New York. A brother-in-law, John Blair Armstrong, came for the services from Chicago, with his son

Young Armstrong. Also present was Gladys McCullagh, the 8-year-old adopted daughter of Mrs. Manion and the late John McCullagh.

McCullagh's death made top headlines across the nation. The Chicago *Tribune* on January 1 devoted most of page 2 to the story of his passing. There were tributes from Chicago newsmen who had known him. The *Tribune* not only credited him with being the "father of the interview" but reprinted the complete text of his interview with President Johnson. The New York *Times* made his death the lead story of the day and devoted more than a column to a review of his career.

Reedy, who in his younger days had been a feature writer for McCullagh and had been fired, and rehired after he sobered up, paid his last respects to "The Chief" in the *Mirror* for January 7, 1897. Pointing out that "tributes to the late Mr. McCullagh are a drug on the market," he wrote: "His position in this community invested him with a certain awe that I believe sometimes overpowered him. There was a good warm heart beating under his somewhat repellent mannerisms. He was as gruff as Dr. Johnson, and had other resemblances to that typical Briton. He did not bear malice. He wielded great power in the city, state and nation and yet he never used that power for an evil end. He never pursued a man, and his paper during all his career never deliberately injured a woman. His paper was clean always. His paper was undignified never. That he was vain in his way would be idle to deny. He affected the 'grand, gloomy and peculiar.' His devotion to his paper was idolatrous. No man ever loved a mistress as he loved the *Globe-Democrat*. He came to be sort of an institution. He grew askance of goodness and gentleness to a certain extent, and his kindly acts, though legion, were done furtively, as if he were afraid of discovery. He never deserted a friend."

McCullagh never made a will. After his death William C. Richardson, the public administrator took charge of the estate. For probate purposes the estate was estimated at approximately $200,000. McCullagh's thirty shares of *Globe-Democrat* stock were valued at $120,000. The remaining items in his safe deposit box included the deed to the property at 3113 West Pine Boulevard, where he lived at one time, and a substantial number of shares of mining stock, reported by the *Globe-Democrat* to have a face value of over $1,000,000, but actually worth about $50. There was a $10,000 life insurance policy and approximately $27,000 in cash in several bank accounts.

That he was able to leave an estate as large as it was is surprising. The *Republic* reported the day after his death that McCullagh's salary "had been for a number of years $150 a week, or $7,500 a year, fully $2,500 a year below salaries paid for similar positions in New York or Chicago." The *Republic* added that McCullagh refused to agree to any increase in salary, explaining he felt it was not right since he was a stockholder.

The news of McCullagh's estate quickly reached Ireland. Hopeful, and distant heirs, filed claims.[7] Before the final settlement was made, claims had been filed from the descendants of nineteen brothers and sisters. McCullagh himself had said he was one of sixteen children. According to the claims he had nine sisters and eleven brothers. Eventually the estate was divided among seven sets of heirs, each group receiving approximately $35,000.

In January 1897 McCullagh's name disappeared from the masthead of the *Globe-Democrat* where it had appeared since he had been named vice president in 1887. On January 17 the board of directors met and named Charles H. McKee to succeed McCullagh as vice president. Houser remained as president and another Houser, William M., became secretary-treasurer.

A JEALOUS MISTRESS

13

"If McCullagh had ever loved a woman, he would have been more human, less Spartan."

This observation,[1] made by Reedy after the editor's death, probably summed up the opinion of those who knew him. No doubt they were puzzled, and sometimes repelled by his gruff manner and apparent snubs. Frequently he would not recognize old friends he met on the street. Rarely did he bother to remove his cigar from his mouth in conversation. In short, he seemed to have none of the saving graces of ordinary politeness a wife might have encouraged.

There was speculation about his lack of romantic interest. Some suggested that a blighted love affair early in his career turned him into a "woman hater." After his death the Louisville *Courier Journal* published, and the *Post-Dispatch* reprinted,[2] a story supporting this speculation. The item read: "Twenty years ago the late Mr. Joseph B. McCullagh was a frequent visitor to Louisville. His love affair was a local one. McCullagh met and fell in love with a most estimable young lady of Louisville and made frequent visits to the city. Their engagement was eventually announced; but the young lady's parents interfered and the match was broken off. The editor, who had just established himself in St. Louis, took the affair much to heart, and it is said he never quite recovered from his chagrin and disappointment. He became very much embittered toward women, and until his last day was known as a thorough woman hater. His Louisville fiancée died a number of years ago."

So far as can be determined, McCullagh never mentioned becoming engaged, or being disappointed in love. The vagueness obvious in the item suggests doubt as to its authenticity, and there is a conspicuous absence of names and dates. Moreover, at that period of his life, McCullagh was devoting seven days a week to his job with the *Globe*.

About the same time there were rumors in St. Louis that he was an admirer of Miss Jennie Brown, the adopted daughter of Joseph Brown, then mayor of St. Louis. The family lived in a fashionable neighborhood on Chouteau Avenue. The romance ended, according to those who circulated the rumor, when Mayor Brown disapproved of the hours McCullagh worked. A short time later, Miss Brown was married to someone else. There was another rumor that he was interested in a young lady in Terre Haute, Indiana. That rumor also died a natural death.[3]

Probably one explanation for the rumors was that McCullagh never took the trouble to discuss them, nor to deny them. His mistress was the *Globe-Democrat* and it claimed his full time and his devotion. He had few intimate friends and virtually no social life. William Hyde, an old adversary and former editor of the *Republican,* recalled that he declined most social invitations and rarely agreed to make speeches.[4] "At the festive board," Hyde wrote, "no voice was merrier, no flow of wit more sparkling than McCullagh's. As an afterdinner speaker, although the opportunities were rare, when he exhibited his talents, few excelled him."

The same reticence that cloaked his romantic interests, if indeed there was any basis of fact for the rumors about them, make his religious views an enigma. Born in Dublin, a predominantly Catholic city, it might be supposed that his parents belonged to that faith. Yet there is no evidence on which to base such a conclusion, just as there is no evidence that he ever formally joined a church in St. Louis. Yet he was obviously a student of the Bible and his interest in spiritualism suggests a deep interest in the hereafter.

In an editorial tribute[5] entitled "McCullagh the Man," Capt.

King admitted that even those with whom he was most closely associated were uncertain. He wrote: "There has been much said about his supposed religious views and tendencies, but it is doubtful if anybody knows what he really believed. Perhaps he did not quite know himself. He frequently talked on the subject, but never in a definitive way, or as one with his mind made up. He made no distinction, but favored them all, and recognized the great value of religious institutions to society."

In his relations with his staff he was aloof and reserved. Dreiser said that "if he ever had a crony, it was not known in the reporters' room.[6] Occasionally he might be seen ambling down the hall to the lavatory, or to the room of his telegraph chief, but mostly it was merely to take his carriage or to walk to the Southern Hotel at 1 for his lunch, or at 6 for his dinner. He was a solitary or an eccentric." Dreiser described him "with a derby hat pulled over his eyes, his white socks gleaming, a cane in his hand and a cigar between his lips." Yet Dreiser insisted that McCullagh "was of immense significance to his staff and the natives. Plainly he was like a god to many of them, the farmers and residents in small towns in states like Texas, Iowa, Missouri, Arkansas and Southern Illinois. He was held in high esteem by his staff, and he was one of the few editors of his day who really deserved to be."

George Windegger remembers that McCullagh "seemed to like printers better than reporters."[7] He frequently stopped to visit with the men in the composing room, though on one occasion he reproved a printer with whom he had been friendly, for using vulgar language. He had a high regard for his foreman's news judgment and for the opinion of one of his proof readers, Harry Fitzgerald, who always had the task of reading proof on Mc-Cullagh's editorials. One reason probably was, Windegger explained, that McCullagh always wrote in long hand and "his writing was not very legible." One of McCullagh's favorite comments was that "A proof reader is a man who keeps editors from making damned fools of themselves."

Reedy declared that McCullagh "was the finest man in St. Louis not to work for.[8] People with ideas of their own could not work under him, but he loved a man who would not fawn to him."

McCullagh was a strict disciplinarian. He once told one of his city editors never to send two or more men on an assignment without placing one of them in charge.

Capt. King's editorial tribute conceded: "He had the reputation of being unsocial and sometimes lacking in courtesy, but this was mainly due to his high sense of duty and his tireless devotion to his daily work. It is true that he was apt to be brusque and forbidding when interrupted without sufficient reason. He was a careful economist of time and never had any of it to waste in idle talk . . . He was a severe disciplinarian but not an unreasonable taskmaster. His subordinates were expected to do their best, to make themselves as useful as possible, but they were never required to do more than he had the right to ask of them. He did not wear his heart on his sleeve and did not invite familiarity; but he liked at times to sit on the edge of a desk and tell an amusing story, or recall some interesting incident of his political or military experience, or to discuss with characteristic pungency and clearness the topics of the times."

In an interview with a reporter for the *Republic* Capt. King said: "I have been here fourteen years and during that time have been intimately associated with Mr. McCullagh. He was not a social being, and his bearing toward his subordinates was always that of a director or manager. He was a great student of Shakespeare and was well posted on the Bible. He was proud of his knowledge and it pleased him to have someone ask him about a quotation."

Underneath his gruff manner he was inclined to be sentimental and generous. Reedy thought that "He grew ashamed of goodness and gentleness to a certain extent, and his friendly acts, though legion, were done furtively, as if he were afraid of discovery . . . he did not care for money. He made more for other people than for himself. He was absurdly generous with his own money, but he kept down newspaper salaries in this city for fifteen years." [9]

Capt. King wrote: "There were springs of kindness and tenderness in his nature that were never known to the world. He was quick to respond to any legitimate appeal to his sympathy, and the list of his modest and often anonymous charities would be a surprise to those who thought him hard or severe." Tammany recalled that he was always a soft touch for printers down on their luck and it was generally known in the composing room that he could be counted on for a loan, which frequently was not repaid.

It was typical of McCullagh that when he read Eugene Field's poetic tribute to him, he never mentioned it either personally or by letter to Field. Instead he sent him a gold watch.[10]

Some insight into the sentimental Irishman that hid behind his austere façade is afforded by two members of the *Globe-Democrat* who came in contact with him over a period of years.[11] Charles S. Webb, who was a reporter and in later years a copy editor, said that on one occasion when he was doubtful about using a news item, he consulted "The Chief." "In stating the case as briefly as I could, since he was always impatient of words, I said something to the effect that a question of tact seemed to be involved. 'Tact, sir?,' he said, looking up quickly, 'decency is tact.'"

Another time, Webb recalled, "when the article in question contained an attack on some man, the Chief said with an air of weariness, 'Oh, well, better leave it out; it's no use to jump on a man just because you've got a newspaper.'" Webb related other incidents:

While Mr. McCullagh appreciated good work, he generally expressed it by a gift or a raise of salary—very seldom by praise. On the morning in 1892 when Cleveland was nominated at Chicago for President, I and those assisting me, did some pretty fast work and scored a first page beat on the opposition paper. I came down in the evening somewhat elated and rather looked for some sort of recognition. When the Chief said nothing, I modestly referred to the matter. The Chief remarked, "Yes, I noticed that. We have some very good printers upstairs."

Of a certain city editor, nervous and excitable by nature, the Chief said: "He is all right, but he thinks the house is afire."

Mr. McCullagh had affection for Charles A. Dana, Henry Watterson and John Sherman. When Sherman was a candidate for the Presidential nomination, the Chief sent him a friendly telegram and signed himself "Your old private secretary." He had once held that position with Mr. Sherman.

A JEALOUS MISTRESS

Something like this was the Chief's comment on a certain writer whom he often employed and as often discharged. The writer had failed to come to the office. The Chief surmised he had been drinking, as usual, and said: "That's the way. If they can write, they drink; and if they don't drink they can't write."

He admired Robert G. Ingersoll, John J. Ingalls, U. S. Grant and Jefferson Davis. He had a high opinion of Mr. Davis as a scholar and a controversialist. He thought that Mr. Davis often had the advantage of General W. T. Sherman and General Wolsely in their points at issue on the Civil War. He would say: "They had better leave Jeff Davis alone."

O. R. Lake, who worked for the *Globe-Democrat* for thirty-seven years and who was telegraph editor for twenty-five years, also had the opportunity to know the Chief well. He told Stevens:

Every man has a dual personality. McCullagh seemed to have a half dozen. Many people said he was gruff and boorish, yet you and I know to the contrary. His so-called gruffness was merely a cloak, which he put on to cover his diffidence, for he was as diffident as an old-fashioned girl in her teens. Few knew of the many kind deeds he did. He was not a man to let his left hand know what his right hand was doing in giving assistance. He was often misjudged, but went serenely on his way doing what was right as far as was in his power.

Three incidents which came under my observation may be of interest. You remember the story of the Eastern potentate who asked who was the most powerful person in his kingdom. The courtiers all responded: "Why you are, Sire." The king replied: "You are wrong. It is a child, my infant son. He rules his mother and she rules me, while I rule the kingdom." It was a child of some five years who caused Mr. McCullagh to reverse himself and to order for the Sunday paper a colored supplement. He always had been opposed to the colored supplement and criticized that feature unsparingly. But he explained his reversal by saying he observed his litle niece every Sunday cried for the colored supplement and would not be appeased until one was given to her. Then he argued to himself that if the child wanted a colored supplement, the mother naturally would buy the paper that had one. And so the *Globe-Democrat* must fall in line with a colored supplement or lose subscribers, or at least, the rival papers would gain an advantage with their colored supplements. The result was that the colored supplement, which the Chief despised, was ordered for the *Globe-Democrat*.

When Jim Butler was a candidate for an office, his mother came to the *Globe-Democrat* and sought a personal interview with Mr. McCullagh. She told the Chief that, as he knew, her husband, Ed Butler, and she had been poor people with little education. They had sent Jim to college and he had graduated in law. They wanted him to have a chance to be a gentleman. They had plenty of money and nothing else. She begged Mr. McCullagh not to ridicule Jim, but to give her boy a chance to bring honor to the family name. The Chief heard the old lady through. Ed Butler, the Democratic politician had been the object of many a good paragraph. You will remember how the Chief used to ring the charge on the Butlers' theater. "The Home of Folly! Two Frolics Daily." The Chief said to Mrs. Butler that while the *Globe-Democrat* could not support Jim Butler against the Republican nominee, he could assure her that for her sake he would see that nothing unkind about her son would appear in the paper during the campaign. And he kept his word, as he always did, when he gave it.

The third incident showed the heart of the man, and I thought at the time it was one of the best revelations I had ever seen of his character. The Chief had a wonderful insight about news. He could foresee events as could no other newspaper man I have ever known. He certainly realized where news was to be found, and had a man there in advance of other papers. He didn't like to miss anything of news value. One night there came over the wires the story of the scandalous misdeeds of a young man. It was a cracking good story of a kind, full of human interest, as we used to say. It came from one of our oldest and most reliable correspondents and was unquestionably true. I had some scruples about the propriety of running the story and took it into the Chief for his judgment. Mr. McCullagh listened while I told him the substance of the special. Then he said: "I wouldn't publish that. The *Globe-Democrat* can get along without it. He may have an old mother."

McCullagh's formal education was meager, but all who knew him agreed that he was a voracious reader.[12] One associate remembered "every hour that he could command found him with his books. He carried a book with him wherever he went. He was probably one of the best-read men in American journalism."

He read poetry and frequently reprinted a column or more of verse in the Sunday editions. His favorite poem, which he often quoted was "The Closing Year," by George D. Prentice.

Stevens, who probably knew McCullagh as well as anyone on the staff, said after McCullagh's death that the Chief's only order always was to "write the situation just as you find it." He could excuse a man for being beaten on a story, Stevens said, but he abhorred the unreliable. "Honest journalism was the cornerstone on which he built." Stevens also recalled that McCullagh once told him "that to do a day's work on a newspaper was enough for any man." [13]

Two years before McCullagh's death, Reedy published a feature story about him in the *Mirror,* on September 2, 1894. There was a full page cartoon showing McCullagh at his desk surrounded by stacks of newspapers. Reedy wrote:

> Mr. Joseph B. McCullagh of the *Globe-Democrat* is undoubtedly the best representative American newspaperman now in existence. There is no managing editor in the world who sees so many different people in each twenty-four hours. Happy in the possession of a remarkable memory and a clear and quick perception, the editor of the *Globe-Democrat* masters situations and solves problems with less waste of time than any man in the profession. During a meeting of the National Sunday School convention, Cliff Sanders had taken a portion of the proceedings and written them out in longhand. A verse of an old hymn was quoted, but no one in the composing room could decipher it. In despair the proof was put on McCullagh's desk with blanks where the words could not be deciphered. Mr. McCullagh took up his pen and wrote it out in full on the proof. "I heard that hymn when I was a small boy in Sunday School," he said.

He had a quick mind and a memory like a sponge. Several of the editorial tributes after his death mentioned his "retentive memory."

The Philadelphia *Ledger* headed its editorial, "A Self Made Man."

The contrast between McCullagh and Charles Dana whom McCullagh admired, in their opinion of college graduates is interesting. Where Dana sought out college men for his staff and emphasized the importance of college training, McCullagh, as we have seen, tended to sneer at college graduates, particularly those from Harvard University. Unconsciously perhaps, he was compensating in his own mind for his lack of formal education. His impatience with the literary errors and writing lapses of others suggests the same conclusion. Perhaps there was personal satisfaction in writing biting editorials chiding those who he thought should know better. For example:[14]

> The pompous and ponderous *Fortnightly Review* has had much to say of late about American English and the ignorance of American writers respecting the great masters of English composition. In its last number, the *Fortnightly* prints an article by Mr. Archibald Forbes, in which the following sentence occurs: "But as the marauding 'Yank' philosophically remarked to General Sherman: 'You can't expect all the cardinal virtues, uncle, for $13 a month.'"
>
> Has the *Fortnightly* ever heard of a man by the name of Samuel Johnson, who figured somewhat as a "master of English style" about a hundred years ago? If so, it will overhaul a book written by a Mr. Boswell and will find in it almost the identical expression above quoted. The subject under discussion was about house servants, and Dr. Johnson observed in extenuation of the faults of a member of that class that you cannot expect all of the cardinal virtues for twenty pounds a year—or words to that effect. An American adaptation of the same idea is related by one who knew the late Edwin Forrest in his palmy days. Mr. Forrest was rehearsing Richelieu in an Eastern theater. It came to the part of a subordinate actor to rush on the stage and exclaim a sentence of which "the Cardinal, Duke de Richelieu" was part. Mr Forrest did not like the young man's orthoepy very well and, turning to him in a rage, asked if he could not say "Cardinal, Dewk de Reech-loo," giving a very difficult and peculiar accent to the last syllable. The undeveloped tragedian stared at the great actor a while and replied: "No sir, if I could, do you suppose I would be playing here for $10 a week?"

Or again, he clucked his tongue at the musical errors of the New York *World* in this paragraph:

> The New York *World*, a noted standard of artistic, literary and musical taste, speaks of Beethoven's Chorus "The Heavens are Falling." We shall probably soon have its opinion of Haydn's "Fidelis" or Mozart's "Messiah" or Handel's "Creation."

He was showing off his own memory when he chided Dana as follows:

> Mr. Dana of the New York *Sun*, who is nothing if not critical in literary matters, ought not to tell his readers in a leading editorial that Talleyrand was the author of the remark that "language is intended to conceal thought." Irving corrects this mistake in his *Life of Goldsmith*, and shows that the expression was used in the *Citizen of the World* several years before it could have been uttered by Talleyrand.

Eugene Field summed up this aspect of McCullagh when he wrote[15] that "His intellectual system's so extensive and so greedy that when it comes to records, he's a walkin' cyclopedy." When Reedy insisted McCullagh was vain in his own way, he probably was referring to the editor's pride in his self-acquired knowledge.

Reading the editorial tributes after his death, there could be no doubt about the esteem with which he was regarded by his peers. It is a human failing to write flatteringly about a man after he is gone, but there is an unmistakable sincerity in the tributes. Orrick Johns,[16] whose comment undoubtedly reflected the opinion of his father, linked McCullagh with two of the great names in American journalism. Horace Greeley, he wrote, had put editorials first and James Gordon Bennett developed news gathering. McCullagh blended the two.

Many of McCullagh's contemporaries regarded him as one of the foremost editors in America. The *Republic*, which had directed many unkind criticisms at McCullagh during his lifetime, declared he was one of the most prominent figures in American journalism and added that his career was more memorable because "in the complex organization of the modern newspaper, the factor of individual influence becomes more and more obscure." It would be a long time, said the *Republic* before there would be "another company of Greeleys, Raymonds and Weeds" and it would be just as long before there was a "counterpart of Joseph B. McCullagh."

The *Post-Dispatch* pointed out that McCullagh had been identified with the journalism of St. Louis for nearly forty years and for "upwards of twenty years, he had been its most conspicuous figure. Among the journalists of the country he was easily in the first rank, and when he was in his prime, few men did more to broaden the scope of newspaper work and enterprise."

The St. Louis *Chronicle* said McCullagh was "the greatest editor in the West. He was one of the select to which Horace Greeley, Murat Halstead and Charles Dana belong."

The *Republic* on January 1, 1897 reprinted in bold face type a quotation from *Reedy's Mirror*: "An institution, says Emerson is the lengthened shadow of one man. Joseph B. McCullagh is the *Globe-Democrat*."

Cincinnati newspapers agreed. The *Commercial-Tribune* called him a "giant in his field" and said "he was one of the rarest of men, a genius who could do hard work and who reveled in it." The *Enquirer* described him as "one of the best known journalists in the United States" and declared that he "had in a high degree the faculty of comprehending the wants of the reading public. When he died, one of the bright lights of journalism went out."

In Kansas City, the *Star* pointed out: "The death of 'Joe' McCullagh, as he was called everywhere, is proof of his nearness to the reading people . . . He was a bright and shining light." Pulitzer's New York *World* called him a "political prophet." Watterson in the Louisville *Courier Journal* said he was a "thorough newspaper man from head to foot." The Omaha *World-Herald* headed its editorial: "Greatest of Newspapermen." The Baltimore *American* described him as "one of the really great men in journalism." The Chicago *Tribune* headed its editorial "A Hater of Sham and Snobbery" and pointed out that "he was instrumental in shaping the careers of many who happened to be under his tutelage." McCullagh, said the *Tribune*,[17] "was the originator of many reforms in the detailed work of preparing a newspaper. Much of his success may be traced to the fact that he was a past master in the business of news gathering." The New York *Times* declared he was a "keen, shrewd, thorough journalist of the type that, at will, plods or soars."

In the opinion of the leading newspapermen of his generation, men like Charles A. Dana of the New York *Sun,* Melville E. Stone of the Chicago *News,* and Henry Watterson of the Louisville *Courier Journal,* McCullagh was one of the trail blazers of the new journalism. Some felt that Pulitzer and Hearst adopted the ideas he demonstrated, to be successful. Certainly in St. Louis there was general agreement that McCullagh was the master and Pulitzer an apt pupil.

Few managing editors could equal his uncanny ability to sense where "hell is likely to break loose next" and to have reporters on the scene to cover a story even before it occurs. He was a master of exploiting controversies. He made the interview a valuable tool in news coverage and his mass interviews anticipated the pollsters by more than half a century. He was among the first to recognize the appeal of illustrations and to use them liberally. He set the pattern for modern courage of political conventions. He was a vigorous crusader, but never did he permit his newspaper to become a common scold. He believed that a newspaper should be a leader in its community and his influence in civic progress and reform was profound.

One of the intriguing questions about McCullagh is why he was so quickly forgotten and the credit for his significant contributions to journalism have been largely attributed to others. One obvious explanation is the man himself. He believed in sounding the praises of the *Globe-Democrat,* but he shrank from calling attention to himself. One of his friends noted that he loved to hear the *Globe-Democrat* talked about, but rarely did he reveal anything about his personal life. He seemed to shun the limelight. He never sought political office and the nearest he ever came to public service was as foreman of a grand jury.

The fact that McCullagh was not a publisher probably was a contributing factor. There has been a tendency on the part of journalism's historians to assume that the guiding genius of great newspapers emanated from their owners. This assumption undoubtedly was valid in appraising the role of James Gordon Bennett, Horace Greeley, Henry Raymond, and others. There is more reason to question it in the role of the two men most often credited with the development of the new journalism: Pulitzer and Hearst. A few writers have raised this question as to how much of Pulitzer's success can be attributed to John Cockerill, Herbert Bayard Swope, and Frank Cobb. Hearst had Arthur Brisbane, Merrill Goddard, and others.

In McCullagh's time and since, New York has been the ultimate goal of most of the noted names in journalism. There has been the assumption, not necessarily valid, that until a newspaperman achieved success in New York, he had not reached stardom. It can be assumed that this factor has influenced the historians of journalism.

Perhaps the most compelling explanation of why McCullagh has all but been forgotten in this century is that he was a prophet ahead of his time. He was a crusading editor, but his crusades were largely limited to local rather than national issues. "Muckraking" had not yet found its way into the language when he died. The exposés of child labor, trusts, white slavery, and the squalor of the tenements came a decade later, and indeed, were sparked first by the magazines rather than by the newspapers. McCullagh exposed political corruption, gambling, and other evils in St. Louis, but the crooks of his day did not achieve the degree of magnitude that characterized Boss Tweed in New York.

By the time he was beginning to make the *Globe-Democrat* nationally recognized, the newspaper giants of the period had passed from the scene: Greeley, the elder Bennett, Raymond, and others. Dana alone of that group remained prominent, and while his contributions to journalism were substantial, they do not compare with the wealth of new ideas McCullagh contributed.

In judging McCullagh with his peers, one other consideration cannot be ignored. Not one of his rivals could equal his ability in as many aspects of his profession. Dana said McCullagh was the best reporter he ever knew. He won a national reputation as a war correspondent, and later as a Washington correspondent. As a managing editor, his acute sense of news and aggressive policies made him the equal of any managing editor of his time. He was recognized as one of the outstanding editorial writers of his generation as well.

A JEALOUS MISTRESS

Eugene Field was not concerned with history's verdict of McCullagh, but he was close to the mark when he wrote:

> For all that sleek, pretentious Eastern editorial pack
> We wouldn't swap the shadow of
> Our little Mack!

The record shows that "the shadow" of Joseph Burbridge McCullagh was a significant and inspiring influence on the profession which was his jealous mistress.

APPENDIX I

The complete interview obtained by McCullagh from President Andrew Johnson as it was published in the Cincinnati *Commercial* on Thursday, February 13, 1868:

WASHINGTON, D.C. Feb. 10, 1868.—I called on the President last evening and had an interview with him of about an hour's duration. From the revival of the impeachment project and the recent correspondence between him and Gen. Grant, which I had been informed, on the authority of several eminently loyal newspapers, was literally "crushing" to A. J., I expected to find His Excellency in a prostrate and enfeebled condition, or perhaps "writhing in the agonies of despair," as Forney's two dailies would express it. But he was not prostrate, and he didn't writhe any. Quite the contrary, I never saw him more cheerful or in better health and spirits.

"They're after you again, Mr. President, with an impeachment," said I. "So I hear," said he, "but I can't get the point they're trying to make against me this time; though, for that matter I haven't taken much trouble to find out."

I explained to him then what I understood to be the charges under consideration in the Reconstruction committee: First, his order to Gen. Grant not to regard Stanton's orders unless he knew they came from the Executive; and second, what was termed a conspiracy on his part to resist the execution of the tenure-of-office act, by arranging with Gen. Grant that he (Grant) should resign the Secretaryship ad interim of the War Department in time for him (Johnson) to put in some man who would refuse to relinquish his portfolio at the bidding of the Senate, in order to test the validity of the tenure-of-office act, before the Supreme Court.

"Is that all?" said the President.

"Yes sir, and I understand that Bingham and other Republicans on the committee think it quite enough to turn you out of office."

"Well, now," said the President, "as to the order about Stanton, I didn't suppose there was a man in Congress who is not aware that I have a perfect right to do what that order directs without making any order at all. Mr. Stanton's orders are of no more force than yours, except upon the presumption that they come direct from me; and I have a perfect right to communicate with Gen. Grant direct, without availing myself to Mr. Stanton, who, in such matters, is a mere clerk for the transmission of orders. As to the charge of conspiracy, it only shows how badly they are off for something to quarrel about. In the first place, if I wanted to do what they make out to be a conspiracy, I could have done it without a conspiracy with Grant or anybody else. I could have removed Grant as Secretary ad interim in time to have put in some man who would test the law. And if I had taken such a course there would be no crime about it unless it be a crime to appeal to a remedy provided by the Constitution for the settlement of disputes between the legislative and executive departments of the government. What else is the Supreme Court for but to settle such controversies?"

"And has the Executive no rights, and no opinions, nothing but blind obedience to the legislative department? If such was the intention of the framers of the government, they wouldn't have created a Supreme Court for it could be of no use. But it was intended as the final arbiter in all such controversies and when it determines a question its decision is binding as much as the Constitution itself."

"Do they seem to be very rabid about impeachment this time—worse than they were before?" inquired the President.

"I think the thing is a little stronger than it was," I replied. "They are getting desperate and they want to put you out so as to put Ben Wade in and get control of the Federal patronage for the next Presidential election. Besides, maybe they want to disqualify you as a candidate against them, for Boutwell and others among them say you will be their most formidable opponent in the next canvass."

"I don't know about that," said the President launghing, "but I hope they'll find somebody formidable enough to beat them. I don't think they expect to do anything with the impeachment unless a few of them may be operating in the gold market."

I replied that previous experience in gold speculation on im-

APPENDIX I

peachment probabilities was not encouraging. Several gentlemen had gone into it in the hope of a rise which never came, and the result had been rather disastrous than otherwise. Nothing short of actual conviction by the Senate would create rise enough to make it pay to buy on a margin.

"Well," said the President, "let them go ahead. When they bring in the charges I'll try to answer them, that's all," and he laughed as if he didn't believe the charges would ever come.

Mr. Johnson referred to that part of Gen. Grant's correspondence in which the General asks him to reduce to writing the order given to him verbally to disregard any order received from Stanton unless he knew it to emanate from the Executive.

"Here," said he, Gen. Grant asserts that I had given him such a verbal order. I never did anything of the kind. It was he himself who first suggested that I could take such a course as to reduce Stanton to a mere clerk, and it was suggestion from him, and not any verbal order from me, that first brought the subject up in that light."

At this point the President produced a letter from Gen. Sherman, dated Saturday evening Jan. 18. "Sherman says that it was the intention of himself and Grant to call on Stanton on the following Monday, to request him, for the good of the country, to resign the office of the Secretary of War; but that he learns Grant must go to Richmond and he to Annapolis, so that they can't call on Stanton on Monday, but will do so at some other time, and insist that he should resign. Then Sherman goes on to say that if Stanton won't resign it will be time enough to look to ulterior considerations."

"Now," said the President, "these ulterior considerations were nothing else than the suggestions of Grant himself that Stanton should be treated as a mere clerk and confined strictly to the execution of the duties imposed upon him by the letter of the law. And yet, after having suggested this and urged it upon me, he writes me a letter asking me to reduce my 'verbal order' to writing. It was his own 'verbal order' not mine. Yet he makes it appear from his letter that the first intimation came from me, and that he never said a word about it until I had spoken of it. That is a fair specimen of the way he has been acting all along. This whole matter is not the first or the only time he has played that part. It is only one of a great many instances in which he has grossly deceived me. I got a dispatch one day from Georgia, telling me that Meade and Jenkins had been in consultation and that it was probable that Meade would remove Jenkins. I sent for Gen. Grant and he came over. I showed him the dispatch and told him I would not like Jenkins to be removed until I could hear something more about the matter. He answered me that he would see to it that Jenkins was not removed. I thought this was enough; but judge of my surprise when the next day I learned that Jenkins was removed. I don't believe Grant interfered at all, though he distinctly promised me he would. That's the kind of game he has been playing all along.''

Just here a little question of veracity occurred to my mind, which I thought it well enough to settle. It was this: Some time in the early part of the winter a paragraph appeared in the *Commercial*'s Washington correspondence to the effect that Col. Hillyer formerly of Gen. Grant's staff, had told a member of the Judiciary committee that he once was present at a conversation between Gen. Grant and the President in which the former took strong grounds in favor of a white man's government and against negro suffrage, saying that this government was made for white men, and none other should have a voice in it—and striking his fist on an adjacent table to show that he meant what he said. When this paragraph appeared it was extensively copied, and about as extensively denied, especially by that large class of newspapers and Grant men who, having no means of ascertaining whether it was true or false, felt all the more sure that it was false, and denounced it as one of ''Mack's'' malicious fabrications.

I called the President's attention to this subject—asked him if he remembered any such conversation with Grant, and if so whether he remembered Grant's remark that this is a white man's government. He promptly replied that he did. He could not repeat Grant's words exactly, but the substance of them was what I had stated, and they were strongly against negro suffrage, which, about that time, it was proposed to introduce into the District of Columbia. Among other things Grant said was that the negroes didn't know enough to vote and that they would vote just as their employers wanted them to. He illustrated by saying that he had a number of negro servants in his house, and that to let them

APPENDIX I

vote would simply be to give him (Grant) so many additional votes, for they would vote just as he told them. He was quite vehement at this time in his denunciations of the radical policy of negro suffrage.

The above, I think, settles the question of veracity as to Grant being a white man's government man. It is pretty well authenticated now.

The subject of finances was next brought up. The President seemed to have given a great deal of attention to the subject, and to have very strong convictions on it. He thought the common sense view of the matter was better than any of the fine spun theories to which the country was so often treated, and which only confused without enlightening anybody.

"The fact is," said he, "that, before the war, there were $3,000,000,000 worth of property in slaves in the South, distributed so as to create an aristocracy, which controlled the South, and through the South the country. The war destroyed both the property and the aristocracy. But now we find that the property only disappeared from the South to appear in the North in another shape, and to create an aristocracy and a political power, in the shape of bondholders more destructive of the government than the slave-holding aristocracy was, because a continued burden upon it—drawing upon the resources of the country to support it, and not adding one cent to the productive interests. The $3,000,000,000 of slave property, while it was an evil, was at the same time a good, for it increased the productive resources of the Nation. But now we find the 4,000,000 negroes a charge upon the country, instead of a benefit to it, and the $3,000,000,000 which they represented has taken the shape of a heavy burden upon the taxpayers, drawing from them all they can rake and scrape to pay a larger rate of interest than can be got out of any other investment."

I asked the President what remedy he would propose for what he considered so great an evil. Would the Western Democratic theory of an illimitable issue of greenbacks do?

"No," he replied, "that would only increase the evil, instead of diminishing it or remedying it. To issue more money might make easy times for a while, but they wouldn't last long. There could be no true prosperity derived from such a course."

"Then what do you think would bring about the desired result?"

"Why, the first thing is to release the South from her present condition and let the people of those ten States have a chance to recover from the effects of the war, to engage in business, and to offer opportunities for absorbing some of the surplus capital which is now invested in government bonds. Let them have a chance and they'll go to work with a will and do their full share. Then reduce the expenses of the government—reduce the army and navy to a peace basis, collect the revenue and take up these bonds as fast as possible. Suppose we issue a hundred millions or a thousand millions of greenbacks, how much better are we off than we were before? The debt is still before us and must be paid. No advantage is gained, but a great evil is done to the laboring interests of the country in the inflation of prices, which laboring men will feel only as it operates against them in making their wages represent less than they did before."

From the above the reader can judge that any attempt made by Congress this winter to inflate the currency or, as Gen. Schenck says, "To make times easy" for the next campaign, will be promptly vetoed by the President.

The subject of the next Presidency came up in the course of the conversation. Mr. Johnson was noncommittal but inquisitive as to candidates. He asked me how Pendleton stood in the West and what strength he had as a candidate. I replied that I thought Mr. Pendleton's principal strength was in his personal popularity among the Ohio Democrats, and that it did not extend much beyond where he was personally known to people, but that Wash McLean was running him very strong, and that Wash was a power in the Democracy of the West, as was manifested by his slaughter of Vallandigham.

"Well," said the President," if the idea is to run Pendleton exclusively on the financial theory it will prove a mistake. Reconstruction is the paramount issue and cannot be absorbed or swallowed up by any other. The radical policy of Congress is an attempt to change our form of government, if not to overthrow it altogether. If that succeeds, it makes very little difference what becomes of the finances, for they will go with the rest and there will be nothing left anywhere."

He did not think the result in the Eighth District looked well

APPENDIX I

for Pendleton. He spoke of McClellan, and asked me how I thought he'd run. I replied that McClellan seemed to have some strength in the East, but I didn't think it would prove very strong in the national convention. The last campaign took all the music out of McClellan's name.

In conclusion on this topic I told the President there were a great many Democrats and a great many who used to act with the Republicans who considered him the strongest and most available candidate to oppose the radicals with. He didn't know about that, but he believed it to be quite possible to find a man who would carry the North against the radicals.

And Nathan said unto David, "Thou art the man."

The President referred to the dissatisfaction which some of the Fenians and their friends in this country felt toward the administration, and especially toward Mr. Seward.

"But," said he, "they don't take into account that we can't do just what we want in these things. As Andrew Johnson I have always sympathized with this movement but a man can't always do officially what he feels unofficially. We must obey certain laws of nations—we must obey the neutrality laws. Still, I think the matter now in controversy will be satisfactorily determined. The other day we sent to Brady and O'Connor of New York to know if they would go to Europe to defend American citizens undergoing trial there. We have received no answer yet, but I think the arrangement can be made with them or some other prominent lawyers, and that's as much as we can do just now."

"Mack"

APPENDIX II

INTERVIEWING CORPS

Mission for the Promulgation of Political History in the Halls of Congress

"No American Education is complete which does not include an accurate knowledge of the political history of this country."—*Charles Sumner*

The column wheeled to the left, and started up Pennsylvania avenue, the scene of many a pageant, but never one that could be called a precedent to this. A little detachment of skirmishers fell off at the junction of Fourteenth street and turned to the right. Its destination was the White House, the great Treasury building, the War, Navy, and State Departments, and the Department of Justice. The corps moved on. At Thirteenth street a second detail turned to the right, and headed for the Department of Agriculture and Uncle Jerry, half a mile away. At Sixth street a third detachment wheeled to the left, and moved on the great public hives in which Secretary Noble and Postmaster General Wanamaker are king bees. But the main corps, full thirty strong, kept right along toward the big white Capitol. Once under the big dome the corps deployed. Up-stairs, down-stairs, everywhere, the interviewers scattered. They stood guard with the Doorkeeper at the House entrance and captured the Democratic Representatives hastening to the caucus. They invaded the committee rooms, where Republican Representatives were talking of the dead-lock and having no end of fun at the expense of the unwieldy majority. They wormed their way through the crowded corridors in search of truant scholars. They sat down to late breakfasts in the restaurants with members who had rushed from their bed rooms to the Capitol, and while this intellectual raid was going on at the south end of the great building the Senate wing of the corps were searching the committee rooms and having interesting experiences with grave and dignified Senators.

It was the first experience of Congress with a *Globe-Democrat* catechism, but everybody took kindly to the innovation. Statesmen who threw up their hands in despair when they fully appreciated the ordeal said it wasn't a bad idea to show Americans how little definite knowledge they really had about big events in their country's history. Representatives like Henry Cabot Lodge, on the Republican side of the House, and like Amos J. Cummings, on the Democratic side, went through the catechism as rapidly as they could write the answers. Others, like Charles H. Mansur of Missouri, and Constantine Buckley Kilgore, took time for reflection and jotted down the answers slowly. Some flew the track at the first suggestion of a test of their historical accuracy. They pleaded lack of time, asked that the cards be left with them or got out of the way as quickly as possible.

There was no place where the visit of the interviewer was better appreciated than at the Civil Service Commission. The Commissioners confessed judgment, and the chief examiner begged a copy of the catechism. Whether he proposes to incorporate it in his next civil service examination papers is a matter of conjecture. One member of the corps had a novel experience. When the Democratic caucus adjourned the corps passed the doorkeepers on the strength of the white badges and gained access to the floor of the House. A very busy half hour was spent. Then the floor was ordered cleared of all but members for the brief session of the House. At this juncture a group of members agreed that any man who could go around with so much political history, even if it was printed on a big card, was entitled to the privilege of the floor. The *Globe-Democrat* representative remained and silently participated in the proceedings.

Perhaps the reader would like to see the catechism which was the sensation of the opening day of the Fifty-second Congress. Here it is; but the newspaper print will fail to do justice to the heavy cardboard and handsome typographical appearance:

ST. LOUIS 𝕲𝖑𝖔𝖇𝖊-𝕯𝖊𝖒𝖔𝖈𝖗𝖆𝖙.
Class in Political History

This card contains a number of questions relating to the Political History of this country. The person to whom it is handed is requested to write out the answers without consultation with any other person.

RETURN TO THE REPORTER

1. How old was George Washington at the time of his retirement, after having served eight years as President?
2. How many officers were included in the Cabinet of George Washington, and what were they?
3. How long did Thomas Jefferson live after the close of his second Presidential term?
4. When was the Navy Department created, and who was the first Secretary of the Navy?
5. When was the Postmaster General made a Cabinet office, and who was the first Postmaster General who was also a Cabinet officer?
6. When was the Interior Department created, and who was the first Secretary of the Interior?
7. Who was the first Chief Justice of the United States?
8. What Chief Justice of the United States served the longest period and how long did he serve?
9. What Speaker of the House of Representatives served the longest in that capacity, and how long did he serve?
10. How many ex-Presidents of the United States died on the Fourth of July, and who were they?
11. Had any President of the United States, previous to his election to that office, been Speaker of the House of Representatives? Give name or names.
12. Who was the first Speaker of the House of Representatives?
13. When were the first ten amendments to the Constitution adopted?
14. What article of the Constitution of the United States prescribes the method of choosing a President by Electors?

Some of the Congressmen called these questions conundrums. They said it was unfair to arouse the curiosity without satisfying it. There was a key to catechism, but it was not revealed until after the interviewing corps was called off. Here is the key:

1. Sixty-five years and eleven days.
2. Four—Secretary of State, Attorney General, Secretary of the Treasury and Secretary of War and Navy. (Secretary of War and Navy one office.)

APPENDIX II

3. 1809 to 1826—17 years and 4 months.
4. In 1798. George Cabot.
5. In 1829. William T. Barry.
6. In 1849. Thomas Ewing.
7. John Jay.
8. John Marshall—34 years, 5 months, 7 days.
9. Henry Clay—10 years.
10. Three—Jefferson, Adams and Monroe.
11. James K. Polk.
12. Fred A. Muhlenberg.
13. 1791.
14. Amendments, Article 12.

NOTES

Chapter 1

1. Walter B. Stevens, "Joseph B. McCullagh," *Missouri Historical Review*, XXV (October 1930), 4.
2. Sara Lockwood Williams, *Twenty Years of Education for Journalism* (Columbia, Mo.: E. W. Stephens Publishing Co., 1929), p. 13.
3. Walter B. Stevens, "Joseph B. McCullagh," *Missouri Historical Review*, XXV (October 1930), 4.
4. Interview with Sam Slawson, St. Louis *Republic,* January 1, 1897.
5. Theodore Dreiser, *A Book About Myself* (New York: Boni & Liveright, Inc., 1922).
6. Louis M. Starn, *Bohemian Brigade* (New York: Alfred A. Knopf, 1954).
7. Walter B. Stevens, "Joseph B. McCullagh," *Missouri Historical Review*, XXV (October 1930), 6.
8. *Ibid.*
9. Franc Wilkie, *Pen and Powder* (Boston: Tichnor & Co., 1888).

Chapter 2

1. Franc Wilkie, *Pen and Powder* (Boston: Tichnor & Co., 1888).
2. Louis M. Starn, *Bohemian Brigade* (New York: Alfred A. Knopf, 1954).
3. Walter B. Stevens, "Mack, War Correspondent," *Missouri Historical Review,* XXV (January 1931).
4. *Ibid.*
5. *Ibid.*
6. *Ibid.*
7. J. Cutler Andrews, *The North Reports the Civil War* (Pittsburgh: University of Pittsburgh Press, 1955).
8. Walter B. Stevens, "Mack, War Correspondent," *Missouri Historical Review,* XXV (January 1931).
9. Chicago *Tribune,* January 1, 1897.
10. Walter B. Stevens, "Mack, War Correspondent," *Missouri Historical Review,* XXV (January 1931).
11. *Ibid.*
12. *Ibid.*
13. *Ibid.*
14. *Ibid.*

Chapter 3

1. Only two of McCullagh's Washington contemporaries survived him, General H. V. Boynton and Major John M. Carson. Reid went to New York as chief editorial writer for the New York *Tribune* in 1868, about the time McCullagh returned to Cincinnati.
2. Walter B. Stevens, "Mack and A. J.," *Missouri Historical Review,* XXV (April 1931).
3. *Ibid.*
4. *Ibid.*
5. During the earlier period of the "party press," a few editors and reporters had direct access to the President. Notable in that select group were the three men who edited the Washington *Globe* during most of the eight years President Andrew Jackson was in the White House. Francis P. Blair, Amos Kendall, and John C. Rives, all from Kentucky, made up the so-called "kitchen cabinet" and were intimate companions of the President. However, the *Globe* was supported by public printing amounting to more than $50,000 a year and openly a partisan publication. McCullagh was the first reporter for an independent newspaper in the sense that it had no official support, to enjoy such a relationship.
6. Walter B. Stevens, "Mack and A. J.," *Missouri Historical Review,* XXV (April 1931).
7. *Ibid.*
8. *Ibid.*
9. *Ibid.*
10. *Ibid.*
11. Jim A. Hart, "The McCullagh-Johnson Interviews: A Closer Look," *Journalism Quarterly,* XXXXV No. 1. While this article points out there had been question and answer interviews previously, it was McCullagh who was the first to interview a President, and that the Washington *Post,* October 10, 1936 reported that the Johnson interview "rocked the land and caused men to see red."
12. Walter B. Stevens, "Mack, Interviewer," *Missouri Historical Review,* XXVI (January 1932).
13. *Ibid.*
14. McCullagh had been sent by the Cincinnati *Commercial* on a tour of the South to report on postwar conditions. The St. Louis *Republic* on January 1, 1897 noted that his report on his visit to Stephens was "the first considerable interview ever published, a three column talk with Alexander H. Stephens."
15. Walter B. Stevens, "Mack and A. J.," *Missouri Historical Review,* XXV (April 1931).
16. *Ibid.*
17. *Ibid.*
18. *Ibid.*

NOTES

19. *Ibid.*
20. *Ibid.*
21. *Ibid.*

Chapter 4

1. Homer W. King, *Pulitzer's Prize Editor* (Durham, N.C.: Duke University Press, 1965).
2. *Ibid.*
3. Franklin W. Scott, *Newspapers and Periodicals of Illinois, 1814–1879* (Springfield, Ill.: Illinois Historical Collection, Vol. IV, Illinois State Historical Library); Melville Stone, *Fifty Years a Journalist* (Garden City, N.Y.: Doubleday, Page and Co., 1923).
4. *Ibid.*
5. Interview of Melville E. Stone with the Chicago *Tribune*, January 1, 1897.
6. Walter B. Stevens, "Mack, Managing Editor," *Missouri Historical Review*, XXVI (April 1932).
7. Melville Stone, *Fifty Years a Journalist* (Garden City, N.Y.: Doubleday, Page and Co., 1923).
8. Walter B. Stevens, "Mack, Managing Editor," *Missouri Historical Review*, XXVI (April 1932).
9. *Ibid.*
10. *Ibid.*
11. *Ibid.*
12. St. Louis *Globe*, July 25, 1872.
13. There is some disagreement as to the price paid for the *Missouri Staats-Zeitung*. W. A. Swanberg in *Pulitzer* (New York: Charles Scribner's Sons, 1967), fixed the price at between $27,000 and $40,000. Jim A. Hart in *A History of the Globe-Democrat* (Columbia, Mo.: University of Missouri Press, 1961), uses the figure "a little in excess of $40,000." Since McCullagh also used it in an editorial, January 11, 1874, this is probably correct.
14. Walter B. Stevens, "Mack, Managing Editor," *Missouri Historical Review*, XXVI (April 1932).
15. *Ibid.*
16. *Ibid.*
17. *Ibid.*
18. McCullagh was given fourteen additional shares to bring his holdings to thirty shares of stock in the new company.
19. Walter B. Stevens, "Mack, Managing Editor," *Missouri Historical Review*, XXVI (April 1932).

Chapter 5

1. Walter B. Stevens wrote that McCullagh "never claimed to be the inventor of the interview." However, other writers are virtually unanimous in crediting McCullagh with originating it. Edwin B. Smith, for example, wrote in the Washington *Post* on October 10, 1936: "Early in his long and notable career, Joseph B. McCullagh invented the interview. Beyond question he originated it. A precedent had been set, all leading journals quickly conformed, and the interview became an institution."
2. Theodore Dreiser, *A Book About Myself* (New York: Boni & Liveright, Inc., 1912).
3. Walter B. Stevens, "Mack, Managing Editor," *Missouri Historical Review*, XXVI (April 1932).
4. *Ibid.*
5. Walter B. Stevens, "Mack and the News," *Missouri Historical Review*, XXVI (July 1932).
6. *Ibid.*
7. *Ibid.*
8. Jim A. Hart, *A History of the St. Louis Globe-Democrat* (Columbia, Mo.: University of Missouri Press, 1961).
9. *Ibid.*
10. St. Louis *Globe-Democrat*, January 25, 1878.
11. Walter B. Stevens, "The New Journalism in Missouri," *Missouri Historical Review*, XVIII (January 1924).
12. *Ibid.*
13. Orrick Johns, *The Time of Our Lives: The Story of My Father and Myself* (New York: Stackpole & Sons, 1937).
14. Walter B. Stevens, "The New Journalism in Missouri," *Missouri Historical Review*, XVIII (January 1924).
15. O. K. Bovard was employed as a bookkeeper for the *Globe-Democrat* from 1892 to 1895. James W. Markham in "Bovard of the *Post-Dispatch*" credits McCullagh with being a decisive influence in Bovard's career. Others who got their start under McCullagh include W. C. Brann, founder of *The Iconoclast,* and Harry B. Martin, who created the "Weather Bird," a feature still used on the *Post-Dispatch*.

Chapter 6

1. St. Louis *Globe-Democrat,* January 12, 1878.
2. Interview of author with Stephen C. Tammany, retired printer of *Globe-Democrat.*
3. Walter B. Stevens, "Mack and the News," *Missouri Historical Review*, XXVI (July 1832).
4. *Ibid.*

NOTES

5. *Ibid.*
6. *Ibid.*
7. Walter B. Stevens, "The New Journalism in Missouri," *Missouri Historical Review,* XXVI (January 1932).
8. *Ibid.*
9. *Ibid.*
10. *Ibid.*
11. Letters from Joseph B. McCullagh to Walter B. Stevens, Missouri Historical Society.

Chapter 7

1. David Kaser, *Joseph Charless: Printer in the Western Country* (Philadelphia, Pa.: University of Pennsylvania Press, 1963).
2. Walter B. Stevens, "A Sensational Half-Decade," *Missouri Historical Review,* XXVI (April 1932).
3. *Ibid.*
4. St. Louis *Globe-Democrat,* December 12, 1878.
5. Julian Rammelkamp, *Pulitzer's Post-Dispatch* (Princeton, N.J.: Princeton University Press, 1967). Mr. Rammelkamp states: "The *Post* and *Dispatch* used the *Globe-Democrat*'s press and office space."
6. Walter B. Stevens, "The Grant Boom," *Missouri Historical Review,* XXVIII (January 1934).
7. *Ibid.*
8. Homer W. King, *Pulitzer's Prize Editor* (Durham, N.C.: Duke University Press, 1965).
9. Walter B. Stevens, "A Sensational Half-Decade," *Missouri Historical Review,* XXVI (April 1932).
10. Conversation of the late E. Lansing Ray, publisher of the St. Louis *Globe-Democrat* with the author.
11. Walter B. Stevens, "Mack, Managing Editor," *Missouri Historical Review,* XXVI (April 1932).
12. Walter B. Stevens, "The Texas Boycott," *Missouri Historical Review,* XXVII (October 1933).
13. *Ibid.*
14. *Ibid.*

Chapter 8

1. Melville E. Stone quoted in interview in the Chicago *Tribune* January 1, 1897.
2. Walter B. Stevens, "The Chief as They Knew Him," *Missouri Historical Review,* XXIX (July 1935).

3. *Ibid.*
4. St. Louis *Globe-Democrat*, May 16, 1892.
5. Walter B. Stevens, "Mack, Paragrapher Extraordinary," *Missouri Historical Review*, XXVII (July 1933).
6. *Ibid.*
7. *Ibid.*
8. Walter B. Stevens, "Mack in Politics," *Missouri Historical Review*, XXVII (October 1932).
9. *Ibid.*
10. St. Louis *Republic*, January 1, 1897.
11. Paul G. Hencke, "Joseph B. McCullagh, an Editor's Editor," *Overset*, I (July 1952).
12. Walter B. Stevens, "The Chief as They Knew Him," *Missouri Historical Review*, XXIX (July 1935).
13. After McCullagh's death the St. Louis *Republic* speculated on who would succeed him and listed three leading candidates: Capt. King, Walter B. Stevens, then Washington correspondent, and Casper S. Yost, then Sunday editor.
14. Walter B. Stevens, "The New Journalism in 1880," *Missouri Historical Review*, XXIX (April 1935).
15. *Reedy's Mirror*, August 22, 1895.
16. Walter B. Stevens, "The New Journalism in 1880," *Missouri Historical Review*, XXIX (April 1935).

Chapter 9

1. Walter B. Stevens, *St. Louis, the Fourth City* (St. Louis, Mo.: S. J. Clark Publishing Co., 1909).
2. *Ibid.*
3. Walter B. Stevens, "The Pitch in Policy," *Missouri Historical Review*, XXIX (January 1935).
4. Walter B. Stevens, *St. Louis, the Fourth City* (St. Louis, Mo.: S. J. Clark Publishing Co., 1909).
5. The railroad referred to in the news story was the Missouri Pacific Railroad.
6. The *Missouri Republican* was purchased in 1888 by Charles H. Jones, who renamed it the St. Louis *Republic*. Jones sold the *Republic* in 1893 to David R. Francis, a former Governor of Missouri and later Ambassador to Russia. In 1919 the *Republic* was purchased by the *Globe-Democrat* and merged with that paper.
7. U.S. Census Office, *The Ninth Census, 1870* (Washington, D.C.: Government Printing Office), Part 1.
8. McCullagh vigorously opposed the action of the Missouri Legislature at the time the city's boundaries were fixed.

NOTES

9. Walter B. Stevens, "The New Journalism in 1880," *Missouri Historical Review,* XXIX (April 1935).
10. Walter B. Stevens, *St. Louis, the Fourth City* (St. Louis, Mo.: S. J. Clark Publishing Co., 1909).

Chapter 10

1. Walter B. Stevens, "The Grant Boom," *Missouri Historical Review,* XXVIII (January 1934).
2. *Ibid.*
3. *Ibid.*
4. *Ibid.*
5. Joseph B. McCullagh, "Recollections of Great Conventions," St. Louis *Globe-Democrat* (June 14, 1896).
6. *Ibid.*
7. Walter B. Stevens, "The Great Boom," *Missouri Historical Review,* XXVIII (January 1934).
8. *Ibid.*
9. *Ibid.*
10. Douglas Martin, who served as promotion manager for the St. Louis *Globe-Democrat* coined the phrase, "Forty-Ninth State," which was used from 1920 until Alaska became the forty-ninth state in 1959.
11. Walter B. Stevens, "Mack in Politics," *Missouri Historical Review,* XXVII (October 1932).
12. Walter B. Stevens, "The Great Boom," *Missouri Historical Review,* XXVIII.

Chapter 11

1. Interview with Steven Tammany, St. Louis *Globe-Democrat* printer.
2. St. Louis *Republic,* January 1, 1897.
3. *Ibid.*
4. Theodore Dreiser, *A Book About Myself* (New York: Boni & Liveright, Inc., 1922)
5. *Ibid.*
6. *Ibid.*
7. *Ibid.*
8. Silas Bent, *Ballyhoo: The Voice of the Press* (New York: Boni & Liveright, Inc., 1922).
9. Interview with George Windigger, retired foreman of the *Globe-Democrat* composing room.
10. Addison Archer, *American Journalism* (New York: Holmes Publishing Co., 1897).

Chapter 12

1. St. Louis *Post-Dispatch,* December 31, 1896.
2. *Ibid.,* January 1, 1897.
3. *Ibid.,* January 3, 1897.
4. *Ibid.,* January 3, 1897.
5. *Ibid.,* January 4, 1897.
6. St. Louis *Globe-Democrat,* January 4, 1897. The St. Louis *Republic* report of the funeral mentioned "almost innumerable floral offerings" and said the funeral was "one of the most imposing corteges in St. Louis history."
7. New York *Times,* February 5, 1897.

Chapter 13

1. *Reedy's Mirror,* January 7, 1897.
2. St. Louis *Post-Dispatch,* January 3, 1897.
3. William Hyde, *Encyclopedia of St. Louis History,* Vol. III. It seems likely that the rumor about the Louisville and the Terre Haute romances may have involved the same young lady.
4. *Ibid.*
5. St. Louis *Globe-Democrat,* January 3, 1897.
6. Theodore Dreiser, *A Book About Myself* (New York: Boni & Liveright, Inc., 1922).
7. Personal interview by the author.
8. *Reedy's Mirror,* January 7, 1897.
9. *Ibid.*
10. Walter B. Stevens, "The Chief as They Knew Him," *Missouri Historical Review,* XXIX (January 1935).
11. *Ibid.*
12. Walter B. Stevens, "He Read to Some Purpose," *Missouri Historical Review,* XXIX (April 1935).
13. St. Louis *Republic,* January 1, 1897.
14. Walter B. Stevens, "He Read to Some Purpose," *Missouri Historical Review,* XXIX (January 1935).
15. Eugene Field, "Little Mack" from *A Little Book of Western Verse* (New York: Charles Scribner's Sons, 1896). Reedy called the poem the "best poem" Field ever wrote.
16. Orrick Johns, *The Time of Our Lives* (New York: Stackpole & Sons, 1937).
17. Chicago *Tribune,* January 2, 1897.

BIBLIOGRAPHY

Books

Anderson, Galusha. *The Story of a Border City During the Civil War.* Boston: Little, Brown & Co., 1908.

Andrews, J. Cutler. *The North Reports the Civil War.* Pittsburgh: University of Pittsburgh Press, 1955.

Archer, Addison. *American Journalism.* New York: Holmes Publishing Co., 1897.

Bent, Silas. *Ballyhoo: The Voice of the Press.* New York: Boni & Liveright, Inc., 1922.

Bleyer, Willard Grosvenor. *Main Currents in the History of American Journalism.* New York: Houghton, Mifflin Co., 1927.

Cincinnati Guide. Ohio Writers Project. Cincinnati: Wiesen-Hart Press, 1943.

Daniels, Jonathan. *They Will Be Heard: America's Crusading Newspaper Editors.* New York: McGraw-Hill, 1965.

Dreiser, Theodore. *A Book About Myself.* New York: Boni & Liveright, Inc., 1922.

Emery, Edwin. *The Press and America.* Englewood Cliffs, N.J.: Prentice-Hall, Inc., 1962.

Field, Eugene. *A Litlte Book of Western Verse.* New York: Charles Scribner's Sons, 1889.

Filley, C. I. *Some More Republican History of Missouri: 1856–1902.* St. Louis: Chutman Printing Co., 1902.

Greve, Charles Theodore. *Centennial History of Cincinnati and Representative Citizens.* 2 vols. Chicago: Biographical Publishing Co., 1904.

Hart, Jim Allee. *A History of the St. Louis Globe-Democrat.* Columbia, Mo.: University of Missouri Press, 1961.

Johns, Orrick. *The Time of Our Lives: The Story of My Father and Myself.* New York: Stackpole & Sons, 1937.

Kaser, David. *Joseph Charless: Printer in the Western Country.* Philadelphia, Pa.: University of Pennsylvania Press, 1963.

King, Homer W. *Pulitzer's Prize Editor: A Biography of John A. Cockerill, 1845–1896.* Durham, N.C.: Duke University Press, 1965.

Kirschten, Ernest. *Catfish and Crystal.* New York: Doubleday & Co., 1960.

Lee, James Melvin. *History of American Journalism.* Boston: Garden City Publishing Co., 1917.

Lyon, William H. *The Pioneer Editor in Missouri, 1808–1860.* Columbia, Mo.: University of Missouri Press, 1965.

Markham, James W. *Bovard of the Post-Dispatch.* Baton Rouge, La.: Louisiana State University Press, 1954.

McReynolds, Edwin. *Missouri: A History of the Crossroads State.* Norman, Okla.: University of Oklahoma Press, 1962.
Missouri: A Guide to the Show Me State. Missouri Writers Project. New York: Duell, Sloan & Pearce, 1941.
Mott, Frank Luther. *American Journalism: A History, 1690–1960.* 3rd ed. New York: The Macmillan Co., 1962.
Putzel, Max. *The Man in the Mirror: William Marion Reedy and His Magazine.* Cambridge, Mass.: The Harvard University Press, 1963.
Rammelkamp, Julian. *Pulitzer's Post-Dispatch.* Princeton, N.J.: Princeton University Press, 1967.
Scharf, J. Thomas. *History of St. Louis City and County.* 2 vols. Philadelphia, Pa.: Louis H. Everts & Co., 1883.
Scott, Franklin William. *Newspapers and Periodicals of Illinois 1814–1879.* Illinois Historical Collection. Vol. VI. Springfield: Illinois Historical Library, 1910.
Shoemaker, Floyd C. *Missouri and Missourians.* 5 vols. Chicago: The Lewis Publishing Co., 1943.
Starr, Louis M. *Bohemian Brigade.* New York: Alfred A. Knopf, 1954.
Stevens, Walter B. *St. Louis, the Fourth City: 1784–1909.* St. Louis, Mo.: S. J. Clark Publishing Co., 1909.
Stevens, Walter B. *Centennial History of Missouri (The Center State), One Hundred Years in the Union.* St. Louis, Mo.: S. J. Clark Publishing Co., 1909.
Stone, Melville. *Fifty Years a Journalist.* Garden City, N.Y.: Doubleday, Page and Co., 1923.
Swanberg, W. A. *Pulitzer.* New York: Charles Scribner's Sons, 1967.
Taft, William H. *Missouri Newspapers.* Columbia, Mo.: University of Missouri Press, 1964.
Wilkie, Franc. *Pen and Powder.* Boston: Tichnor & Co. 1888.
Williams, Sara Lockwood. *Twenty Years of Education for Journalism: A History of the School of Journalism of the University of Missouri.* Columbia, Mo.: E. W. Stephens Publishing Co. 1929.
Williams, Walter. *The State of Missouri: An Autobiography.* Columbia, Mo.: E. W. Stephens Co. 1904.

Periodicals and Pamphlets

Clevenger, Homer. "Railroads in Missouri Politics," *Missouri Historical Review,* XLIII (April 1949).
The Globe-Democrat Story. St. Louis *Globe-Democrat,* 1967.
Grissom, David M. "Personal Recollections of Distinguished Missourians," *Missouri Historical Review,* XIX (April 1925).
Guese, Lucius E. "St. Louis and the Great Whiskey Ring," *Missouri Historical Review,* XXXVI (January 1942).

Hart, Jim A. "The McCullagh-Johnson Interview: A Closer Look," *Journalism Quarterly*, XLV, No. 1.
Hencke, Paul G. "E. Lansing Ray and the Globe-Democrat's Contributions to World History," *Overset*, I (May 1952).
Hencke, Paul G. "The Globe-Democrat Comes Into Its Own," *Overset*, I (April 1952).
Hencke, Paul G. "Joseph B. McCullagh, an Editor's Editor," *Overset*, I (July 1952).
Historical Sketch of the St. Louis Globe-Democrat. St. Louis Globe-Democrat, 1935.
Mills, George. "On History of St. Louis Newspapers," *American Journalist*, September 15, 1883.
Riegel, Robert E. "The Missouri Pacific Railroad, 1879–1900," *Missouri Historical Review*, XVIII (January 1924).
"St. Louis Globe-Democrat Takes Bow on 100th Birthday," *Editor and Publisher*, November 8, 1952.
Stevens, Walter B. "Joseph B. McCullagh," *Missouri Historical Review*, XXV (October 1930); XXV (January 1931); XXV (April 1931); XXV (July 1931); XXVI (October 1931); XXVI (January 1932); XXVI (April 1932); XXVI (July 1932); XXVII (October 1932); XXVII (January 1933); XXVII (April 1933); XXVII (July 1933); XXVIII (October 1933); XXVIII (January 1934); XXVIII (April 1934).
Stevens, Walter B. "The New Journalism in Missouri," *Missouri Historical Review*, XVII (April 1923); XVII (July 1923); XVIII (October 1923); XVIII (January 1924); XVIII (April 1924); XVIII (July 1924); XIX (October 1924); XIX (January 1925); XIX (April 1925); XIX (July 1925).
White, E. L. "Western Journailsm," *Harper's New Monthly Magazine*, LXXXVII (October 1888).
Willier, Robert A. "The *Globe-Democrat*'s Golden Century," *St. Louis Globe-Democrat Sunday Magazine*, November 9, 1952.
Wilson, Harry. "McCullagh of the *Globe-Democrat*," *Page One*. St. Louis Newspaper Guild, 1948.

Reference Works

Dictionary of American Biography, eds. Allen Johnson and Dumas Malone. 18 vols. New York: Charles Scribner's Sons, 1933.
Encyclopaedia of the City of St. Louis. 2 vols. New York: The Southern History Co., 1899.
Gould's St. Louis Directory, 1874–1880.
American Newspaper Annual and Directory, 1880–1896. N. W. Ayer and Sons.

INDEX

American Society of Newspaper Editors, 95, 107, 207
Anderson, Finley, 29
Andrews, J. Cutler, 31
Archer, Addison, 211, 212, 213
Armstrong, John Blair, 221
Associated Press, 65, 67, 68, 69, 74, 75, 76, 97, 98, 115, 187, 220

Baltimore *American*, 234
Baltimore *Gazette*, 133
Beaman, George W., 9
Beecher, Henry Ward, 80, 111
Bennett, James Gordon, 165, 233, 235, 236
Bent, Silas, 207, 208
Blaine, James, 192, 198, 199
Bodman, Albert H., 29
Bohle, Louis C., 217
Boston *Herald*, 106
Bovard, O. K., 107
Boyd, W. W., 217, 219, 221
Boynton, H. V., 220
Brisbane, Arthur, 236
Browne, Junius Henri, 9
Butler, Benjamin, 63, 64
Byars, William Vincent, 183

Chicago *Daily News*, 149, 235
Chicago *Globe*, 106
Chicago *Inter-Ocean*, 69
Chicago *Morning Post*, 67
Chicago *Republican*, 67, 68, 69
Chicago *Times*, 68, 145, 146
Chicago *Times-Herald*, 150
Chicago *Tribune*, 17, 18, 21, 29, 33, 39, 67, 95, 96, 145, 146, 175, 211, 219, 222, 234, 235
Chicago World's Fair, 175, 176
Christian Advocate, Galveston, 118
Christian Advocate, St. Louis, 3, 4
Cincinnati *Commercial*, 7, 18, 19, 21, 22, 31, 32, 33, 38, 41, 44, 45, 46, 49, 53, 57, 62, 64, 65, 66, 126, 189
Cincinnati *Commercial-Tribune*, 234
Cincinnati *Enquirer*, 9, 51, 66, 67, 68, 76, 95, 96, 107, 133, 138, 234
Cincinnati *Gazette*, 7, 8, 9, 10, 11, 17, 18, 19, 20, 41, 67
Cleveland, Grover, 163, 184, 195, 197
Cleveland *Leader*, 17
Cobb, Frank, 236
Cockerill, John A., 66, 67, 76, 107, 133, 135, 136, 137, 142, 143, 150, 236
Colburn, Richard T., 9
Commercial Travelers Association, 124
Crane, Newton, 72, 79

INDEX

Dana, Charles A., 1, 67, 68, 74, 106, 148, 228, 232, 233, 234, 235, 236
Danford, Homer A., 108
Davis, Charles R., 71, 73
Davis, Jefferson, 53, 54, 229
Denslow, V. B., 67
Denver Tribune, 149
Dillon, John A., 106, 107, 132, 133
Dreiser, Theodore, 6, 90, 106, 204, 205, 206, 207, 226

Field, Eugene, 85, 149, 228, 233, 237
Filley, Chauncey I., 155, 156, 157, 158, 198, 221
Fishback, George W., 7, 18, 69, 70, 72, 73, 74, 75, 76, 79, 81, 82, 83, 85, 99, 100, 102
Fishback, William P., 18, 21, 72
Fitzgerald, Harry, 226
Foote, Andrew H., 12, 13, 37
Freeman's Journal, 2
Fremont, John Charles, 6, 8, 9, 10

Galveston *News*, 116, 117
Garrett, Thomas E., 130
Goddard, Merill, 236
Gould, Jay, 78, 170, 171
Grant, Ulysses S., 12, 17, 21, 22, 23, 24, 27, 29, 30, 33, 35, 48, 49, 50, 61, 78, 99, 100, 155, 167, 185, 186, 190, 191, 192, 193, 194, 195, 229
Greeley, Horace, 41, 193, 194, 195, 233, 234, 235, 236
Grissom, Daniel M., 130
Grosvenor, William M., 69, 70, 79, 82, 101

Halstead, Murat, 11, 18, 19, 234
Harper's New Monthly Magazine, 137
Harper's Weekly, 9, 190
Harvey, Charles M., 164, 221
Hearst, William Rondolph, 86, 87, 99, 185, 235, 236
Hilbard, Homer N., 68
Houser, Daniel M., 69, 70, 71, 72, 74, 75, 79, 82, 83, 84, 85, 91, 97, 100, 101, 133, 170, 203, 212
Houser, William M., 223
Hughes, Charles Hamilton, 216, 217, 218, 220
Hyde, William, 130, 139, 199, 200, 219, 225

Ingersoll, Robert G., 111, 112, 113, 128, 229
Interview, 42, 44, 46, 49, 50, 51, 52, 53, 56, 62

Johns, George S., 104, 105, 150, 219
Johns, Orrick, 150, 233
Johnson, Andrew, 7, 42, 43, 44, 45, 48, 49, 50, 51, 55, 56, 57, 60, 61, 62, 63, 222
Jones, Charles H., 219
Journalist's Creed, 95

Kansas City *Star*, 234
Kansas City *Times*, 149, 183
King, Henry, 1, 4, 164, 165, 202, 221, 226, 227
King, Homer W., 67
Knapp, Charles, 103, 129, 139, 219
Knapp, George, 103, 129, 139, 144
Knapp, John J., 200
Knights of Labor, 170
Koenigsberg, M., 103
Kurtin, Joseph, 221

Lake, O. R., 221, 229
Lawson, Victor F., 86
Lincoln, Abraham, 10, 41, 54, 60, 67, 156, 216
Logan, John Alexander, 37, 38, 39
Louisville *Courier-Journal*, 189, 221, 225, 234, 235
Love, Henri, 9

McAnally, David Rice, 3
McAnally, David Rice, Jr., 3, 125, 151

INDEX

McCormick, Richard C., 11
McCullagh, Gladys, 222
McCullagh, John, 68, 204, 222
McEnnis, John T., 106
McKee, Charles H., 223
McKee, Henry, 84
McKee, William, 5, 69, 70, 71, 72, 74, 75, 79, 82, 83, 84, 90, 99, 100, 101, 102, 103, 130, 201, 221
McKinley, William, 208, 209, 214
McLean, Washington, 66
Manion, Mrs. Peter, 204, 217, 218, 221, 222
Miller, J. W., 221
Missouri Democrat, 8, 9, 17, 69, 70, 71, 72, 73, 74, 75, 76, 77, 78, 79, 80, 81, 82, 83, 84, 85, 87, 99, 100, 101, 106, 129, 194, 211
Missouri *Editor,* 149
Missouri *Gazette,* 131
Missouri Republican, 39, 70, 71, 75, 77, 81, 87, 88, 102, 103, 105, 111, 114, 115, 116, 117, 118, 126, 129, 130, 131, 132, 136, 137, 139, 140, 141, 144, 145, 157, 158, 185, 199, 200, 225
Missouri *Staats-Zeitung,* 74, 75, 76
Mott, Frank Luther, 86
Mumford, Morris, 183

National Intelligencer, 45
Nelson, William Rockhill, 86
New York *Herald,* 29, 39, 106, 154, 211
New York *Sun,* 106, 211, 235
New York *Times,* 17, 31, 41, 44, 107, 186, 187, 235
New York *Tribune,* 9, 31, 32, 41, 193
New York *World,* 9, 86, 138, 147, 150, 152, 233, 234
Noonan, E. A., 161, 162, 181, 182

Ochs, Adolph, 107
Ochs, George S., 107
Omaha *Bee,* 220
Omaha *World-Herald,* 234
O'Neil, Frank R., 130, 219

Philadelphia *Ledger,* 106, 231
Pulitzer, Joseph, 74, 75, 86, 87, 99, 107, 132, 134, 135, 142, 143, 145, 147, 150, 152, 155, 185, 234, 235

Ray, E. Lansing, 142
Ray, Simeon, 84
Raymond, Henry, 235, 236
Redpath, James, 11
Reedy, William Marion, 107, 130, 209, 210, 220, 222, 224, 226, 227, 231, 233
Reedy's Mirror, 107, 154, 166, 209, 220, 222, 231, 234
Reid, Whitelaw, 17, 18, 41
Rosewater, Victor, 220
Ryan, P. J., Bishop, 109

St. Louis, population of, 3, 87, 89, 168, 177
St. Louis *Chronicle,* 153
St. Louis *Dispatch,* 71, 75, 77, 81, 102, 105, 107, 132, 133
St. Louis *Evening Chronicle,* 207, 234
St. Louis *Evening Journal,* 101, 105
St. Louis *Evening Post,* 106, 107, 133
St. Louis *Globe,* 71, 72, 73, 74, 75, 76, 77, 78, 79, 80, 81, 82, 83, 84, 85, 87, 99, 100, 106, 111, 129, 211, 225
St. Louis *Globe-Democrat:* Towline, 80, 161, 167, 178, 192, 193, 195; rules of reporting, 91, 92, 93, 94, 95, 96, 98, 126; society news, 98; Great Religious Controversy, 109, 110, 111, 113; Texas boycott, 114, 115, 116, 117, 118, 119; catechism, 119, 120, 121, 122, 123, 124, 126; Commercial Travelers Column, 124, 125; unspoken speeches, 125; human interest features, snake dept., 126; spiritualists, 127; school news, 146, 147; railroad dept., 169, 170, 171, 172, 173, 174; political conventions, 187, 188, 189, 190, 191, 192, 193, 208, 209

St. Louis *Hornet*, 159
St. Louis *Post-Dispatch*, 104, 107, 125, 133, 134, 135, 136, 137, 138, 139, 142, 143, 144, 150, 152, 166, 181, 185, 205, 206, 211, 212, 213, 217, 218, 219, 221, 224, 234
St. Louis *Republic*, 171, 202, 207, 212, 219, 223, 227, 233, 234
St. Louis *Star-Sayings*, 153
St. Louis *Times*, 71, 73, 102, 105, 144
St. Louis *Times-Journal*, 196
Schurz, Carl, 78, 155, 156, 186, 193, 194
Schuyler, William H., 68
Seward, William H., 7
Sherman, John T., 42, 152, 191, 228
Sherman, William Tecumseh, 21, 33, 38, 39, 40, 155, 229
Simplot, Alexander, 9
Slawson, Sam, 4, 5
Slayback, Alonzo, 135, 136, 137, 139
Smith, Richard, 7, 17
Souter, Mrs. Rachel, 221
Springfield (Mass.), *Republican*, 154
Stanley, Henry M., 11, 69
Starn, Louis M., 12
Stephens, Alexander, 53, 54
Stevens, Walter B., 17, 104, 120, 121, 122, 125, 126, 127, 164, 169, 196, 199, 229, 231
Stone, Melville E., 68, 149, 150, 220, 235
Storey, Wilbur F., 146

Swift, William H., 130
Swope, Herbert Bayard, 236

Tammany, Stephen C., 113, 203, 227
Thornton, W. J., 221
Tilden, Samuel J., 189, 190
Trumbull, Lyman, 7

Upton, George P., 33

Walbridge, Cyrus P., 221
Walsh, John R., 67
Watterson, Henry, 86, 189, 221, 228, 234, 235
Webb, Charles S., 108, 228
Western Associated Press, 71, 74, 91
Westliche Post, 155, 186
Whiskey Ring, 83, 99, 100
White, Z. L., 137
Wilkie, Franc B., 8, 9, 10, 31
Williams, George F., 11
Williams, Walter, 95, 104, 119, 149
Windegger, George E., 209, 226
Witter, Martin R. H., 165, 170, 221

Yost, Casper S., 107, 127, 207, 208, 219